DECISION BY OBJECTIVES

HOW TO CONVINCE OTHERS THAT YOU ARE RIGHT

DECISION BY OBJECTIVES

HOW TO CONVINCE OTHERS THAT YOU ARE RIGHT

Ernest H. Forman
The George Washington University, Washington, D.C., USA

Mary Ann Selly
Expert Choice, Inc., Pittsburgh, Pasadena, USA

World Scientific
New Jersey • London • Singapore • Hong Kong

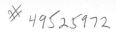

Published by

World Scientific Publishing Co. Pte. Ltd.

P O Box 128, Farrer Road, Singapore 912805

USA office: Suite 1B, 1060 Main Street, River Edge, NJ 07661

UK office: 57 Shelton Street, Covent Garden, London WC2H 9HE

British Library Cataloguing-in-Publication Data
A catalogue record for this book is available from the British Library.

DECISION BY OBJECTIVES
How to Convince Others that You are Right

ISBN   981-02-4142-9
ISBN   981-02-4143-7 (pbk)

Not everything that counts can be counted and not everything that can be counted, counts

Albert Einstein

Dedication/Acknowledgments

To our family, friends, colleagues, teachers and students.

We dedicate this book to, and acknowledge those who have come before us; those whose paths have crossed ours, both directly and indirectly; and those who have shared their ideas with us and have permitted us to share our ideas with them.

Contents

Preface xvii

Chapter 1
Introduction: Management Decision-Making Today 1
   The Need for Better Decision-Making 2
   Tradeoffs 5
   BOGSAT 5
   Cognitive Limitations 6
   Satisficing 6
   Common Simplistic Strategies 7
   Cognitive Decision Rules 8
   Unimportant vs. Crucial Decisions 10
   Resistance to Change 11
   Requisites for Change 11
   The Analytic Hierarchy Process 13

Chapter 2
Problem Solving and Decision-Making 15
   Problem Solving 15
   Decision Making 18
      Intelligence, Design, Choice 18
      Decision-Making is a Process 21
      Analysis vs. Synthesis 22
      Quantitative vs. Qualitative 22
      Objectivity vs. Subjectivity 24
      Linear versus Non-Linear 25

Chapter 3
Decision-Making Concepts & Methodologies 27
   Alternatives — Pros and Cons 27
   Misuse of Numbers 31
   Levels of Measurement 32

Nominal 32
Ordinal 33
Interval 33
Ratio 34
Weights and Scores 37
Channel Capacity and Short Term Memory 38
Need for Hierarchical Structure 39
Orders of Magnitude 39
Arbitrary Assignment 40
Absolute Versus Relative 40
Words Instead of Numbers 40

Chapter 4

The Analytic Hierarchy Process and Expert Choice 43
The Analytic Hierarchy Process 43
Beyond Weights and Scores 45
Inconsistency 46
Causes of Inconsistency 47
Clerical Error 47
Lack of Information 47
Lack of Concentration 48
Real World is not Always Consistent 48
Inadequate Model Structure 48
Compensatory and Non-Compensatory Decision-Making 49
Principles and Axioms of the Analytic Hierarchy Process 50
Expert Choice 53
Developing a Decision Hierarchy 54
Goal 54
Objectives 55
Alternatives 55
More Complex Hierarchies 56
Establishing Priorities 62
Pairwise Comparisons 62
Eigenvalues and Eigenvectors 63
Numerical Judgments 67

Graphical Judgments..68
Verbal Judgments 68
Synthesis...78
Sensitivity...79
A Typical Application of AHP/EXPERT CHOICE............................82
Seven Step Process for Choice...109
Other Decision-Making "Recipes"...111
Musts and Wants 111
Summary of the Benefits of AHP..113
Incremental Improvement 113

Chapter 5
From Brainstorming to Structuring to Evaluation and Choice 127
Brainstorming..127
Creativity..128
Narrowing Down...129
Categorizing and Combining..129
Voting...130
Multiple Choice 130
Rating...131
Considering Multiple Objectives 132
Structuring...133
Top Down Structuring 134
Bottom Up Structuring..134
From Pros/Cons to Objectives 136
Evaluation and Choice...137

Chapter 6
Other Topics / Refinements 139
Missing Judgments...139
Using Hard Data...140
Converting to Pairwise...141
Transformation of Data..141
Artificial Clustering of Elements — Linking Clusters.....................143
Ratings Approach...144

Absolute vs. Relative Measurement 144
An Overview of a Ratings Model 146
Creating the Ratings Model from Evaluation and Choice 147
Using Ranges for Intensities 148
Using the Same Intensities for All Objectives 149
From Absolute to Relative Measurement 150
Ideal and Distributive Synthesis Modes (Preventing or Allowing
Rank Reversals) 151
The Cause of Rank Adjustment 153
Closed and Open Systems — Scarcity and Abundance 154
Closed and Open Synthesis Modes with AHP. 156
Illustrative Example 162
When is Scarcity Germane? 173
Summary 174
Structural Adjustment / Product Adjustment 175
Structural Adjustment 175
Product Adjustment 177
Complete Hierarchy 179
Benefit/Cost 181
Benefit/Cost/Risk 184
Pairwise Comparisons Versus MAUT Swing Weights 187
Integrating with Quantitative Methodologies 190
Linear Programming 190
Queueing Models 198
Critical Path Method 202
Forecasting 205
Integer Programming 205

Chapter 7
Forecasting — The Forward Process 213
Illustration 1 — Synthesizing Forecasting Methods for a
Composite Forecast 215
Illustration 2 — Selecting a Forecasting Method 217
Illustration 3 — Deriving Probability Distributions 218
Illustration 4 — Forecasting Alternative Outcomes 222

Illustration 5 — Forecasting Models Interacting with Choice
Model(s). 226
Illustration 6 — Deriving Scenario Likelihoods 228
Illustration 7 — Analytical Planning (The Forward/Backward
Process) 230

Chapter 8
Resource Allocation.. 235
  Methodology Overview.. 239
    Identify/Design Alternatives.. 240
    Identify and Structure the Organization's Goals and
    Objectives 241
    Prioritize the Objectives and Sub-Objectives 242
    Measure Alternatives' Contributions 243
    Find the Best Combination of Alternatives 243
  Discrete Alternative Resource Allocation 244
    Benefit/Cost Ratios — Sort and Allocate 251
    Maximizing Benefits — Optimization 253
    Flexibility of Benefits Optimization Approach 267
    Constraints for Dependencies 267
    Constraints Representing Synergy... 268
    Orders of Magnitude Considerations... 273
    Summary of B/C Ratios vs. Optimization of Benefits................. 274
  Activity Level Resource Allocation 276
    Benefit/Cost Ratios... 278
    Maximizing Benefits — Optimization... 283
  Resource Allocation Summary... 287

Chapter 9
Meetings, Meeting Facilitation and Group Support Systems (GSS) 291
  Groups and Meetings... 291
  Dissatisfaction with Outcomes of Meetings.................................... 300
  What is a Meeting?... 300
  Meeting Model 301
  Meeting Outcomes: Relational as well as Task................................ 302

A Meeting Facilitation Framework 303
Facilitation Activities by Meeting Stage 305
    Pre-Meeting Activities 305
    During Meeting Activities 306

Chapter 10
Feedback 309
    Intuitive and Formal Feedback 309
    Top Down Evaluation of Bridge Selection AHP Model 311
    Top Down and Bottom Up 314
    AHP with Feedback — A More Formal Mechanism 316
        Iterating for Feedback 318
        Supermatrix for Feedback 322
        Intuitive Versus Formal Feedback 322
    The Analytic Network Process 324
        A Car Buying Example with Feedback 325
        Links in a Feedback Network Model 328
        Summary of Steps in Building a Feedback Network 330

Chapter 11
Empowered for the Future 331
    Everything That Counts 331
    Beyond Buzzwords 331
    Empowered 332

Appendix I
Contemporary Management Trends 333
    Strategic Planning 333
    Total Quality Management 334
        Malcom Baldridge Award 338
        Assessing the Voice of the Customer 340
        Value Based Value Pricing 344
        Value Pricing 345
        Competitive Value Analysis 347
        Competitive Value Pricing 348

Planning for Value 352
Quality Loss Function... 352
Prioritizing Defects and Evaluating Solutions with AHP 357
Quality Function Deployment and the House of Quality 360
Benchmarking.. 365
Benchmarking Effort Results.. 368
Cause and Effect or Fishbone Diagrams.................................... 371

Appendix II
Case Studies... 375
   AHP at the Inter-American Development Bank............................ 375
      Introduction... 375
      The Account Reconciliation Project 376
      Decision Support Environment... 377
      Intelligence Phase 378
      Design Phase... 379
      Choice Phase... 379
   AHP For Future Navy Sea-Based Platforms 386
      Carrier Attribute Prioritization.. 390
      Step 1 — Determine Appropriate CVX Tasks............................ 391
      Step 2 — Prioritize CVX Tasks... 391
      Step 3 — Develop CVX Attributes 396
      Step 4 — Prioritize CVX Attributes 397

Index.. 401

Preface

Although management decision-making books abound, ***Decision By Objectives*** takes decision-makers down a new and exciting path – a path that focuses on methods and processes to structure complexity, derive ratio measures for both qualitative as well as quantitative factors, and synthesize in ways never before possible.

In the first three chapters, we discuss decision-making concepts and methodologies. Then, in Chapter 4, we focus on the Analytic Hierarchy Process, developed by Thomas L. Saaty while at the Wharton School of Business. A decision hierarchy, containing a goal or mission statement, objectives or criteria, and alternatives of choice, is evaluated by deriving ratio scale priorities from pairwise judgments. A synthesis of the derived priorities produces a recommended course of action. Sensitivity analyses are performed to see how well the alternatives perform with respect to each of the objectives and how sensitive the alternatives are to changes in the importance of the objectives.

In Chapter 5 we illustrate a progression from brainstorming, to structuring, to evaluation and choice – improving measurement quality along the way. A variety of other topics and refinements are presented in Chapter 6.

Forecasting, a frequent adjunct to decision-making, is discussed in Chapter 7. Illustrations are presented for synthesizing forecasting methods into a composite forecast; selecting a forecasting method; deriving probability distributions; forecasting alternative outcomes; combining forecasting models with choice models; deriving scenario likelihoods; and performing analytical planning.

Resource allocation is one of the most difficult and politically charged activities in any organization. A rational approach to resource allocation, based on the achievement of objectives, is presented in Chapter 8. Two resource allocations formulations are presented – discrete activity resource allocation and activity level resource allocation.

Meetings, meeting facilitation and group decision support systems are discussed in Chapter 9. Feedback from lower levels in the hierarchy to upper levels is discussed in Chapter 10. Chapter 11, Empowerment for the Future, and Appendix I, Contemporary Management Trends, summarize the modern era of decision-making.

Two case studies are presented that show how the methods presented herein were used by the Inter-American Development Bank in large-scale procurements and the United States Navy in planning for future sea-based aircraft platforms.

Chapter 1

Introduction: Management Decision-Making Today

Decision-making is a process of choosing among alternative courses of action in order to attain goals and objectives. Nobel laureate Herbert Simon wrote that the whole process of managerial decision-making is synonymous with the practice of management.[1] Decision-making is at the core of all managerial functions. Planning, for example, involves deciding what should be done? When? How? Where? By whom? Other managerial functions, such as organizing, implementing, and controlling rely heavily on decision-making.

Today's fast changing and global environment dictates that a successful enterprise have a rich decision-making process. This means not only gathering and processing data, but also making decisions with the support of state-of-the-art decision methods. Decision-making is the very foundation of an enterprise, and sound decision-making is absolutely necessary for gaining and maintaining a competitive advantage.

In many enterprises the decision process entails great time and effort in gathering and analyzing information. Much less time and effort go into evaluating alternative courses of action. The results of the analyses (there are often many, for example financial, marketing, operations, and so on) are intuitively synthesized to reach a decision. Research has shown that although the vast majority of everyday decisions made intuitively are adequate, intuition alone is not sufficient for making complex, crucial decisions. Organizations that use modern decision support methods can gain and maintain a competitive edge in leading and managing global business relationships that are influenced by fast changing technologies and complicated by complex interrelationships between business and governments.

---

[1] Herbert A. Simon, *The New Science of Management Decision* (New York: Harper & Row, 1960), pp. 40 - 43.

This book will help you learn and apply methods to gain and maintain a competitive edge.

Specifically, this book will help you to:

Prioritize
Evaluate alternatives
Allocate resources
Deliver powerful presentations
Justify/defend recommendations
Make meetings more effective
Improve communications
Achieve consensus
Eliminate fifty percent of your business worries

The Need for Better Decision-making

Few people today would doubt the importance of relevant information when making vital decisions.

Yet many people are unaware of the need for a logical approach to the decision itself. They consider it sufficient to collect data, analyze the data, and then simply "think hard" in order to arrive at a good decision. They use seat of the pants approaches or simplistic strategies for analyzing their decisions. In his book, Crucial Decisions, Irving Janis provided evidence that "A poor-quality decision-making process (which characterizes simplistic strategies) is more likely than a high-quality process to lead to undesirable outcomes (including disastrous fiascoes)."[2] He asserted "When all vital decisions are made on the basis of a simplistic strategy, the gross misperceptions and miscalculations that remain uncorrected are likely to lead to disaster sooner or later — usually sooner rather than later."[3]

There are some who have already recognized the need for what Janis called vigilant decision-making. Janis stated: "When executives are asked how they go about making the most consequential decisions, some of them

---

[2] Irving L. Janis, *Crucial Decisions — Leadership in Policymaking and Crisis Management* (New York: The Free Press, 1989), p 287.
[3] Janis, *Crucial Decisions*, p. 89.

acknowledge that when they believe the stakes are really very high, they do not stick to the seat-of-the pants approach that they ordinarily use in daily decision-making. In fact, their accounts of what they do in such circumstances are not very different from the analytic problem-solving approach recommended in most standard textbooks in management sciences." One of the difficulties in using the analytical problem solving approaches found in management science textbooks, however, is that they are predominantly quantitative approaches — incapable of incorporating the qualitative factors so important in vital decisions. We will, in this book, look at and resolve the quandary posed by the need to synthesize quantitative and qualitative factors in a decision process. We will come to understand what Albert Einstein meant when he said (in a letter to President Roosevelt) "Not everything that counts can be counted and not everything that can be counted, counts."

Decision-making ability is the most important business skill

Decision-making is undoubtedly the most difficult and most essential task a manager performs[4]. Executives rate decision-making ability as the most important business skill, but few people have the training they need to make good decisions consistently. In their excellent book, *Decision Traps*[5], Russo and Shoemaker point out that becoming a good decision-maker requires coaching just like becoming a good athlete. Coaches have learned that excellent athletic performance depends on techniques that *can* be taught. Some of these techniques are counter intuitive and therefore extremely difficult to learn by trial and error. Experienced golfers love to watch athletic baseball players step up to the tee and swing as hard as they can, only to miss the ball completely. A golf instructor can quickly teach the athletic baseball player what is not intuitive — that the left arm (for a right-hander) should be kept almost straight, unlike during a baseball swing, and that swinging easier will usually make the golf ball go further. Techniques like 'keeping your head down' (or 'eyes on the ball'), work well in several

---

[4] C. H. Kepner and B. B. Tregoe, B.B. *The Rational Manager: A Systematic Approach to Problem Solving and Decbision-Making,* McGraw Hill, New York, NY, 1965.

[5] Russo, J. Edward and Shoemaker, Paul J. H., *Decision Traps*, Doubleday, New York, N.Y., 1989.

been using it as well – so you may not have yet been at a competitive disadvantage. However, times are changing and many organizations have been abandoning the BOGSAT in favor of more capable methods. Before looking at these methods, lets first consider why BOGSAT decision-making is inadequate.

Cognitive limitations

Psychologists have proven time and time again that the human brain is limited in both its short-term memory capacity and its discrimination ability (channel capacity) to about seven things.[9] A BOGSAT discussion typically involves dozens of 'things', e.g., issues, alternatives, pros, cons, objectives, criteria, etc. Then what do we do?

Satisficing

Bazerman[10] points out that the economist's model of the rationality assumes that decision-makers following the following logical steps with perfect judgment:
1. Perfectly defining the problem
2. Knowing all relevant information
3. Identifying all criteria
4. Accurately weighting all the criteria according to his/her goals.
5. Accurately accessing each alternative on each criterion.
6. Accurately calculating and choosing the alternative with the highest value

However, Herbert Simon claims that humans lack both the knowledge and computational skills necessary to make decisions in a manner compatible with economic notions of rational behavior[11]. Simon refers to this as bounded rationality.

We argue that decision-making for *every* complex, crucial decision takes place under constraints of human information-processing limitations.

---

[9] See discussion on page 6.

[10] Max Bazerman, Max H., Max H., Max H., Max H., Max H. *Judgment In Managerial Decision Making*, John Wiley & Sons, 1986.

[11] Hogarth, Robin, *Judgment and Choice*, John Wiley & Sons, New York, 1987. p62.

What do people do when confronted with these limitations? Hogarth explains:

> "Simon has suggested several strategies that people use to reduce the cognitive demands of decision-making in order to make 'reasonable' decisions. First, people delimit the scope of the decision problem by imposing constraints, that, conceptually at least, can be thought of as eliminating whole regions of the payoff matrix. In other words, people consider only part of the total decision problem. Second, people simplify the evaluation of outcomes by, in essence, seeking to characterize whether outcomes are or are not acceptable. The key concept is that of an *aspiration level*. That is, prior to learning of the levels of outcomes that can be reached by taking different actions, the decision-maker is assumed to fix a level to which he or she aspires and which is acceptable. It is important to note that adopting aspiration levels reduces the need to search for information to evaluate alternatives and possible states of the world. This strategy therefore considerably reduces the need for and processing of information."

> "The use of aspiration levels is thus the primary mechanism by which people can reduce the costs of information processing and yet still act in a purposeful manner. However, the use of aspiration levels is not without its costs. In Simon's model, the aspiration level is a device used to simplify choice. Its use suggests a willingness to balance the quality of a decision against the cost, and frequently impossibility, of being able to engage in more extensive analysis."

The use of aspiration levels, or what Simon referred to as *satisficing*, is a non-compensatory decision-making approach because an alternative that does not meet one of the aspiration levels cannot compensate with superior performance with respect to other objectives. Satisficing is but one of the common simplistic strategies identified by Irving Janis, in his book *Crucial Decisions - Leadership in Policymaking and Crisis Management* [12].

Common Simplistic Strategies

Janis identified different categories of rules that people use as strategies to cope with their constraints. These include cognitive decision rules, affiliative decision rules, and self-serving / emotive rules.

---

[12] Irving L. Janis, *Crucial Decisions - Leadership in Policymaking and Crisis Management*, The Free Press, New York, N.Y., 1989.

Cognitive Decision Rules

Cognitive decision rules are used to cope with cognitive limitations of the human mind, insufficient time for deliberation, limited organizational resources for information gathering, and related problem-solving constraints. These rules, which simplify the intellectual tasks posed by complicated problems that confront executives who make important decisions, include:

Satisficing

Satisficing entails establishing aspiration levels and then settling for an alternative (often the first) that satisfies those aspiration levels. Suppose you were to relocate from the Midwest to the San Francisco area and wanted to purchase a house somewhat comparable to what you now have — a five bedroom, three bathroom house, on a 2 acre piece of land, 5 minute drive from work, in a very good school district. The estimated value of your house is $175K. You realize that a comparable house in San Francisco would be much more expensive, but your salary will be a bit larger after the move. When you visit San Francisco to look for a house, you are really disappointed. Four bedroom houses within a 15-minute commute are selling for $400K and up. So you begin adjusting your aspiration levels. Four bedroom houses within a 30-minute commute are selling for $350K and up. You really don't want to pay more than $300K. A Realtor shows you some houses priced around $300K, but they are 45 minutes drive from your new office. You say that is too far, how about three bedroom houses? You continue to adjust your aspiration levels, as a function of what you see available. When you 'finally' see a house that satisfies those aspiration levels, you make an offer (the Realtor tells you that if you don't make an offer right away, the house is likely to be sold to someone else.) A better strategy would be to continue to look until you find *several* houses that meet your objectives in different ways. One might be larger, but further from the office. Another might be newer but cost more. A decision considering the tradeoffs of alternatives is almost certain to result in a better choice.

Analogs and Adages

Why don't we do something similar to what we did last time a similar decision was made? Or, when in doubt, go with your first hunch. How often are crucial decisions made this way? What if the circumstances or the business environment has changed enough so that the analogy is no longer valid? What if the analogy is still valid, but the last decision was actually a poor choice that worked out well only by chance?

Nutshell Briefing

Busy top-level executives often ask for a 'nutshell' briefing, and then decide. How much can you fit in a nutshell? Perhaps not enough for a particularly crucial decision.

Incremental Change

Its very easy and comforting to stick closely to the last decision bearing on an issue, making only slight changes to take care of the most urgent aspects of the problem currently at hand. Easy, but dangerous for crucial decisions.

Consensus

It is desirable to achieve consensus on a decision so that those involved will make strong efforts to implement the decision. But for crucial decisions, consensus might not be enough to overcome the choice of a bad alternative.

Affiliative Decision Rules

Affiliative decision rules like avoiding punishment (the old CYA principle), following the party line, rigging meetings to suppress the opposition[13], and preserving group harmony are sometimes helpful for everyday decisions, but not for crucial decisions.

---

[13] The opposition might have some important insights that are valuable during the decision formulation and structuring stages — but not during the alternative evaluation stage.

Self Serving and Emotive Rules

Self serving and emotive rules like rely on gut feelings, retaliating (don't get mad, get even), we can do it! (even if its not the best thing to do), or Wow! Grab it before the opposition does it – are dangerous rules to use for crucial decisions.

Unimportant vs. Crucial Decisions

Janis concluded that "Relying on a few such rules of thumb might generally work out fairly well when making routine choices or dealing with minor relatively unimportant decisions; however, when executives rely upon such rules to make important decisions, they save time and effort at the cost of risking being stuck with an ill-conceived choice entailing disastrous consequences that could have been avoided."[14] We are not advising that the above common simplistic strategies be abandoned – many of them are not only useful, but also essential for the thousands of minor decisions each of us makes every day. However for *CRUCIAL DECISIONS*, they should be carefully avoided. This requires a *change* in the way crucial decisions are made in most organizations.

Unfreeze, change, refreeze

According to Lewin[15], in order for a *change* in a system to occur and last over time, it is necessary to (1) get the system to "unfreeze" (from existing processes), (2) change, and (3) "refreeze," making the change part of the system's standard repertoire. Without unfreezing and refreezing, change is not expected to take place successfully and last over time. In working with a Vice President of a Fortune 500 industrial firm, we helped initiate a change to the way resources were allocated to proposed R&D projects. The VP, while personally satisfied with the change, asked his staff what they thought of the new process. Most of the comments were "It's OK, but that's not the way we do things around here." Sticking with the new process, the

---

[14] Irving L. Janis, *Crucial Decisions*, Op. Cit.
[15] K. Lewin, (1947) Group decision and social change. In T. M. Newcomb and E.L. Hartley (Eds.), *Readings in social psychology*, New York: Holt, Rinehart and Winston.

next year comments changed to "Good process – we did it that way last year." The third year comments were "Fine – that's the way we've always done it."

Resistance to Change

But it is not easy to bring about change in the way executives address crucial decisions. Bazerman[16] noted that because many successful executives rose to the top using their intuitive strategies they are resistant to any information that his/her judgment is deficient in some observable manner. This judgment has usually included the intuitive use of common simplistic strategies for crucial decisions. Thus, while improving intuition should be an important activity for successful managers, cognitive resistance to change is a predictable pattern. Can this resistance be overcome? If so, how?

Requisites for Change

A crisis is necessary to induce successful, busy executives to change the way decisions are made. Unfortunately, crises are often not appreciated until it is too late. The number of Fortune 500 companies of twenty years ago that are no longer on the list, some of which are no longer in *existence*, is ample evidence. But the crises of today and tomorrow abound, such as budget cutbacks, increased competition from abroad, technological innovations, changing demographics and lifestyles.

Change to what? A methodological process that focuses on the *achievement of objectives*

It's easy to say we should change the way we make crucial decisions as individuals or in groups, but what should we change to? After studying the decision-making research and applications conducted over the past fifty years or so, the methodology that has emerged as theoretically sound,

---

[16] Max H. Bazerman, *Judgment In Managerial Decision Making*, John Wiley & Sons, 1986

practical, and widely successful, and the methodology we will focus on in this book, is called the Analytic Hierarchy Process (AHP).

In the late 1960's, Thomas Saaty, a world renowned mathematician, one of the pioneers of Operations Research, and author of the first Mathematical Methods of Operations Research textbook and the first queuing textbook, was directing research projects for the Arms Control and Disarmament Agency in the Department of State. His very generous budget allowed him to recruit some of the world's leading economists and game and utility theorists[17]. Saaty later recalled[18]:

> Two things stand out in my mind from that experience. The first is that the theories and models of the scientists were often too general and abstract to be adaptable to particular weapon tradeoff needs. It was difficult for those who prepared the U.S. position to include their diverse concerns and to come up with practical and sharp answers. The second is that the U.S. position was prepared by lawyers who had a great understanding of legal matters, but [who] were not better than the scientists in accessing the value of the weapon systems to be traded off.

Years later, Saaty was troubled by the communication difficulties he had observed between the scientists and lawyers and by the lack of any practical systematic approach for priority setting and decision-making. Having seen the difficulty experienced by the world's best scientists and lawyers, Saaty was motivated to attempt to develop a *simple* way to help ordinary people make complex decisions. The result was the Analytic Hierarchy Process (AHP). The most difficult thing about AHP is its title, so lets look at the meaning of each of three words, Analytic, Hierarchy, Process.

AHP focuses on *the achievement of objectives*. Its use will lead to "rational decisions" according to the following definition: A rational decision is one which best achieves the multitude of *objectives* of the decision maker(s). The key will be to focus on *objectives*, rather than alternatives, criteria or attributes.

---

[17] Three of whom, Gerard Debreu, John Harsanyi, and Reinhard Selten, have since won the Nobel Prize.
[18] Saaty, Thomas L., *Decision Making with Dependence and Feedback*, RWS Publications, Pittsburgh, PA, 1996, p 12.

The Analytic Hierarchy Process

Analytic

Analytic is a form of the word analysis, which means the separating of any material or abstract entity into its constituent elements. Analysis is the opposite of synthesis, which involves putting together or combining parts into a whole. Many organizations have departments or divisions with the word analysis in their title. We speak of financial analysis, marketing analysis, and process analysis. Organizations have become quite good at doing analysis. Few organizations, however, know how to synthesize! In a sense, AHP should really be called the *Synthesis* Hierarchy Process because at its core, AHP helps us measure and synthesize the multitude of factors involved in complex decisions.

Hierarchy

How can humans best deal with complexity? Herbert Simon, father of the field of Artificial Intelligence and Nobel laureate, writes:[19]

> "Large organizations are almost universally hierarchical in structure. That is to say, they are divided into units which are subdivided into smaller units, which are, in turn, subdivided and so on. Hierarchical subdivision is not a characteristic that is peculiar to human organizations. It is common to virtually all complex systems of which we have knowledge. The near universality of hierarchy in the composition of complex systems suggest that there is something fundamental in this structural principle that goes beyond the peculiarities of human organization. An organization will tend to assume hierarchical form whenever the task environment is complex relative to the problem-solving and communicating powers of the organization members and their tools. Hierarchy is the adaptive form for finite intelligence to assume in the face of complexity."

In his book on "Hierarchical Structures" L.L. Whyte expressed this thought as follows:

> "The immense scope of hierarchical classification is clear. It is the most powerful method of classification used by the human brain-mind in ordering experience, observations, entities and information. The use of

---

[19] Simon, Herbert A., *"The New Science of Management Decision"*, Harper and Brothers, New York, N.Y., 1960.

hierarchical ordering must be as old as human thought, conscious and unconscious." [20]

Process

A process is a series of actions, changes, or functions that bring about an end or result. The Analytic Hierarchy Process (AHP) is *not* a magic formula or model that finds the 'right' answer. Rather it is a process that helps decision-makers to find the 'best' answer. We will discuss AHP in more detail shortly.

---

[20] L.L. Whyte, *Hierarchical Structures*, American Elsevier, New York, N.Y., 1969.

Chapter 2

Problem Solving and Decision-Making

Problem Solving

For some, problems are opportunities in disguise. For others, problems cause worry. In his book, *How to Stop Worrying and Start Living,* Dale Carnegie included a chapter entitled "How to Eliminate Fifty Percent of Your Business Worries."[1] Rather than tell a story about a Mr. Jones, or a Mr. X, Carnegie relates the experience of a real person, Leon Shimkin, in Shimkin's own words. (Shimkin was a former partner and general manager of one of the foremost publishing houses in the United States: Simon and Schuster.)

"For fifteen years I spent almost half of every business day holding conferences, discussing problems. Should we do this or that—or nothing at all? We would get tense; twist in our chairs; walk the floor; argue and go around in circles. When night came, I would be utterly exhausted. I fully expected to go on doing this sort of thing for the rest of my life. I had been doing it for fifteen years, and it never occurred to me that there was a better way of doing it. If anyone had told me that I could eliminate three-fourths of the all the time I spent in those worried conferences, and three fourths of my nervous strain – I would have thought he was a wild-eyed, slap-happy, armchair optimist. Yet I devised a plan that did just that. I have been using this plan for eight years. It has performed wonders for my efficiency, my health, and my happiness. It sounds like magic – but like all magic tricks, it is extremely simple when you see how it is done.

Here is the secret: First, I immediately stopped the procedure I had been using in my conferences for fifteen years – a procedure that began with my troubled associates reciting all of the details of what had gone wrong, and ending up by asking: 'What shall we do?' Second, I made a new rule – a rule that everyone who wishes to present a problem to me must first prepare and submit a memorandum answering these four questions:

Question 1: *What is the problem?* (In the old days we used to spend an hour or two in a worried conference without anyone knowing specifically and concretely what the real problem was. We used to work ourselves into a lather discussing our troubles without ever trying to write out specifically what our problem was.)

---

[1] Carnegie, Dale, How to Stop Worrying and Start Living, 1944,1984 Pocket Books, New York, N.Y.

Question 2: *What is the cause of the problem?* (As I look back over my career, I am appalled at the wasted hours I have spent in worried conferences without every trying to find out clearly the conditions, which lay at the root of the problem).

Question 3: *What are all possible solutions of the problem?* (In the old days, one man in the conference would suggest one solution. Someone else would argue with him. Tempers would flare. We would often get clear off the subject, and at the end of the conference no one would have written down all the various things we could do to attack the problem.)

Question 4: *What solution do you suggest?* (I used to go into a conference with a man who had spent hours worrying about a situation and going around in circles without ever once thinking through all possible solutions and then writing down, 'This is the solution I recommend.')

My associates rarely come to me now with their problems. Why? Because they have discovered that in order to answer those four questions they have to get all the facts and think their problems through. And after they have done that they find, in three fourths of the cases, they don't have to consult me at all, because the proper solution has popped out like a piece of bread popping out from an electric toaster. Even in those cases where consultation is necessary, the discussion takes about one third the time formerly required, because it proceeds along an orderly, logical path to a reasoned conclusion."

Not only will better problem skills result in less worry; they will lead to more successful problem solving. In *Building Team Power*[2], Thomas Kayser suggests six steps for achieving problem solving success. The methodologies we present here will help you implement parts or all of these steps:

Step 1) Defining and selecting the problem. View the problem as a GAP or difference between the current condition (as is) and some future condition (what should be).

- DO specify the extent of the problem.
- DON'T include causes or solutions (yet).

---

[2] Thomas Kayser, Building Team Power, CRM Films, Carlsbad, CA, 1994, pp 223 -226.

Have the group brainstorm for 'as is' conditions that might be viewed as problems. Brainstorming and simple voting tools can be helpful here. More elaborate methodologies like AHP with criteria (objectives) such as control, importance, difficulty, time, return on investment, resources can be useful to prioritize the as is conditions.

Step 2) Analyzing the problem. Identify, collect, and analyze data to confirm the problem is real. Identify and prioritize possible causes for what exists. The use of fishbone diagrams and AHP models can be helpful.

Step 3) Generating potential solutions. This can be done many ways, including brainstorming, research (secondary and/or primary), and design activities. What "should be", expressed as objectives, should guide the generation of potential solutions. Creativity is important in this step. Never stop with only one solution – two or hopefully more potential solutions should be generated.

Step 4) Selecting and planning the solution. Deciding which solution to select should be based on the achievement of objectives. The use of AHP will be instrumental in this step.

Step 5) Implementing the solution. This step often leads to an embedded decision process—generating potential ways to implement the solution and selecting an implementation alternative based on the achievement of objectives.

Step 6) Evaluating the solution. Was the problem 'solved'? If so, was the problem solving process effective? If the problem was not solved, was it due to a deficiency in the problem solving process or to the occurrence of an unforeseen event? In retrospect, was the unforeseen event unlikely to have happened or should it have been considered in the problem solving process?

Decision Making

Decision-making, the focus of this book, is a part of almost all human endeavors. While most decisions are connected with problem solving, many are not. Managers may decide to take actions that will set entirely new standards of performance or decide to attain some new goal or establish a new direction for their companies[3]. We will see that most managerial activities such as problem solving, strategic planning, and resource allocation, involve one or more components of what we will now define as the decision-making process.

Intelligence, Design, Choice

We will follow what is perhaps the most widely accepted categorization of the decision-making process first introduced by Herbert Simon[4]. Simon's categorization of the decision-making process consists of three *phases*:
- Intelligence,
- Design, and
- Choice

The INTELLIGENCE phase involves the identification of the problem or opportunity.

The intelligence phase – identifying problems or opportunities – can involve a wide variety of activities, such as listening to people (your customers, competitors, employees, suppliers, etc.); environmental scanning and the query of internal or external data bases, either intermittently or continuously; brainstorming for gaps between current conditions (as is) and some future conditions (what should be); or performing an analysis of your organization's strengths, weaknesses, opportunities, and threats (SWOT). Operationally, it will make no difference whether you view something as a problem or an opportunity – what some people view as a problem; others might view as an opportunity. What some may view as a headache, others

---

[3] C. H. Kepner and B. B. Tregoe, B.B. The Rational Manager: A Systematic Approach to Problem Solving and Decision Making, McGraw Hill, New York, NY, 1965.
[4] Herbert A Simon, The New Science of Management Decision, (New York: Harper and Brothers, 1960), pp. 40-43.

design phase), a benefit-cost analysis[12] was conducted. The group that performed the analysis reported their results in the form of benefit/cost ratios. They were satisfied with their study, and were careful to point out in their report that the benefit-cost analysis included only those factors that could be quantified. (Qualitative factors tend to get relegated to footnotes.)

The decision-makers were left in a quandary. They understood that the benefit-cost analysis included only the quantitative factors, but knew instinctively that the "best" alternative according to the benefit-cost analysis was not the best for their purposes. The discrepancy arose because the qualitative considerations could not be included in the study and the decision-makers did not know how to synthesize their qualitative considerations with the quantitative benefit-cost analysis.

You have probably been involved in a decision where the numbers told you to do one thing but your intuition told you something else. As an individual you have the luxury to dismiss the numbers and "go with your intuition."[13] A corporate decision-making group or a U.S. Government agency cannot do this. What can they do?

One thing they can do is to "re-evaluate" the quantitative factors, collect more data, and hopefully find a way to have the quantitative results coincide with their intuition. Some may view this as cheating. It is not! Quantitative factors are not the only considerations. Qualitative factors may be just as important, or even more important than the quantitative factors. Decision-makers would be shirking their responsibility by deciding on the basis of the quantitative factors alone.

The other alternative is to dismiss the benefit-cost analysis and start all over again. The frustration at having to do this stems from the lack of ability to synthesize quantitative and qualitative factors.

---

[12]Benefit-Cost analysis is becoming a more popular expression than Cost-Benefit analysis. A tongue in cheek reason for the change in terminology is that it is impossible to divide by zero.

[13]There are also times when our intuition is wrong. T.L. Saaty gives the following example. Suppose we were to wrap a string snugly around the earth. The string would be about 25,000 miles long. Now suppose we cut the string and spliced in a ten-foot section and raised the string an equal distance above the earth all around its circumference. Would there be enough room for a mouse to crawl under the string? Most people's intuition would say no. A numerical calculation would tell you that not only would there be enough space for a mouse to crawl under the string anywhere around the circumference, but the string would be about 19 inches off the ground, enabling you to crawl under as well.

Many decision-makers resist having to conduct benefit-cost analyses. They argue that the time and expense of a benefit-cost study is not justified. This is only true for relatively small decisions. A second reason is that they view the study as necessary for satisfying some other department's purpose, but not really helpful in making the decision. Still another reason for such resistance is the hidden fear that the study may result in the quantitative supremacy of an alternative that the decision-makers "do not like." They (somewhat justifiably) view the benefit-cost analysis as a number crunching roulette wheel (sophisticated with present value calculations and the like) that could put them in an uncomfortable position. Consequently decision-makers turn their backs on benefit-cost analysis and attempt to make decisions using an intuitive synthesis of non-discounted costs and qualitative considerations. This fear would vanish if decision-makers had the ability to synthesize the quantitative benefit-cost analysis *with* their qualitative considerations. They would be able to capitalize on both the information generated by the benefit-cost analysis, and their knowledge and experience about the qualitative considerations. Thus, the ability to synthesize quantitative and qualitative factors in a decision is extremely important. We will see how this can be done shortly.

Objectivity vs. Subjectivity

Organizations like to think they make 'objective' decisions. Did you ever hear an executive tell someone "I'd like you to study this issue and give me a *subjective* recommendation?" Of course not. We use the word objective as if it meant correct. We claim that there are no objective crucial decisions! The proof is simple. As noted earlier, we have found that all important or crucial decisions have more than one objective. Economists like to think of measuring everything in dollars or dollar equivalents to try to force things into one dimension, but in practice, that doesn't work very well. The next time you are tempted to think of a decision on the basis of just one objective, say dollars, ask yourself, does time matter? What if you choose a low cost alternative but the time to implement is rather long? Does quality matter? Does public opinion matter?

In a decision with more than one objective, the relative importance of the objectives will influence the choice of the best alternative. Since every important decision has more than one objective, and since the relative importance of the objectives is *subjective,* every important decision is *subjective!* While this might at first seem contrary to what we were taught to believe, it is not inconsistent with other popular beliefs. Most people agree that *values* are subjective. What we are saying here is that all important decisions are influenced by our values (determining the relative importance of the objectives) and hence are subjective. Furthermore, many organizations recognize that hiring top quality people is important in being competitive. When we hire good people and pay them good salaries, why in the world would we ask them to make a decision or recommendation that is 'objective'? Wouldn't we want to capitalize on their 'subjectivity'?

Thomas Saaty, creator of the Analytic Hierarchy Process claims, (only half tongue in cheek), that objectivity is nothing more than agreed upon subjectivity!

Linear versus Non-Linear

Another aspect of decision-making that is often overlooked is the need to take into account non-linearities. Instead of a mathematical definition or example, consider the following situation. A hungry teenager goes to the Pizza shop for lunch. The first slice of pizza tastes great. The second slice tastes almost as good as the first, but not quite. The third slice is not nearly as good tasting as the second. Even for a hungry teenager, there comes a point when additional slices or pizza have no utility.

Two dollars, to most people, can buy twice what one dollar can, four dollars can buy twice what two dollars can, and so the 'utility' curve for money is linear when we consider small amounts. But what happens when we consider 2 million dollars versus 1 million dollars? Or 2 billion dollars compared to 1 billion? Eventually, the utility curve becomes non-linear. Even the U.S. Government would most likely have a non-linear utility curve at dollar values in the tens of trillions!

There is a tendency, when making decisions, to put too much emphasis on 'hard data'. Data, from a scientific instrument, for example, may have been costly to obtain and is 'objective', so why 'corrupt' it with human judgment? This is generally short-sighted and should be avoided.

We have defined a rational decision as one that best meets our objectives. In the process of evaluating alternatives to see which is best, we will have to consider the utility (we will call it preference) of each alternative relative to each of our objectives. In general, these utilities will be non-linear and whatever methodology we use must take this into account. Note, that this is yet another reason why important decisions are always subjective—the utility of an alternative with respect to a given objective is often (perhaps always?) subjective!

Chapter 3

Decision-making Concepts & Methodologies

Alternatives - Pros and Cons

Perhaps the most common 'formal' approach to making a choice among alternatives is to list the pros and cons of each alternative. A list of pros and cons is often embedded in a memorandum with a format shown below:

From:
To:
Issue: (i.e. problem or opportunity)
Alternative 1:
Pros:
Cons:
Alternative 2:
Pros:
Cons:

A meeting is then held to discuss the alternatives and their pros and cons.[1]

The meeting is relatively unstructured and the discussion jumps from topic to topic in a haphazard way. Some relevant points are discussed several times, some not at all. Frustration develops as "strong" members of the group dominate the discussion, often far beyond the level justified by their knowledge and experience. Shy members of the group may fail to speak at all, even though they may have important information to convey.

A decision is "made" either when it appears that no more progress is forthcoming, or when it is time to go to another meeting (or lunch), or time to go home for the day. This haphazard approach to decision-making is far too common. Even a small change in the decision process to a structured discussion of each alternative's pros and cons would be a vast improvement. Time would not be wasted by jumping back and forth, discussing some

---

[1] Decisions are often made without even this much preparation. A meeting may be held to make a decision without any serious attempt to identify alternatives or list their pros, and cons.

points over and over again, and inadvertently failing to discuss some issues at all.

However, even if we conducted a structured discussion, it is still not clear how to make the decision. Certainly it would be <u>wrong</u> to calculate the net number of pros over cons for each alternative and then select the alternative with the largest net number because the relative importance of the pros and cons differ. How then can one proceed?

Benjamin Franklin considered this problem over two hundred fifty years ago.

In a letter addressed to Priestly[2], Franklin explained how he analyzed his decisions:

> Dear Sir: In the affair of so much importance to you, where in you ask my advice, I cannot, for want of sufficient premises, advise you what to determine, but if you please I will tell you how. When those difficult cases occur, they are difficult, chiefly because while we have them under consideration, all the reasons pro and con are not present to the mind at the same time; but sometimes one set present themselves, and at other times another, the first being out of sight. Hence the various purposes or information that alternatively prevail, and the uncertainty that perplexes us. To get over this, my way is to divide a sheet of paper by a line into two columns; writing over the one Pro, and over the other Con. Then, during three or four days consideration, I put down under the different heads short hints of the different motives, that at different times occur to me, for or against the measure. When I have thus got them all together in one view, I endeavor to estimate their respective weights; and when I find two, one on each side, that seem equal, I strike them both out. If I find a reason pro equal to some two reasons con, I strike out the three. If I judge some two reasons con, equal to three reasons pro, I strike out the five; and thus proceeding I find at length where the balance lies; and if, after a day or two of further consideration, nothing new that is of importance occurs on either side, I come to a determination accordingly. And, though the weight of the reasons cannot betaken with the precision of algebraic quantities, yet when each is thus considered, separately and comparatively, and the whole lies before me, I think I can judge better, and am less liable to make a rash step, and in fact I have found great advantage from this kind of equation, and what might be called moral or

---

[2] Letter from Benjamin Franklin to Joseph Priestly in 1772, is taken from: "Letter to Joseph Priestly", Benjamin Franklin Sampler, (1956).

```
┌─────────────────────────────────────────────────────────────────┐
│                                                                   │
│            A Fighter Aircraft Selection Problem                   │
│                                                                   │
│                           Attributes                              │
│                                                                   │
│                                                                   │
│  Alternatives        Maximum  Ferry    Acquisition Reliability    Maneuverability │
│             speed    range    payload  cost                       │
│                                                                   │
│  (Al)       (Mach)   (NM)     (pounds) ($ x 10 7) (high-low) (high-low) │
│  A1         2.0      1500     20000    5.5        average   very high │
│  A2         2.5      2700     18000    6.5        low       average  │
│  A3         1.8      2000     21000    4.5        high      high    │
│  A4         2.2      1800     20000    5.0        average   average │
│                                                                   │
└─────────────────────────────────────────────────────────────────┘
```

Alternatives	speed (Mach)	Maximum range (NM)	Ferry payload (pounds)	Acquisition cost ($ x 10^7)	Reliability (high-low)	Maneuverability (high-low)
(Al)	(Mach)	(NM)	(pounds)	($ x 10^7)	(high-low)	(high-low)
A1	2.0	1500	20000	5.5	average	very high
A2	2.5	2700	18000	6.5	low	average
A3	1.8	2000	21000	4.5	high	high
A4	2.2	1800	20000	5.0	average	average

Figure 1 – Fighter Aircraft Selection Problem

prudential algebra. Wishing sincerely that you may determine for the best, I am ever, my dear friend, yours most affectionately.

Franklin's insights were far beyond his time. He sensed that the human brain is limited in the number of factors that can be kept in mind at any one time. Psychologists discovered this in the mid twentieth century. He knew enough not to rush an important decision, but to devote several days to the study of the pros and cons, attempting to make tradeoffs based on relative importance.[3] And he tried to develop a "moral or prudential" algebra, recognizing that some way of measuring qualitative as well as quantitative factors was necessary in the decision process. Not only was Franklin far ahead of his time, but his decision process is superior to that used by the vast majority of today's decision makers who fool themselves into thinking that they can make a good decision after a few hours of unstructured discussion and some "hard" thought.

---

[3] Relative comparisons are a key component of the Analytic Hierarchy Process (AHP), developed two hundred fifty years later.

Although Franklin was able to reduce the number of factors (pros and cons) under consideration by a process of cancellation, he could not complete a decision analysis because of his inability to "measure" the remaining factors. We have had significant advancements in the meaning and use of numbers and measurement since Franklin's time. However, our use of numbers and measurement can sometimes be misleading or even *wrong*.

Consider the Fighter Aircraft Selection Problem illustrated in Figure 1.

Attributes[4] are shown for four fighter alternatives. How would you decide which alternative is best? Of course, the answer depends on many things not specified, such as who your enemies are, how far away are they, what planes do they have or are expected to have, and so on. But even if you knew all of these things, how would you decide? How would you 'weight' the importance of each attribute? Can you use the 'data' without applying judgment? Is a plane that can fly 2.5 Mach only 2.5/2.2 times as preferable with respect to speed as one that can fly 2.2 Mach? How would you combine performance on speed, range, payload and cost? Many people erroneously think that just by normalizing each attribute on a similar scale, such as 0 to 100, they can just multiply attribute values by weights and add. What would you do with the qualitative attributes, such as maneuverability?

Consider the following study by a Washington D.C. based think tank:

The study attempted to evaluate 100 cities in the United States in terms of their attractiveness to minorities. The evaluation was performed with a matrix of seven columns and 100 rows. Each column represented a factor, such as employment or housing. Each row represented a city. The study (somehow) ranked each of the 100 cities for each of the factors. The city considered best for a particular factor was "given" a 1 while the city considered the worst was "given" a 100. The numbers in each row were then added to obtain a total score for each city. The cities were then ranked by their "attractiveness" scores, with a low score being more attractive than a high score.

---

[4] We will deviate from this approach and focus on objectives rather than attributes

Several things are wrong with this "evaluation". Take a minute and write down what you think is wrong.

Most people will immediately note that the factors received equal weight. While this is indeed generally inappropriate (we will consider how factors can be "weighted" later) there are even more serious errors involving the misuse of numbers.

Misuse of Numbers

Not weighting the factors was an error of omission and is often fairly obvious. A more serious error, one of commission rather than omission, and one that is more likely to go unnoticed, is the inappropriate addition of ranks. The "scores" in the above example are "ordinal" numbers, representing rank, but nothing more. It is just plain wrong to add these numbers. Any results are meaningless!

How can we identify such mistakes? By thinking about the meaning of the numbers. A city "scoring" a 1 on salary is ranked better than a city "scoring" a 2, but how much better? Is the interval between cities ranked 1 and 2 the same as the interval between cities ranked 21 and 22? Not necessarily. The city ranked first might be ten thousand dollars higher than the city ranked second, while the interval between the 21st and 22nd cities might be only fifty dollars. The numbers in this study are, according to Stevens' classification scheme[5,6,7], ordinal in nature and cannot be added.

In the 1990 edition of *Retirement Places Rated*, author David Savageau ranked 151 retirement places on each of seven criteria and then added the ranks to determine an overall ranking. Using this methodology, Las Vegas Nevada came in 105th. In the next (1994) edition of *Retirement Places Rated* Savageau improved his methodology by 'scoring' (instead of ranking) 183 cities on the seven criteria and then averaging the scores to determine an overall score. This time, Las Vegas came in first! (See page 115 for details).

[5] S.S. Stevens, "On the Theory of Scales of Measurement", Science, (103, 1946), pp. 677-680.
[6] F.S. Roberts, Measurement Theory with Applications to decision-making, Utility and the Social Sciences, (London, Addison Wesley, 1979).
[7] Jean Claude Vansnick, "Measurement Theory and Decision Aid", Proceedings of the Third International Summer School on Multiple Criteria Decision Methods, Applications and Software, (Monte Estoril, Portugal: July 1988).

The misuse of numbers is one reason that numerical analyses are sometimes flawed. Unfortunately, decision models based on flawed numerical reasoning[8] may go undetected, leaving the decision-maker left wondering why the results do not make sense. It is any wonder that some of our top-level executives are somewhat suspicious of numerical analyses such as this? But the misuse of numbers is not a reason to forego using them. We just must be careful that a sound theoretical foundation exists for whatever we do.

In order to avoid making such errors, we will take a brief detour and review what is known as levels of measurement. Let us briefly look at Stevens' categorization.

Levels of Measurement

According to Stevens' categorization, there are four levels of measurement. The levels, ranging from lowest to highest are Nominal, Ordinal, Interval, and Ratio. Each level has all of the meaning of the levels below plus additional meaning.

Nominal[9]

Nominal numbers, the lowest level in terms of the meaning conveyed, are just numerical representations for names. Nominal numbers are used for identification purposes only and imply nothing about the ordering. Telephone numbers and social security numbers are nominal. Are you 'older' or 'better' than someone else because your telephone number is higher? Obviously not, and people rarely make mistakes with nominal numbers. However, errors arising from the misuse of ordinal numbers are not so rare as we will see next.

---

[8] Tom R. Houston, "Why Models Go Wrong", Byte Magazine, (October 1985), pp. 151.
[9] A mathematical definition of nominal is: admits any one - to - one substitution of assigned numbers.

Ordinal[10]

Ordinal numbers[11], as the name suggests, implies an order or ranking among elements. The order may be either increasing or decreasing depending on the application. For example, we could order or rank cities based on population by ranking the city with the highest population as #1, or by ranking the city with the lowest population #1. A ranking implies an ordering among elements but nothing more. It does not imply anything about the differences (or intervals) between items. For example, if we know only that a professional baseball team finished in second place at the end of the season, we do not know if the team was one game behind the first place team or twenty games behind. Care must be taken not to add or multiply ordinal data. Errors arising from the addition of ordinal data are far too common.

Interval[12]

Interval scale data possesses the meaning of Nominal and Ordinal data, as well as having meaning about the intervals between objects. Corresponding intervals on different parts of an interval scale have the same meaning. If we have interval level data then we can infer that the interval between two objects with values of 20 and 5 (an interval of 15) is equivalent to the interval between two objects with values of 80 and 65. Interval level data can be used in arithmetic operations such as addition and multiplication. However, after adding interval level data, one can not infer that a total of 100 is twice as good as a total of 50. If one were to allocate resources based on this inference, then the allocation would be incorrect.

---

[10] A mathematical definition of ordinal is: can be transformed by any increasing monotonic function.
[11] Ordinal numbers are sometimes referred to as rank numbers. Likert scales used in many marketing studies are ordinal numbers.
[12] A mathematical definition of interval is: can be subjected to a linear transformation, or is invariant under the transformation $Y = a X + b$.

Ratio[13]

Ratio level data (sometimes called ratio scale) is the highest level, having Nominal, Ordinal, and Interval properties, as well as the property of ratios. Corresponding ratios on different parts of a ratio scale have the same meaning. If we have ratio scale data, then the ratio between two objects with values of 100 and 50 is equivalent to the ratio of two objects with values of 6 and 3. A ratio scale is often defined as one having a true zero point. However, for our purposes, it is easier to think of a ratio scale as one for which equivalent ratios are considered equal. Temperature measured on the Fahrenheit scale is <u>not</u> a ratio measure, since there we would be wrong to infer that there is twice as much heat when the temperature is 80 degrees as when the temperature is 40 degrees. (If we used the Kelvin scale, which has the ratio property, then such an inference would be correct.)

Numbers at the Racetrack[14]

Suppose the owner of a horse-racing stable is interested in buying a particular horse. He studies the results of the horse's last five races. Let's consider the numbers used to designate the results of a particular race.

The number worn on the horse and jockey is *nominal*—it identified the horse so that people at the track could look in the racing form to see the horse's name, owner, etc. The number conveys no information about the horse's *order* of finish in the race.

The finishing position for each horse is *ordinal*. The first place horse finished ahead of the second place horse, the second place horse finished ahead of the third place horse, and so on. Knowing that this horse finished first, however conveys no information about how far in front, or the *interval* to the second place horse.

The number of lengths to the next finisher is an *interval* measure. Knowing that the horse finished first by 15 lengths as opposed to 5 lengths is important information not conveyed by the order of finish alone. However, even this measure may not tell us as much as what we want to know.

---

[13] A mathematical definition of ratio is: admits multiplication by a constant, or is invariant under the transformation $Y = a X$. A ratio scale is said to have a true 'zero', however the true zero can be conceptual and need not be observable.

[14] Thanks to Chuck Cox of Compass Associates for this example.

Suppose the horse finished first by 15 lengths in a 2-½ mile race. Is this as strong as finishing first by 15 lengths in a ½ mile race? No. More information would be conveyed if we knew the *ratios* of the times of the first and second place finishes.

Mathematical operations allowed:

Nominal, ordinal, interval, ratio – succeeding scales have additional meaning and can be used in more arithmetic operations as summarized below:

- Addition/subtraction and multiplication/division require at least interval level meaning.
- An interval level number can be multiplied by a constant or a ratio level number but cannot be multiplied by another interval level number.
- There are no restrictions when using ratio level numbers.
- A decision method that produces ratio scale numbers is the most flexible and accurate.

How can you know the level of measure in your numbers?

Although measurements from scientific instruments are often ratio scale, the level of measurement in most social and decision contexts depends on the intent of the subject responding to a question or making a judgment. One need not take a college course to learn how to tell the difference between Nominal, Ordinal, Interval, and Ratio scales. Rather, one needs to ask the question: *What meaning does this data have for the purpose at hand?* For example, if you asked someone to express a preference on a scale of 1 to 5, and they specify a 4 for one item, a 3 for a second item, a 2 for a third item, and a 1 for a fourth item, you can easily infer that the values possess the ordinal property. Whether or not the data possesses the interval property depends on the respondent's intent and understanding of the numbers. The scores would have the interval property only if the subject's intent or understanding was that corresponding intervals are equivalent, e.g., the interval between 1 and 2 is equal to the interval between 4 and 5. Likewise the scores would have the ratio property only if the respondent's intent was, for example, that a score of 5 is five times better than a score of 1. If the respondent's intent was not interval or ratio, the numerical response possesses only the ordinal property. Interval or ratio properties are often assumed for scales with little or no justification. In most graduate schools the letter grade of 'A' represents excellent work, 'B' represents good work, while 'C' is almost failing. The implied interval between an 'A' and a 'B' is much smaller than the interval between a 'B' and a 'C'. But grade point averages are calculated by assigning 4 to an A, 3 to a B, and 2 to a C - which incorrectly measures the interval between an 'A' and 'B' as the same as between a 'B' and 'C'. Furthermore, the grade point average assumes that a 'A' is 1.333 times better than a 'B' and that an 'A' is twice as good as a 'C'. While the former ratio might be reasonable, the latter certainly is not - a 'A' is probably more like 10 or 50 times better than a 'C'. The only conclusion we can draw is that the grade point average calculation is mathematically meaningless! Later we will show how easy it is to obtain ratio level measurement for both quantitative as well as qualitative factors using the Analytic Hierarchy Process.

Let's pause to see where we are and where we are going. We looked at what is perhaps the most common approach to making a choice among alternatives, listing their pros and cons. We then looked at how Benjamin Franklin ingeniously traded off some of the pros and cons, reducing the problem to one of more manageable size. We took a small detour and looked at how we might be lured into misusing numbers if, in an attempt to carry the evaluation process further, we introduce and manipulate numbers without regard to their underlying level of measurement. Let's continue and see how numbers can be used (with care) in a scheme often referred to as weights and scores.

Table 1 – Typical Weights and Scores Matrix

	Crit. 1	Crit. 2	Crit. 3	Crit. 4	Crit. 5	Crit. 6	...	Crit. 7
Weights	80	40	25	90	3	1	...	17
Alt. 1	5	10	2	9	etc.			
Alt. 2								
Alt. 3								
Alt. 4								
....								

Weights and Scores

The typical weights and scores approach consists of a matrix with criteria as column headings and alternatives as rows[15] as shown in Table 1. Criteria are "assigned" weights using a scale such as 0 to 10 or 0 to 100. Then each alternative is scored against each criterion in a similar fashion. The alternative scores for each criterion are then multiplied by the weight for the criterion and summed to give a total score for each alternative

This score represents the overall preference for or performance of the alternative. *If* used carefully, weights and scores can be an effective methodology. There are, however, several practical difficulties:

First of all, when assigning weights, what do the numbers really mean? On a scale of 0 to 100, what is an 80, or what is a 40? When you "give" an 80 to one criterion and "give" a 40 to another, do you really mean that the 80 is twice as important as the 40? If the answer is yes, then the weights possess the ratio scale property. But how can you be consistent enough to insure this if you are dealing with 20, 30 or 100 criteria? If you assigned an 80 to the first criterion and later assign a weight of 10 to the 95th criterion, can you remember what you did earlier and do you really mean that the 95th criterion is only one eighth as important as the first criterion?

---

[15] Sometimes criteria are shown in rows and alternatives in columns.

Channel capacity and short term memory

Experiments have proven time and time again that the human brain is limited in both its short-term memory capacity and its discrimination ability (channel capacity) to about seven things.

According to James Martin[16], if a person "has to choose from a range of 20 alternatives, he will give inaccurate answers because the range exceeds the bandwidth of his channel for perception. In many cases, seven alternatives are the approximate limit of his channel capacity." Martin's conclusion is based on the results of numerous psychological experiments, including the well known study "The Magical Number Seven, Plus or Minus Two: Some Limits on Our Capacity for Information Processing," by G. A. Miller.[17] It has been demonstrated time and time again that humans are not capable of dealing accurately with more than about seven to nine things at a time, and we are just fooling ourselves if we try. To demonstrate this to yourself, have a friend make up a seven digit number and read the digits to you. After hearing the last digit, try to write down each of the seven digits in sequence. You will probably be able to do so without a mistake. Now try it with nine digits. You probably will <u>not</u> be able to recall the digits without a mistake. (If you did, you are above average as only about 11% of the population can recall 9 items from their short term memory — now try it with eleven digits!). Although we do not like to admit it, our brains are quite limited in certain respects.

Not only have psychologists demonstrated that humans have difficulty dealing with more than about seven plus or minus two factors at a time, but there is a mathematical basis for this phenomenon. Thomas Saaty, has shown that to maintain reasonable consistency when deriving priorities from

---

[16] James Martin, *Design of Man*-Computer *Dialogues*, (Englewood Cliffs, New Jersey: Prentice-Hall, Inc., 1973).

[17] G.A. Miller, "The Magical Number Seven, Plus or Minus Two: Some Limits on Our Capacity for Information Processing." *Psychological Review*, (Vol. 63, No. 2, March 1956), pp. 81-97. The distribution is a bell shaped curve with an average of 7. Obviously some people can recall more than seven, some fewer. But only about 11 percent of the population can recall 9 things from their short term memory, still fewer 10 things, and so on.

paired comparisons, n, the number of factors being considered must be less or equal to nine.[18]

Need for Hierarchical Structure

Suppose we try to assign weights to 20, 30 or 100 columns; there are bound to be many mistakes! We can cope with this complexity as we do with other complex situations - by arranging the criteria into groups[19], each group having sub-groups, and so on. This "hierarchical" arrangement has been found to be the best way for human beings to cope with complexity. (See page 13).

Humans have had to <u>learn</u> how to deal with complexity. We discover this time and time again. For example, if you try to recall a sequence of nine or eleven digits as someone reads them, you will probably find yourself grouping (psychologists call this chunking) the digits into groups in an effort to overcome the limitations of your short-term memory. If you prepare a presentation with ten or fifteen bullet items, you will probably find yourself organizing them into categories and sub-categories each with nine or fewer elements so that you do not lose your audience).

Orders of magnitude

Another problem arises when a weights and scores approach involves more than a handful of criteria (columns). Some of the criteria might be "orders of magnitude" more important than others. For example, if one criterion is assigned a .02 on a scale of 0 to 10, and another is assigned a 9, do we really mean that one is 450 times more important than another? Our ability to accurately compare things that differ by orders of magnitude is not nearly as good as our ability to compare things that differ by less than an order of magnitude. A hierarchical grouping avoids this problem as well.

---

[18] Saaty, T.L., The Analytic Hierarchy Process, New York, N.Y., McGraw Hill, 1980, reprinted by RWS Publications, Pittsburgh, 1996, p. 195.
[19] Groups of seven or fewer if we do not want to exceed our capabilities.

Arbitrary assignment

Another difficulty with the weights and scores methodology stems from the "assignment" of weights and scores in what often appears to be an arbitrary fashion. How can we justify that a criterion (such as customer perception) was "given" an 8? What does the 8 really mean? Certainly, we can refer to studies and experience with similar decisions to show how important the criterion is, but why "assign" an 8? Why not a 7, or a 9? Similarly, when scoring a particular alternative with respect to a criterion such as customer perception, we may refer to customer interview studies and past experience and "assign" a 3. But what does the 3 really mean?

Absolute versus relative

This difficulty is due to two causes. The first is the weighing and scoring in an absolute fashion rather than a relative fashion[20]. The second is the implied precision of numbers in situations where we know the precision is not justified. We can lift two objects, one in each hand and estimate that one is 2.7 times heavier than the other, or we can look at two houses and estimate that one house should cost 1.5 times the other. But do we expect that the implied precision of our estimates (e.g. 2.7 rather than 2.5 or 2.8) is appropriate or justifiable? And suppose we had to compare the relative importance of employee moral with customer satisfaction. How can we justify <u>any</u> specific number that we might think of?

Words instead of numbers

Justification would be much easier if we use a less precise way of expressing judgments, such as words instead of numbers. Suppose we were to use words instead of numbers. Words are often easier to justify than numbers. For example, if you say that, with respect to corporate image, alternative A is 3 times more preferable than alternative B, can you justify why it is exactly 3? Why not 2.9, or 3.1? But if you said, instead, that A is

---

[20] Martin observed that there are several ways of increasing our effective channel capacity. One of these is to enable the subject to make relative rather than absolute judgments.

"moderately" more preferable than B, this can be justified with a variety of arguments, including, perhaps, some hard data.

But what can you do with the 'words'?

But what then do you do with verbal judgments such as "moderate"? Words have different meanings to different people. True, anyone can put arbitrary numbers behind words in a computer program. But will the numbers "accurately" reflect the meaning the words had to the individual or group making the judgments?

Even if the decision-maker specifies numerical equivalencies for words, will he or a group of his colleagues consistently remember the assignments accurately enough to insure that the results reflect their actual judgments? Will "errors" due to the use of imprecise words be a problem?

Chapter 4

The Analytic Hierarchy Process and Expert Choice

The Analytic Hierarchy Process

The analytic hierarchy process (AHP), developed at the Wharton School of Business by Thomas Saaty[1], allows decision makers to model a complex problem in a hierarchical structure showing the relationships of the goal, objectives (criteria), sub-objectives, and alternatives (See Figure 1). Uncertainties and other influencing factors can also be included.

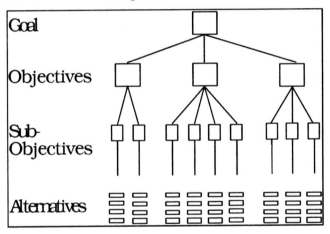

Figure 1 – Decision Hierarchy

AHP allows for the application of data, experience, insight, and intuition in a logical and thorough way. AHP enables decision-makers to *derive* ratio scale priorities or weights as opposed to arbitrarily *assigning* them. In so doing, AHP not only supports decision-makers by enabling them to structure complexity and exercise judgment, but allows them to incorporate both

[1] Saaty, T.L., The Analytic Hierarchy Process, New York, N.Y., McGraw Hill, 1980, reprinted by RWS Publications, Pittsburgh, 1996.

objective and subjective considerations in the decision process[2]. AHP is a compensatory decision methodology because alternatives that are deficient with respect to one or more objectives can compensate by their performance with respect to other objectives. AHP is composed of several previously existing but unassociated concepts and techniques such as hierarchical structuring of complexity, pairwise comparisons, redundant judgments, an eigenvector[3] method for deriving weights, and consistency considerations. Although each of these concepts and techniques were useful in and of themselves, Saaty's synergistic combination of the concepts and techniques (along with some new developments) produced a process whose power is indeed far more than the sum of its parts.

With the introduction of its PC implementation, Expert Choice[4], the number and diversity of AHP applications has grown rapidly[5]. As of 1995, Expert Choice was being used in 57 countries throughout the world and there were over 1000 journal and other citations about AHP. The International Society of the Analytic Hierarchy Process[6] conducts meetings every two or three years throughout the world (the first meeting was held in Tianjin, China).

The ability for AHP to enhance the (evaluation and) choice phase of decision-making is well known. What is not as well known, however, is AHP's utility in *any* facet of problem solving and decision-making that involves evaluation and measurement. Forecasting is one such area. In the process of evaluating the alternatives to a decision, it often becomes apparent that the outcomes of one or more of alternative courses of action are uncertain. AHP can be used to measure the relative impact of numerous influencing factors on the possible outcomes and, in so doing, forecast (derive the distribution of relative likelihoods of) outcomes. These forecasts are then used when evaluating the alternative courses of action. Another

---

[2] Forman, E.H., "The Analytic Hierarchy Process as a Decision Support System," *Proceedings of the IEEE Computer Society* (Fall, 1983).
[3] Eigenvectors will be discussed later.
[4] Ernest H. Forman, Thomas L, Saaty, Mary Ann Selly, Rozann Waldron, *Expert Choice*, Decision Support Software, McLean, VA, 1983.
[5] F. Zahedi, The Analytic Hierarchy Process- A Survey of the Method and its Applications. *Interfaces*, (Vol. 16, 1986), pp. 96-108.
[6] Located on the Internet at http://ahp.net/www/ahp/support/ahp_disc.html

area of application of AHP beyond the choice phase of decision-making is in resource allocation. These, as well as other applications, will be addressed in this book.

Beyond Weights and Scores

The Analytic Hierarchy Process overcomes the problems with weights and scores approaches discussed above. This is done by structuring complexity as a hierarchy and by deriving ratio scale measures through pairwise *relative* comparisons. The pairwise comparison process can be performed using words, numbers, or graphical bars, and typically incorporates redundancy, which results in a reduction of measurement error as well as producing a measure of consistency of the comparison judgments.

Humans are much more capable of making relative rather than absolute judgments. The use of redundancy permits accurate priorities to be <u>derived</u> from verbal judgments even though the words themselves are not very accurate[7]. This opens up a new world of possibilities—we can use words to compare qualitative factors and derive ratio scale priorities that can be combined with quantitative factors!

Weights or priorities are not arbitrarily "assigned".

By using the AHP pairwise comparison process, weights or priorities are <u>derived</u> from a set of judgments[8]. While it is difficult to justify weights that are arbitrarily assigned, it is relatively easy to justify judgments and the basis (hard data, knowledge, experience) for the judgments. These weights or priorities are ratio level measures[9], not counts. In a Wall Street Journal article, "We Need to Measure, Not Count", Peter Drucker emphasized the need for measuring as opposed to counting[10]:

---

[7] Expert Choice also has a numerical mode, which, for numerical aspects of a problem would be even more "accurate". But it is not always appropriate to use numbers in such a direct fashion because priorities derived directly from accurately measured factors do not take into account the decision makers utility!

[8] Expressed either verbally, numerically, or graphically.

[9] See pages 34.

[10] Peter F. Drucker, "We Need to Measure, Not Count", *The Wall Street Journal* *Tuesday*, April 13, 1993.

"Quantification has been the rage in business and economics these past 50 years. Accountants have proliferated as fast as lawyers. Yet we do not have the measurements we need.

Neither our concepts nor our tools are adequate for the control of operations, or for managerial control. And, so far, there are neither the concepts nor the tools for business control - i.e., for economic decision-making. In the past few years, however, we have become increasingly aware of the need for such measurements...".

Furthermore, the priorities that are derived from judgments automatically incorporate the necessary non-linearities in measuring utility. For example, when considering a vehicle for city driving, the preference for a vehicle with a top speed of 40 miles per hour is probably more than twice that of a vehicle with a top speed of 20 miles per hour. But the preference for a vehicle with a top speed of 100 miles per hour would be much less than twice as preferable than a vehicle with a top speed of 50 miles per hour. When organizations lack the ability to measure, including non-linearities and utilities, they sometimes resort to counting as a poor substitute. "How many articles do I need for tenure?", a junior faculty member often asks. Depending on the contribution, perhaps just one, a wise Full Professor answers! The Analytic Hierarchy Process provides the ability to measure.

Inconsistency

The theory of AHP does <u>not</u> demand perfect consistency.

AHP allows inconsistency, but provides a measure of the inconsistency in each set of judgments. This measure is an important by-product of the process of deriving priorities based on pairwise comparisons. It is natural for people to want to be consistent. Being consistent is often thought of as a prerequisite to clear thinking. However, the real world is hardly ever perfectly consistent and we can learn new things only by allowing for some inconsistency with what we already know.

If we are perfectly consistent (as measured with an AHP inconsistency ratio of zero), we can <u>not</u> say that our judgments are good, just as we can not say that there is nothing wrong with us physically if our body temperature is 98.6 degrees. On the other hand, if our inconsistency is say 40 or 50% (an inconsistency ratio of 100% is equivalent to random judgments), we <u>can</u> say there is something wrong, just as we can say that there is something wrong if our body temperature is 104 degrees.

An inconsistency ratio of about 10% or less is usually considered "acceptable", but the particular circumstance may warrant the acceptance of a higher value[11]. Let us look at some of the reasons why inconsistency occurs as well as the useful information that the inconsistency ratio conveys, and ways to reduce it.

Causes of Inconsistency

Clerical Error

The most common cause of inconsistency is a clerical error. When entering one or more judgments into a computer, the wrong value, or perhaps the inverse of what was intended is entered. Clerical errors can be very detrimental and often go undetected in many computer analyses[12]. When using Expert Choice, one can easily find and correct such errors.

Lack of Information

A second cause of inconsistency is lack of information. .If one has little or no information about the factors being compared, then judgments will appear to be random and a high inconsistency ratio will result[13]. Sometimes we fool ourselves into thinking that we know more than we really do. It is useful to find out that a lack of information exists, although sometimes we might be willing to proceed without immediately spending time and money gathering additional information in order to ascertain if the additional information is likely to have a significant impact on the decision.

---

[11] For example, a body temperature of 100 degrees may be taken as normal if we know that the person has just completed a 26 mile marathon on a hot, sunny day.

[12] For example, just one clerical error in a multiple regression of one million data points can cause the resulting regression parameter estimates to be considerably different.

[13] That is unless one <u>attempts</u> to hide the lack of information by making judgments that appear to be consistent. One is reminded of Ralph Waldo Emerson's saying, "Foolish consistency is the hobgoblin of small minds".

Lack of Concentration

Another cause of inconsistency is lack of concentration during the judgment process. This can happen if the people making judgments become fatigued[14] or are not really interested in the decision.

Real World Is Not Always Consistent

Still another cause of a high inconsistency ratio is an actual lack of consistency in whatever is being modeled. The real world is rarely perfectly consistent and is sometimes fairly inconsistent. Professional sports is a good example. It is not too uncommon for Team A to defeat Team B, after which Team B defeats Team C, after which Team C defeats Team A! Inconsistencies such as this may be explained as being due to random fluctuations, or to underlying causes (such as match-ups of personnel), or to a combination. Regardless of the reasons, real world inconsistencies do exist and thus will appear in our judgments.

Inadequate Model Structure

A final cause of inconsistency is "inadequate" model structure. Ideally, one would structure a complex decision in a hierarchical fashion such that factors at any level are comparable, within an order of magnitude or so, of other factors at that level. Practical considerations might preclude such a structuring and it is still possible to get meaningful results. Suppose for example, we compared several items that differed by as much as two orders of magnitude. One might erroneously conclude that the AHP scale is incapable of capturing the differences since the scale ranges[15] from 1 to 9. However, because the resulting priorities are based on second, third, and higher order dominances, AHP can produce priorities far beyond an order of magnitude[16]. A higher than usual inconsistency ratio will result because of the extreme judgments necessary. If one recognizes this as the cause,

---

[14] At which point it is time to stop and resume at a later time.

[15] Actually 9.9 using the Expert Choice numerical mode.

[16] For example, if A is nine times B, and B is nine times C, then the second order dominance of A over C is 81 times.

(rather than a clerical error for example), one can accept the inconsistency ratio even though it is greater than 10%.

Necessary but not sufficient

It is important that a low inconsistency <u>not</u> become the goal of the decision-making process. A low inconsistency is necessary but not sufficient for a good decision. It is possible to be perfectly consistent but consistently wrong. It is more important to be accurate than consistent.

Compensatory and Non-Compensatory Decision-making

As mentioned above, AHP is a compensatory decision methodology because alternatives that are deficient with respect to one or more objectives can compensate by their performance with respect to other objectives. Hogarth[17] has categorized 'decision rules' for choice into two groups:

(1) strategies that confront the conflicts inherent in the choice situation; and
(2) strategies that avoid the conflicts. Conflict-confronting strategies are compensatory. That is, they allow you to trade off a low value on one dimension against a high value on another. Conflict-avoiding strategies, on the other hand, are non-compensatory. That is, they do not allow trade-offs.

According to Hogarth, the most straightforward, and in many ways most comprehensive strategy (for choice), is the so-called linear compensatory model.

Under a set of not too restrictive assumptions, this (the linear compensatory model) is quite a good choice model from a normative viewpoint. At a descriptive level, the linear model has been shown to be remarkably accurate in predicting individual judgments in both laboratory and applied settings.[18]

---

[17] Robin Hogarth *Judgment and Choice*, John Wiley & Sons, New York, 1987, p. 72.
[18] Ibid., p74.

Up until recently, the linear model as a choice process has been inadequate because, as Hogarth points out, it implies a process of explicit calculations and the trading off of dimensions, which, when there are many alternatives and dimensions, is not feasible for unaided judgment. Even when the number of dimensions and number of alternatives are small, people may still avoid compensatory strategies in making choices. According to Hogarth[19]

> A number of studies have shown, for instance, that preferences based on holistic or intuitive judgment differ from those constructed by use of a linear model; however, the latter are more consistent in the sense that final judgments show less disagreement between different individuals than intuitive evaluations. Intuitive judgment has two sources of inconsistency: in the application of weights attributed to dimensions, and in the aggregation of information across dimensions.

Today, with AHP and readily available computer technology, we can take advantage of the linear compensatory model[20].

Principles and Axioms of the Analytic Hierarchy Process

AHP is built on a solid yet simple theoretical foundation. The basic 'model' is one that almost every executive is familiar with — a pie chart. If we draw a pie chart, the whole of the chart represents the goal of the decision problem. The pie is organized into wedges, where each wedge represents an objective contributing to the goal. AHP helps determine the relative importance of each wedge of the pie. Each wedge can then be further decomposed into smaller wedges representing sub-objectives. And so on. Finally, wedges corresponding to the lowest level sub-objectives are broken down into alternative wedges, where each alternative wedge represents how much the alternative contributes to that sub-objective. By adding up the priority for the wedges for the alternatives, we determine how much the alternatives contribute to the organization's objectives.

---

[19] Ibid., 74.
[20] The AHP is actually more elaborate than a simple linear model because the multiplication of priorities from one level to the next results in what mathematicians refer to as a multilinear model.

AHP is based on three basic principles: decomposition, comparative judgments, and hierarchic composition or synthesis of priorities.[21]   The decomposition principle is applied to structure a complex problem into a hierarchy of clusters, sub-clusters, sub-sub clusters and so on. The principle of comparative judgments is applied to construct pairwise comparisons of all combinations of elements in a cluster with respect to the parent of the cluster. These pairwise comparisons are used to derive 'local' priorities of the elements in a cluster with respect to their parent. The principle of hierarchic composition or synthesis is applied to multiply the local priorities of elements in a cluster by the 'global' priority of the parent element, producing global priorities throughout the hierarchy and then adding the global priorities for the lowest level elements (the alternatives).

All theories are based on axioms. The simpler and fewer the axioms, the more general and applicable is the theory. Originally AHP was based on three relatively simple axioms. The first axiom, the reciprocal axiom, requires that, if $P_C(E_A, E_B)$ is a paired comparison of elements A and B with respect to their parent, element C, representing how many times more the element A possesses a property than does element B, then $P_C(E_B, E_A) = 1/P_C(E_A, E_B)$. For example, if A is 5 times larger than B, then B is one fifth as large as A.

The second, or homogeneity axiom, states that the elements being compared should not differ by too much, else there will tend to be larger errors in judgment. When constructing a hierarchy of objectives, one should attempt to arrange elements in a cluster so that they do not differ by more than an order of magnitude. (The AHP verbal scale ranges from 1 to 9, or about an order of magnitude. The numerical and graphical modes of Expert Choice accommodate almost two orders of magnitude, allowing a relaxation of this axiom. Judgments beyond an order of magnitude generally result in a decrease in accuracy and increase in inconsistency).

The third axiom states that judgments about, or the priorities of, the elements in a hierarchy do not depend on lower level elements. This axiom is required for the principle of hierarchic composition to apply. While the

---

[21] T. L. Saaty, *Fundamentals of Decision Making and Priority Theory with the Analytic Hierarchy Process*, RWS Publications, Pittsburgh PA., 1994, p 337.

first two axioms are always consonant with real world applications, this axiom requires careful examination, as it is not uncommon for it to be violated.   Thus, while the preference for alternatives is almost always dependent on higher level elements, the objectives, the importance of the objectives might or might not be dependent on lower level elements, the alternatives.   For example, in choosing a laptop computer, the relative importance of speed vs. weight might depend on the specific alternatives being considered—if the alternatives were about the same weight but differed greatly in speed, then speed might be more important. We say there is feedback from the alternatives to the objectives.   There are two basic ways to proceed in those situations where this axiom does *not* apply, that is, when there is feedback. The first involves a formal application of feedback and a supermatrix calculation for synthesis rather than hierarchic composition.   This approach is called the Analytic Network Process.   For simple feedback (between adjacent levels only), this is equivalent to deriving priorities for the objectives with respect to each alternative, in addition to deriving priorities for the alternatives with respect to each objective.   The resulting priorities are processed in a supermatrix, which is equivalent to the convergence of iterative hierarchical compositions.   While this approach is extremely powerful and flexible (feedback within levels and between nonadjacent levels can also be accommodated), a simpler approach that usually works well is to make judgments for lower levels of the hierarchy first (or to reconsider judgments at the upper levels after making judgments at the lower level).   In so doing, the brain performs the feedback function by considering what was learned at lower levels of the hierarchy when making judgments for upper levels.   Thus, an important rule of thumb is to make judgments in a hierarchy from the bottom up, unless one is sure that there is no feedback, or one already has a good understanding of the alternatives and their tradeoffs. Even if this is *not* done, adherence to AHP's fourth axiom (below) as well as the process notion of AHP, can usually lead to appropriate judgments, since an examination of the priorities after a first iteration of the model will highlight those areas where judgments should be revised based on what has been learned.

A fourth axiom, introduced later by Saaty, says that individuals who have reasons for their beliefs should make sure that their ideas are adequately represented for the outcome to match these expectations. While this axiom might sound a bit vague, it is very important because the generality of AHP makes it possible to apply AHP in a variety of ways and adherence to this axiom prevents applying AHP in inappropriate ways. We will illustrate this a bit later.

The simplicity and generality of AHP fit nicely with Ockham's razor, which contends that the simplest of two or more competing theories is preferable. Not only do we contend that AHP's axioms are simpler and more realistic than other decision theories, but that the ratio scale measures that it produces makes AHP more powerful as well.

Expert Choice

We will illustrate AHP and Expert Choice with a simple site location problem. Assume that we want to determine the best retail site within a geographic area for a small ice cream store catering to young children and families. We have narrowed down the site alternatives to three locations: the first one is a suburban shopping center. The second site is in the main business district area of the city, and the third is a suburban mall location. Details regarding each of these alternative sites are presented below:

Suburban Shopping Center

A vacant store location that was formerly a pizza shop is available for $28/sq. ft. per month in a neighborhood "strip" shopping center at a busy highway intersection. The area is populated with 45,000 (mostly middle income, young family) residents of a community who live in townhouses and single family dwellings. The strip center is constantly busy with retail customers of the major supermarket chain, a drug store, a hardware store, a hair stylist/barber shop, and several other small businesses sharing the location. No ice cream shops are located in the community.

The Mall

This location would cost $75/sq. ft. per month. We would be in the main food area of a major suburban mall with 75 retail shops and three "magnet" stores (Sears and two large department stores). The mall is frequented by teens, young mothers, and families usually on weekend days and weekday nights. There are three ice cream stores at various locations within the mall.

Main Street

For $50/sq. ft. per month we can locate our ice-cream store in the ground level of a large high rise office and retail complex. The shop would be in a moderately out of the way corner of the building. The majority of the people frequenting the building and the surrounding area are young professionals who are in the area Monday through Friday only. There is one ice cream store within a ten-block radius of this location.

The information on the three candidate sites can be used to build a basic model. There can be many variations to this model depending on how you choose to structure the problem. There is no one specific right or wrong way to model any decision problem. A basic approach to modeling the site location problem is outlined next.

Developing a Decision Hierarchy

Step 1. Decompose the Problem

The first step in using AHP and the Expert Choice software is to develop a hierarchy by breaking the problem down into its components. The three major levels of the hierarchy (shown in alternative views in Figure 2 and Figure 3) are the goal, objectives, and alternatives.

Goal

The goal is a statement of the overall objective. In our example, to Select the Best Retail Site

Objectives

What are we trying to achieve in selecting the site? In our example: Cost(low), Visibility, Customer Fit, Competition (lack of).

Alternatives

We consider the feasible alternatives that are available to reach the ultimate goal. In our example the alternatives that have been identified are a Suburban Shopping Center, The Mall, and Main Street.

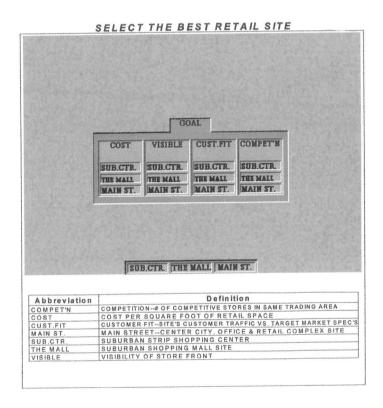

Abbreviation	Definition
COMPET'N	COMPETITION--# OF COMPETITIVE STORES IN SAME TRADING AREA
COST	COST PER SQUARE FOOT OF RETAIL SPACE
CUST.FIT	CUSTOMER FIT--SITE'S CUSTOMER TRAFFIC VS. TARGET MARKET SPEC'S
MAIN ST.	MAIN STREET--CENTER CITY, OFFICE & RETAIL COMPLEX SITE
SUB.CTR.	SUBURBAN STRIP SHOPPING CENTER
THE MALL	SUBURBAN SHOPPING MALL SITE
VISIBLE	VISIBILITY OF STORE FRONT

Figure 2 – Basic EC Model with Goal, Objectives and Alternatives

More Complex Hierarchies

Expert Choice can easily support more complex hierarchies containing sub-objectives, scenarios or uncertainties, and players. Another variation, the ratings approach, can be used to evaluate a large number of alternatives.

Sub-objectives—

This allows more specificity in the model. By adding sub-objectives you can detail your objectives. Figure 4 shows the model with sub-objectives added for COST, CUSTOMER FIT and COMPETITION.

Figure 3 – Basic EC Model: An Alternative View

Scenarios or Uncertainties—

The importance of different objectives and alternatives may depend on the specific future conditions, which are often difficult to predict. Scenarios can be modeled with Expert Choice allowing you to consider decision alternatives under a variety of circumstances. Scenarios representing the three possible states of the economy, Gloomy Economy, Boom Economy, and Status Quo are shown in Figure 5.

SELECT BEST RETAIL SITE

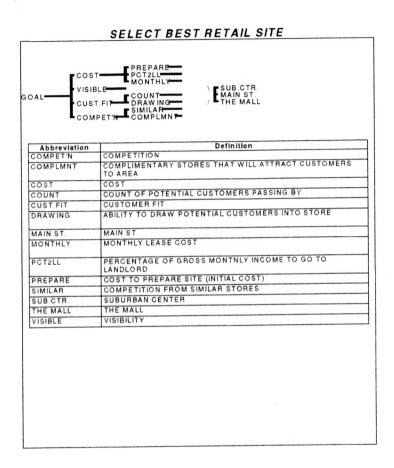

Abbreviation	Definition
COMPET'N	COMPETITION
COMPLMNT	COMPLIMENTARY STORES THAT WILL ATTRACT CUSTOMERS TO AREA
COST	COST
COUNT	COUNT OF POTENTIAL CUSTOMERS PASSING BY
CUST.FIT	CUSTOMER FIT
DRAWING	ABILITY TO DRAW POTENTIAL CUSTOMERS INTO STORE
MAIN ST.	MAIN ST
MONTHLY	MONTHLY LEASE COST
PCT2LL	PERCENTAGE OF GROSS MONTNLY INCOME TO GO TO LANDLORD
PREPARE	COST TO PREPARE SITE (INITIAL COST)
SIMILAR	COMPETITION FROM SIMILAR STORES
SUB.CTR.	SUBURBAN CENTER
THE MALL	THE MALL
VISIBLE	VISIBILITY

Figure 4 – Model with Sub-objectives

SELECT BEST RETAIL SITE

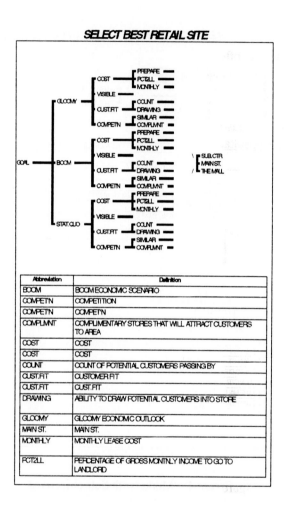

Abbreviation	Definition
BOOM	BOOM ECONOMIC SCENARIO
COMPET'N	COMPETITION
COMPET'N	COMPET'N
COMPLMNT	COMPLIMENTARY STORES THAT WILL ATTRACT CUSTOMERS TO AREA
COST	COST
COST	COST
COUNT	COUNT OF POTENTIAL CUSTOMERS PASSING BY
CUST.FIT	CUSTOMER FIT
CUST.FIT	CUST.FIT
DRAWING	ABILITY TO DRAW POTENTIAL CUSTOMERS INTO STORE
GLOOMY	GLOOMY ECONOMIC OUTLOOK
MAIN ST.	MAIN ST.
MONTHLY	MONTHLY LEASE COST
PCT2LL	PERCENTAGE OF GROSS MONTHLY INCOME TO GO TO LANDLORD

Figure 5 – Model with Scenarios

Players—

Decisions are often made through group consensus, yet it is often difficult for all members of a group to meet, or for each member's opinions to be heard during a meeting. By including a level for players in an EC model, each member's views can be incorporated into the decision-making process. Figure 6 illustrates players that include a <u>Vice-President</u>, <u>Marketing Director</u>, and <u>Consultant</u>

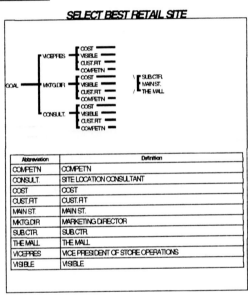

Abbreviation	Definition
COMPET'N	COMPET'N
CONSULT.	SITE LOCATION CONSULTANT
COST	COST
CUST.FIT	CUST.FIT
MAIN ST.	MAIN ST.
MKTG.DIR	MARKETING DIRECTOR
SUB.CTR.	SUB.CTR.
THE MALL	THE MALL
VICEPRES	VICE PRESIDENT OF STORE OPERATIONS
VISIBLE	VISIBLE

Figure 6 – EC Model with Company Players

Ratings Approach for A Large Number of Alternatives—

Some decisions inherently involve a large number of alternatives, which need to be considered. When this is true, the Expert Choice ratings approach easily accommodates a large number of alternatives, such as dozens (or even thousands) of potential sites to compare in a large metropolitan area. Figure 7 and Figure 8 illustrate the ratings approach.

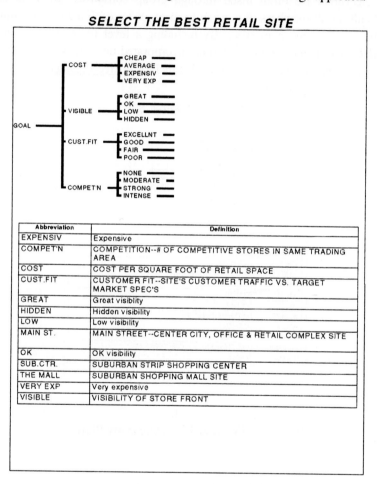

SELECT THE BEST RETAIL SITE

Abbreviation	Definition
EXPENSIV	Expensive
COMPET'N	COMPETITION--# OF COMPETITIVE STORES IN SAME TRADING AREA
COST	COST PER SQUARE FOOT OF RETAIL SPACE
CUST.FIT	CUSTOMER FIT--SITE'S CUSTOMER TRAFFIC VS. TARGET MARKET SPEC'S
GREAT	Great visiblity
HIDDEN	Hidden visibility
LOW	Low visibility
MAIN ST.	MAIN STREET--CENTER CITY, OFFICE & RETAIL COMPLEX SITE
OK	OK visibility
SUB.CTR.	SUBURBAN STRIP SHOPPING CENTER
THE MALL	SUBURBAN SHOPPING MALL SITE
VERY EXP	Very expensive
VISIBLE	VISIBILITY OF STORE FRONT

Figure 7 – EC Model with Large Number of Alternatives

The ratings approach consists of defining "intensities" of achievement or preference with respect to each of the objectives. These intensities are used in place of alternatives in the first stage of the evaluation. For example, instead of comparing the relative preference for two specific alternatives with respect to VISIBILITY, we would compare the relative preference for a non-specific alternative that possesses GREAT visibility to some other alternative that has LOW visibility. This results in measures of preference for the intensities. A ratings "spreadsheet" is then used to evaluate each alternative as to its intensity on each objective. With the ratings approach, pairwise comparisons are made for the objectives, as well as for the intensities under each objective. The results are ratio scale priorities for the importance of each objective, as well as ratio scale priorities for the intensities below each objective. Then, using the ratings "spreadsheet", each alternative is evaluated as to its intensity for each objective. The ratio scale priorities are then summed to give an overall ratio scale measure of the preference for the alternatives.

	COST	VISIBLE	CUST.FIT	COMPET'N	
	.	.	.	.	
	.	.	.	.	
	.	.	.	.	
/INTENSITIES/	0.5088	0.2427	0.1550	0.0935	Total
SUBURBAN CNTR#1	CHEAP	OK	GOOD	STRONG	0.7733
SUBURBAN CNTR#2	CHEAP	LOW	GOOD	MODERATE	0.7192
OLD TOWN AREA	VERY EXP	GREAT	EXCELLNT	INTENSE	0.4581
THE MALL	VERY EXP	GREAT	EXCELLNT	STRONG	0.4775
MAINST/HI RISE	EXPENSIV	OK	GOOD	STRONG	0.4341
NEAR APT. CLUSTER	AVERAGE	LOW	GOOD	MODERATE	0.5041
OFF INTERSTATE	EXPENSIV	OK	EXCELLNT	MODERATE	0.5069
SUBURBAN CNTR#3	AVERAGE	HIDDEN	FAIR	MODERATE	0.4493

Figure 8 – Ratings for a Large Number of Alternatives

Establishing Priorities

After arranging the problem in a hierarchical fashion, the next step is to establish priorities. Each node is evaluated against each of its peers in relation to its parent node; these evaluations are called pairwise comparisons. Referring back to the our basic site selection model in Figure 2:

> SELECTING THE BEST RETAIL SITE is the *parent* node of
> COST, VISIBILITY, CUSTOMER FIT, AND COMPETITION.
> COST is a *parent* to
> MAIN STREET, THE MALL, and SUBURBAN CENTER.
>
> COST, VISIBILITY, CUSTOMER FIT, and COMPETITION are *peers*.
>
> MAIN STREET, THE MALL, and SUBURBAN CENTER are *peers*.

Pairwise Comparisons

Pairwise comparisons of the elements at each level of an EC model are made in terms of either:

- Importance—when comparing objectives or players with respect to their relative importance.

- Preference—when comparing the preference for alternatives with respect to an objective.

- Likelihood—when comparing uncertain events or scenarios with respect to the probability of their occurrence.

Pairwise comparisons are basic to the AHP methodology. When comparing a pair of "factors"[22], a ratio of relative importance, preference or likelihood of the factors can be established. This ratio need not be based on some standard scale such as feet or meters but merely represents the relationship of the two "factors" being compared. For example, when looking at two lights, we can judge (without any scientific measurement) that one light is

---

[22] Factors may be objectives, sub-objectives, scenarios, players, or alternatives.

brighter, or perhaps twice as bright as the other. This may be a subjective judgment, but the two lights can be compared as such.

Most individuals would question the accuracy of any judgment made without using a standard scale. Yet, it has been verified that a number of these pairwise comparisons taken together form a sort of average, the results of which are very accurate. This "average" is calculated through a complex mathematical process using eigenvalues and eigenvectors. The results of this method have been tested experimentally and have been found to be extremely accurate. This method is used in AHP and Expert Choice allowing one to use both subjective and objective data in making pairwise comparisons.

Eigenvalues and Eigenvectors

A little of the Math—Why AHP Uses Eigenvalues and Eigenvectors

Suppose we already knew the relative weights of a set of physical objects like n rocks. We can express them in a pairwise comparison matrix as follows:

$$\underline{A} = \begin{bmatrix} w_1/w_1 & w_1/w_2 & w_1/w_3 & \ldots & w_1/w_n \\ w_2/w_1 & w_2/w_2 & w_2/w_3 & \ldots & w_2/w_n \\ w_3/w_1 & w_3/w_2 & w_3/w_3 & \ldots & w_3/w_n \\ \ldots & \ldots & \ldots & \ldots & \ldots \\ \ldots & \ldots & \ldots & \ldots & \ldots \\ \ldots & \ldots & \ldots & \ldots & \ldots \\ w_n/w_1 & w_n/w_2 & w_n/w_3 & \ldots & w_n/w_n \end{bmatrix}$$

If we wanted to "recover" or find the vector of weights, [w_1, w_2, w_3, ... w_n] given these ratios, we can take the matrix product of the matrix A with the vector w to obtain[23]:

---

[23] The matrix product is formed by multiplying, element by element, each row of the first factor, $\underline{A}$, by corresponding elements of the second factor, $\underline{w}$, and adding. Thus, the first element of the product would be:

$$\begin{bmatrix} w_1/w_1 & w_1/w_2 & w_1/w_3 & ... & w_1/w_n \\ w_2/w_1 & w_2/w_2 & w_2/w_3 & ... & w_2/w_n \\ w_3/w_1 & w_3/w_2 & w_3/w_3 & ... & w_3/w_n \\ ... & ... & ... & ... & ... \\ ... & ... & ... & ... & ... \\ ... & ... & ... & ... & ... \\ w_n/w_1 & w_n/w_2 & w_n/w_3 & ... & w_n/w_n \end{bmatrix} * \begin{bmatrix} w_1 \\ w_2 \\ w_3 \\ ... \\ ... \\ ... \\ w_n \end{bmatrix} = \begin{bmatrix} nw_1 \\ nw_2 \\ nw_3 \\ ... \\ ... \\ ... \\ nw_n \end{bmatrix}$$

$$\underline{A} \qquad\qquad\qquad * \underline{w} \;=\; n\,\underline{w}$$

If we knew A, but not w, we could solve the above for w. The problem of solving for a nonzero solution to this set of equations is very common in engineering and physics and is known as an eigenvalue problem:

$$\underline{A}\ \underline{w} = \lambda\ \underline{w}$$

The solution to this set of equations is, in general found by solving an nth order equation for l. Thus, in general, there can be up to n unique values for l, with an associated w vector for each of the n values.

In this case however, the matrix A has a special form since each row is a constant multiple of the first row. For such a matrix, the rank of the matrix is one, and all the eigenvalues of A are zero, except one. Since the sum of the eigenvalues of a positive matrix is equal to the trace of the matrix (the sum of the diagonal elements), the non zero eigenvalue has a value of n, the size of the matrix. This eigenvalue is referred to as λ_{max}.

Notice that each column of $\underline{A}$ is a constant multiple of $\underline{w}$. Thus, $\underline{w}$ can be found by normalizing any column of $\underline{A}$.

The matrix $\underline{A}$ is said to be strongly consistent in that

$a_{ik}a_{kj} = a_{ij}$ for all i,j.

$(w_1/w_1)*w_1 + (w_1/w_2)*w_2 + ... + (w_1/w_n)*w_n = nw_1$. Similarly, the second element would be $(w_2/w_1)*w_1 + (w_2/w_2)*w_2 + ... + (w_2/w_n)*w_n = nw_2$. The nth element would be nw_n. Thus, the resulting vector would be $n\underline{w}$.

Now let us consider the case where we do *not* know $\underline{w}$, and where we have only estimates of the a_{ij}'s in the matrix $\underline{A}$ and the strong consistency property most likely does not hold. (This allows for small errors and inconsistencies in judgments). It has been shown that for any matrix, small perturbations in the entries imply similar perturbations in the eigenvalues, thus the eigenvalue problem for the inconsistent case is:

$$\underline{A} \ \underline{w} = \lambda_{max} \ \underline{w},$$

where λ_{max} will be close to n (actually greater than or equal to n) and the other λ's will be close to zero. The estimates of the weights for the activities can be found by normalizing the eigenvector corresponding to the largest eigenvalue in the above matrix equation.

The closer λ_{max} is to n, the more consistent the judgments. Thus, the difference, $\lambda_{max} - n$, can be used as a measure of inconsistency (this difference will be zero for perfect consistency). Instead of using this difference directly, Saaty defined a consistency index as:

$$(\lambda_{max} - n)/(n-1)$$

since it represents the average of the remaining eigenvalues.

In order to derive a meaningful interpretation of either the difference or the consistency index, Saaty simulated random pairwise comparisons for different size matrices, calculating the consistency indices, and arriving at an average consistency index for random judgments for each size matrix. He then defined the consistency ratio as the ratio of the consistency index for a particular set of judgments, to the average consistency index for random comparisons for a matrix of the same size. Forman[24] performed additional simulations and calculated indices for cases with missing judgments.

Since a set of perfectly consistent judgments produces a consistency index of 0, the consistency ratio will also be zero. A consistency ratio of 1 indicates consistency akin to that, which would be achieved if judgments were not made intelligently, but rather at random. This ratio is called the inconsistency ratio in Expert Choice since the larger the value, the more inconsistent the judgments.

---

[24] E. H. Forman, "Random Indices for Incomplete Pairwise Comparison Matrices" *European Journal of Operations Research* Vol. 48, #1, 1990, pp. 153-155

Note: Other methods to estimate activity weights, such as least squares and log least squares have been suggested. While these methods produce results that are similar to the eigenvector approach, no other method maintains the reciprocal property of the pairwise comparison matrix (known as weak consistency), nor produces a comparable measure of inconsistency.

Note: An approximation to the Eigenvector method suitable for hand calculations is available (for example, Dyer and Forman[25]). While this approximation is reasonable when the judgments are relatively consistent, it may not be so for inconsistent judgments and is thus not recommended unless a computer and software are not available.

Because of the reciprocal property of the comparison matrix, the eigenvector problem can be solved by raising the matrix to the nth power, and taking the limit as n approaches infinity. The matrix will always converge. Saaty has shown that this corresponds to the concept of dominance walks. The dominance of each alternative along all walks of length k, as k goes to infinity, is given by the solution to the eigenvalue problem[26].

Three pairwise comparison modes

Expert Choice allows you to enter judgments in either numerical, graphical, or verbal modes. Each judgment expresses the ratio of one element compared to another element. When making comparisons in a social, psychological, or political context, you may wish to use the verbal comparison mode. Verbal judgments are easier to make, and for qualitative or value driven comparisons, easier to justify. When comparing economic or other measurable factors, the numerical or graphical comparison modes may be preferred, although it is perfectly acceptable to use the verbal mode in that case as well[27].

---

[25] Dyer, Robert F. and Forman, Ernest H., *An Analytic Approach to Marketing Decisions*, Prentice Hall 1991,pp. 92-93.
[26] For further information, see Saaty pp. 78-121.
[27] The verbal mode is not as accurate and typically requires more judgments than the numerical or graphical mode in order to improve accuracy.

Numerical judgments

When comparing properties that lend themselves naturally to a numerical scale, one can use the numerical mode to enter the judgments. In the numerical scale, 1.0 implies that the elements are equally important, 2.0 that one element is twice as important as the other, and 9.0 that one element is nine times as important as the other. These are absolute numbers that tell us, for example, which of two stones is the heavier and how much heavier it is. Thus, a numerical judgment of 5.0 says that the first stone is five times heavier than the second. If the disparity between elements in a group is so great that they are not of the same "order of magnitude" that is, some elements in the group are more than 9.0 times greater than some other elements in the group, they should be put into clusters of like elements. Alternatively, Expert Choice allows expansion of the numerical scale to a ratio of 99.9 to 1; however people are not as accurate in making judgments when the elements differ by ratios of 10 to 1 or more.

Graphical judgments

The graphical pairwise comparison scale can be used to express the relationships between two elements as the ratio of the lengths of two bars. Judgments are entered in the graphical mode by dragging and adjusting the relative lengths of the two bars (each representing one of the factors in the pairwise comparison). A pie chart changes to reflect the same relative proportion as you drag the bars (see Figure 9).

Verbal judgments

The nine point verbal scale used in Expert Choice is presented in Table 1.

Table 1 – EC Pairwise Comparison Scale.

Numerical Value	Verbal Scale	Explanation
1.0	Equal importance of both elements	Two elements contribute equally
3.0	Moderate importance of one element over another	Experience and judgment favor one element over another
5.0	Strong importance of one element over another	An element is strongly favored
7.0	Very strong importance of one element over another	An element is very strongly dominant
9.0	Extreme importance of one element over another	An element is favored by at least an order of magnitude
2.0, 4.0, 6.0, 8.0	Intermediate values	Used to compromise between two judgments

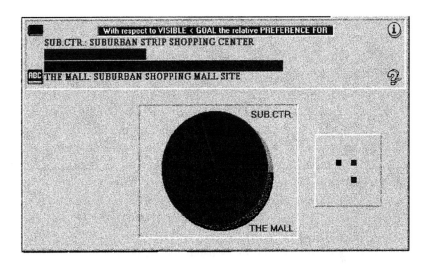

Figure 9 – Pairwise Graphical Comparison

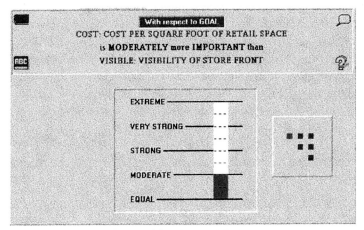

Figure 10 – Verbal Judgment

A verbal judgment in Expert Choice is shown in Figure 10.

Whereas numerical and graphical judgments are in and of themselves ratios and hence possess the ratio level of measurement, the same is not true for the verbal scale. The verbal scale is essentially an ordinal scale. When a decision maker judges A to be Strongly more important than B we know that A is 'more' important than B, but we do not know the interval between A and B or the Ratio of A to B. Studies have shown that relative (pairwise) *verbal* judgments can produce accurate, ratio scale priorities from what are basically imprecise, ordinal judgments, provided that redundant judgments are included in the calculations. Redundancy helps to reduce the average effect of errors in a manner analogous to the way that taking the average of a sample of measurements will produce an estimate of the mean that is likely to be closer to the true mean than only one judgment (i.e., no redundancy.) In addition to reducing the effect of the usual type of errors in measurement, this procedure also reduces the effect of the fuzzy nature of the ordinal scale and different interpretations of the scale by different decision-makers.

While relative pairwise judgments can be made numerically or graphically, verbal judgments are important in decision-making because humans have learned to use and are comfortable in using words to measure the intensity of feelings and understanding with respect to the presence of a property. For example, one might be more comfortable in saying that one fruit tastes moderately sweeter than another fruit than in saying that one fruit tastes three times sweeter than another fruit. Because complex crucial decision situations often involve too many dimensions for humans to synthesize intuitively, we need a way to synthesize over the many dimensions of such decisions. The derivation of ratio scale priorities from verbal judgments makes this possible.

How do we know that this method for deriving the priorities is accurate?

First because it is based on a sound mathematical foundation discussed above, and second by numerous validation experiments. Saaty performed many such experiments, with members of his family, visitors to his house, colleagues at work, and people attending seminars. It was standard practice for a visitor to the Saaty household to be asked to pairwise compare the weights of different size rocks or different suitcases. In one experiment Saaty placed chairs at various distances (9, 15, 21, and 28 yards) from a light source in his back yard to see if his wife and young children, standing at the light source, could judge the relative brightness of the chairs.[28] The results achieved with pairwise verbal judgments (see Table 2) were in very close agreement with the inverse square law of optics, which says that relative brightness is inversely proportional to the square of the distance of the object from the light source.

Table 2 – Results of Brightness of light on Chairs Experiment

Chair	Estimates from Wife's Judgments	Estimates from Sons' Judgments	Results from applying Inverse Square Law of Physics
1	0.61	0.62	0.61
2	0.24	0.22	0.22
3	0.10	0.10	0.11
4	0.05	0.06	0.06

Wedley has performed validation studies estimating the relative color intensities of objects. An Area Validation Study has shown not only is it possible to derive fairly accurate ratio scale priorities from verbal judgments, but that the redundancy in the pairwise process increases accuracy significantly. Consider the following analogy. Suppose you were allocating funds for environmental quality purposes and wanted to determine the relative funding for clean air, clean water, noise reduction, industrial dumps, and acid rain. As the analogy, suppose your insight about the relative needs coincide with the areas of the five objects in Figure 11.

---

[28] Saaty *The Analytic Hierarchy Process*, p. 39.

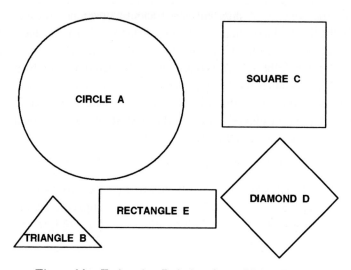

Figure 11 – Estimating Relative Areas Using Words

In this analogy you could look at these objects and estimate their relative sizes numerically, but the analogy is meant to show how words, instead of numbers, can be used to derive accurate priorities for qualitative factors. Using the <u>words</u>, moderate, strong, very strong, and extreme[29], many individuals and groups have made judgments about the relative sizes of these five objects. For example, the verbal judgments made by a group at one organization are shown in Figure 11.

A was judged to be Very Strongly larger than B (represented by a 7), Moderately larger than C (represented by a 3), and so on. The matrix of judgments corresponding to these verbal judgments and used to find the principle right hand eigenvector is shown in Figure 13.

---

[29] In pairwise relative comparisons, with redundancy.

Area Validation -- March 21, 1991

Node: 0

Compare the relative IMPORTANCE with respect to: GOAL

1=EQUAL   3=MODERATE   5=STRONG   7=VERY STRONG   9=EXTREME

#		9	8	7	6	5	4	3	2	1	2	3	4	5	6	7	8	9	
1	A	9	8	(7)	6	5	4	3	2	1	2	3	4	5	6	7	8	9	B
2	A	9	8	7	6	5	4	(3)	2	1	2	3	4	5	6	7	8	9	C
3	A	9	8	7	6	5	(4)	3	2	1	2	3	4	5	6	7	8	9	D
4	A	9	8	7	(6)	5	4	3	2	1	2	3	4	5	6	7	8	9	E
5	B	9	8	7	6	5	4	3	2	1	2	3	(4)	5	6	7	8	9	C
6	B	9	8	7	6	5	4	3	2	1	2	3	(4)	5	6	7	8	9	D
7	B	9	8	7	6	5	4	3	2	1	2	(3)	4	5	6	7	8	9	E
8	C	9	8	7	6	5	4	3	(2)	1	2	3	4	5	6	7	8	9	D
9	C	9	8	7	6	5	(4)	3	2	1	2	3	4	5	6	7	8	9	E
10	D	9	8	7	6	5	4	(3)	2	1	2	3	4	5	6	7	8	9	E

Abbreviation	Definition
Goal	Area Validation -- March 21, 1991
A	Circle
B	Triangle
C	Circle
D	Diamond
E	Rectangle

Figure 12 – Area Validation

However, the numeric values in the matrix can *not* be assumed to be accurate since they represent imprecise verbal judgments (really only an ordinal level of measure).

Algebraically, a minimum of n-1 or 4 comparisons is required to derive the relative areas. Any four judgments that "span" each of the elements being compared are sufficient. For example, *if* one assumes that the numerical representations of the verbal judgments shown in the first row of the matrix are accurate, the resulting priorities would be[30] A = 52.8%; B = 7.5%; C = 17.6%; D = 13.2%; and E = 8.8%. Priorities derived as the normalized values of the eigenvector corresponding to the normalized largest eigenvalue of the full

---

[30] Calculated by solving simultaneous equations: A = 7B, A=3C, A=4D, A=5E, A+B+C+D+E = 1.

$$A = \begin{bmatrix} 1 & 7 & 3 & 4 & 6 \\ 1/7 & 1 & 1/4 & 1/4 & 1/3 \\ 1/3 & 4 & 1 & 2 & 4 \\ 1/4 & 4 & 1/2 & 1 & 3 \\ 1/6 & 3 & 1/4 & 1/3 & 1 \end{bmatrix}$$

Figure 13 – Numerical Representation of Verbal Judgments

pairwise comparison matrix are almost always more accurate than results based on the minimal number of required judgments. This is indeed the case for the set of judgments shown in Figure 13, as can be seen in Table 3 by comparing the priorities derived from the minimal set of judgments (without redundancy) to the actual priorities and then comparing the priorities derived from the full set of judgments to the actual priorities.

Table 3 – Comparisons of Estimated vs. Actual Priorities

FIGURE	Estimates from Verbal Judgments W/O Redundancy	Estimates from Verbal Judgments With Redundancy	Actual
A	52.8	49.4	47.5
B	7.5	4.5	4.9
C	17.6	22.9	23.2
D	13.2	15.4	15.1
E	8.8	7.8	9.3

The sum of squares of the error in the priorities derived from the full set of judgments (those shown in) is 6.2 while the sum of squares of the error in the priorities derived from just the top row of judgments is 70.07. Notice the priorities derived from the full set of judgments do *not* necessarily agree with the numerical representation of any one judgment. For example, the ratio of the derived priorities of Circle-A and Triangle-B is about 10.9, which is closer to the true ratio of 9.7 than is the 7.0 numerical representation of the verbal judgment VERY STRONG.

We will conclude our discussion of priority derivation with two observations. Priorities derived for the five areas in this validation example from numerical or graphical judgments should be even closer since this is an objective problem with known answers. However, verbal judgments are often more appropriate when judging qualitative factors and all crucial decisions have qualitative factors that must be evaluated. Secondly, we have noted that both numerical and graphical judgments are in and of themselves ratios and hence possess the ratio level of measurement, the verbal scale is essentially an ordinal scale, which *can* be used to produce accurate ratio scale priorities. Do not, however, take this for granted! There may be cases where intervals or ratios of the priorities resulting from verbal judgments do not adequately represent the decision maker(s) feelings. It is incumbent upon the decision maker(s) to examine the resulting priorities and if they do not adequately represent the decision maker(s) feelings, to revise the judgments in either the graphical or numerical modes, preferably the former.

Preference of Alternatives with respect to Objectives

We usually evaluate the preference for the alternatives with respect to the objectives before evaluating the importance of the objectives. This 'bottom up' approach is recommended so that we get a better understanding of the alternatives just in case our judgments about the importance of the objectives are dependent on the alternatives (see discussion of AHP's third axiom on page 51). In our example, we would determine our preferences for MAIN STREET, THE MALL, and SUBURBAN CENTER with respect each of the four objectives. Considering COST, we might proceed as follows. Since cost is an 'objective' objective, we can refer to financial data. Monthly rent on MAIN STREET is $50 per square foot, while rent in THE MALL is $75 per square foot, and the SUBURBAN CENTER is $28 per square foot. While we could enter this data directly, we can also factor in

our subjective interpretation of these costs, reflecting a 'non-linear utility function'. Even though THE MALL is about 2.6 times more costly than the

Figure 14 – Preference for Alternatives with Respect to Cost

SUBURBAN CENTER (based on the actual cost data), we might judge that our *preference* for a cost of $28 per square foot per month is perhaps six times more preferable than $50 per square foot per month. Similarly, even though the SUBURBAN CENTER is 1.8 times more preferable than MAIN STREET based on a linear interpretation of the actual data, we might judge that a rent of $28 per square foot is three times more preferable than a rent of $50 per square foot. Finally, we might judge MAIN STREET to be about 1.5 times more preferable than THE MALL, a judgment that corresponds to a linear interpolation of the ratio of the respective costs. These judgments and resulting priorities are shown in Figure 14.

After judgments about the preferences for the alternatives have been made with respect to the COST objective, we derive priorities for the alternative sites with respect to each of the remaining objectives using either numerical, graphical, or verbal judgments pairwise judgments, or actual data.

Importance of the Objectives with Respect to the Goal

Verbal judgments about the relative importance of each objective are shown in Figure 15. In this example, we judged COST to be moderately more important to us than VISIBILITY with respect to their parent node, the GOAL of CHOOSING THE BEST RETAIL SITE. In other words, it is moderately more important to us to have an affordable location than one that is highly visible. This judgment can be based on our intuition—we know that people will find our shop, due to other factors (promotion, word of mouth, and so on) even if the storefront lacks high visibility; or we can base our judgment on objective data. Our financial analysis, which includes the rent of the sites, makes it clear that COST is more important since we would

Figure 15 – Judgments about Importance of Objectives and Resulting Priorities.

be in financial difficulty if we were to choose the high visibility location which is very costly. Each objective is evaluated with respect to every other objective in a similar fashion, using relevant subjective or objective judgments. The result of these judgments is a prioritization (or weighting) of the objectives as shown in Figure 15.

Synthesis

Once judgments have been entered for each part of the model, the information is synthesized to achieve an overall preference. The synthesis produces a report, which ranks the alternatives in relation to the overall goal. This report includes a detailed ranking showing how each alternative was evaluated with respect to each objective. Figure 16 shows the details followed by a ranking of the alternatives.

For our example, the Synthesis shows SUBURBAN CENTER to be the BEST RETAIL SITE. We can examine the details of this decision to see that this site alternative was chosen because it offered better customer fit at a lower cost and with less competition, thus favorably satisfying three of the objectives. Although THE MALL location provided better visibility, it was very expensive and had heavier competition. Expert Choice has helped us determine that the better visibility was not worth the added cost. It is important to note that it would be wrong to conclude that the SUBURBAN CENTER was best overall because it was better on three out of the four objectives. If cost were less important, THE MALL might be best overall as we can see with a sensitivity analysis.

SELECT THE BEST RETAIL SITE

Synthesis of Leaf Nodes with respect to GOAL
Ideal Mode
OVERALL INCONSISTENCY INDEX = 0.07

LEVEL 1	LEVEL 2	LEVEL 3	LEVEL 4	LEVEL 5
COST = .509				
	SUB.CTR.= .509			
	THE MALL=.093			
	MAIN ST.= .154			
VISIBLE =.243				
	SUB.CTR.= .104			
	THE MALL= .243			
	MAIN ST.= .027			
CUST.FIT= .155				
	SUB.CTR.= .155			
	THE MALL= .155			
	MAIN ST.= .031			
COMPET'N=.094				
	SUB.CTR.= .094			
	THE MALL=.016			
	MAIN ST.=.055			

SUB.CTR.   .527 ████████████████████████████████
THE MALL .310 ███████████████████
MAIN ST.   .163 █████████

Abbreviation	Definition
GOAL	
COMPET'N	COMPETITION--# OF COMPETITIVE STORES IN SAME TRADING AREA
COST	COST PER SQUARE FOOT OF RETAIL SPACE
CUST.FIT	CUSTOMER FIT--SITE'S CUSTOMER TRAFFIC VS. TARGET MARKET SPEC'S
MAIN ST.	MAIN STREET--CENTER CITY, OFFICE & RETAIL COMPLEX SITE
SUB.CTR.	SUBURBAN STRIP SHOPPING CENTER

Figure 16 – Synthesis for Site Location Problem[31]

Sensitivity

Sensitivity analyses can be performed to see how well the alternatives performed with respect to each of the objectives as well as how sensitive the alternatives are to changes in the importance of the objectives.

---

[31] Ideal and Distributive modes of synthesis are discussed on page 151.

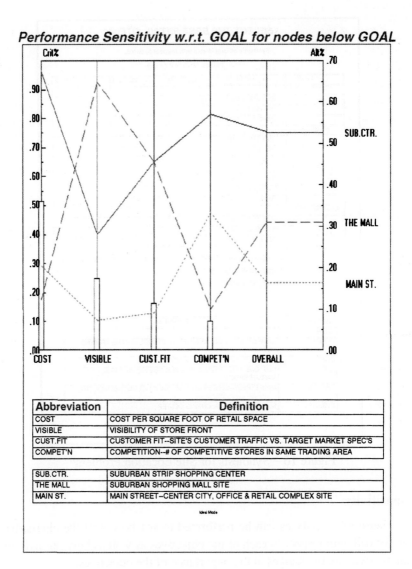

Figure 17 – Performance Sensitivity

The performance sensitivity shows (see Figure 17) the relative importance of each of the objectives as bars , and the relative preference for each alternative with respect to each objective as the intersection of the alternatives' curves with the vertical line for each objective. The overall alternative preferences are shown at the right. As with all AHP priorities, these priorities are ratio scale priorities meaning that not only do the priorities show order, but differences and ratios are meaningful as well. The SUB.CTR is best on three of the four objectives, and best overall. If however, VISIBILITY were to become more important, then The MALL might become the preferred alternative.

Figure 18 shows a gradient sensitivity analysis of the results with respect to the importance of the VISIBILITY objective. The graph shows that the current priority for VISIBILITY is a little less than .25 (see vertical solid red line). The height of the intersection of this dashed line with the alternative lines shows the alternatives' priorities. Thus, SUB. CTR. is the preferred alternative. If VISIBILITY were to become more important, then your overall preference for SUB.CTR decreases while that of THE MALL increases. If the priority of VISIBILITY were to increase above .53, then THE MALL would be the preferred alternative. However, since it would take a significant change in the priority of VISIBILITY in order to change the ranking of the alternatives, we can say that the results are not very sensitive to small changes in the priority of VISIBILITY. Other types of sensitivity analysis will be discussed later.

A Typical Application of AHP/EXPERT CHOICE

Choosing a Coast Guard Weapon Patrol Boat Fleet – Background

The United States Coast Guard was operating an aging fleet of small weapon patrol boats (WPBs)[32]. The fleet of WPBs was between twenty and twenty five years old. The original projected life span of these vessels was twenty years; however, several hulls had renovations enabling the useful life to exceed the original projections. Still, the time had come when patching the existing hulls was no longer a reasonable alternative and the fleet had to be replaced. The fleet size was 76 boats but the Coast Guard felt it had obtain at least 90 hulls to provide the necessary level of service required by their operational missions. Regardless of the type of vessel

---

[32] This study was performed by Edward Hotard and Benjamin Keck, officers in the U.S. Coast Guard assigned to graduate studies at George Washington University. The analysis and conclusions reflect their personal opinions and should in no way be construed as being the opinion of the Commandant of the Coast Guard or the official opinion of any member of the U.S. Coast Guard.

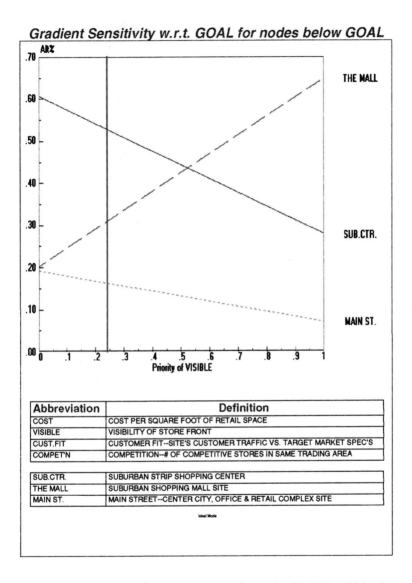

Figure 18 – Gradient Sensitivity Analysis for the Visibility Objective

purchased, each of the replacements would cost at least five million dollars and the projected system life cycle cost was expected to exceed one billion dollars.

The Office of Management and Budget (OMB) requires that major system procurements follow a set of guidelines (entitled OMB A-109) specifying that all reasonable alternatives be investigated before a new or replacement system is selected. The Department of Transportation had designated the Coast Guard WPB acquisition project as a major system acquisition, which came under the purview of OMB A-109. In accordance with OMB A-109 the Coast Guard had determined that the alternatives consisted of several advanced hull forms. The criteria by which the alternative hulls were to be judged were not specified by OMB A-109 and the agency was left with considerable latitude in determining the criteria they wished to use.

Alternatives

The alternative vessel types that were identified for consideration included: a hydrofoil, a small water area twin hull ship (SWATH), a surface effect ship (SES), a planing hull, and a monohull. The present hull form, WPB-95, was included at the request of the Acquisition Project Officer as a baseline in order to observe any anticipated improvements that would result by replacing existing craft with more advanced hull forms.

HYDROFOIL – The hydrofoil was the most technologically advanced of the six candidates. It relied on submerged foils to provide lift to the hull in the same manner that a wing provides lift to an airplane. With less hull surface in contact with the water, the friction or drag of the water against the surface of the hull is reduced allowing for greater speed. Hydrofoils typically have a gas turbine main propulsion plant. The use of a gas turbine requires high speed reduction gears which adds a great deal of complexity to the propulsion drive train. Hydrofoils are very fast, often capable of exceeding 60 knots, an important consideration for use in the war against drug smugglers. Since much of the hull is not in contact with the water the motion of the boat due to wave motions is reduced and a very stable platform results. However, the high speeds require specially designed cavitating screws, more sophisticated control systems, and highly skilled operational and maintenance personnel. The hydrofoil is also one of the more expensive alternatives.

SWATH – A Small Water Area Twin Hull vessel at first glance appears to be similar to a recreational pontoon boat. The pontoons of the SWATH ride not on but beneath the water's surface. The advantage of this type of hull form is that the vessel's center of buoyancy is placed below the surface wave action resulting in a dramatically more stable vessel. The twin hulls however, increase the wetted surface and drag on the hull. Consequently this hull form requires more power per knot than conventional single hull concepts. In addition, the reduced waterplane area produces a vessel that sits deeper in the water and draws a relatively greater draft than the other hulls being considered. While the catamaran style is highly stable over most sea conditions, there are dynamic stability questions that must be resolved when the vessel operates in heavy seas. Unlike single hull designs, its righting arm is comparatively great until it reaches a limiting angle of heel; at this point the righting arm vanishes much more quickly than in other types of hulls and the vessel is subject to being capsized.

SES – The Surface Effect Ship is similar to a hovercraft. The main difference between hovercraft and an SES are the rigid side hulls of the SES. Like the hovercraft, the SES relies on a cushion of air beneath the hull to lift a portion of the hull out of the water, thereby reducing the drag, which results in increased speed. There are, however, several major flaws in this concept. The air under the hull acts as an undampened spring, resulting in a poor ride when sea waves approach the natural frequency of the vessel. In addition, auxiliary motors and fans are required to create the air cushion to lift the vessel out of the water, which adds to the complexity, weight and cost of the ship.

PLANING – The planing hull concept is an evolution of present hull forms that improves dynamic lift and reduces drag. By reducing the resistance of the hull as it is forced through the water the vessel can obtain greater speed and fuel efficiency. The use of aluminum to reduce weight and turbo-charged diesel engines for power, are part of the evolution of ship design that the planing hull has embraced. The main advantages of the planing hull are that it deals with a known technology, has a lesser draft, a high speed in low to moderate seas and moderate cost. The main disadvantages are speed degradation in higher sea states and poor ride quality overall in comparison to some of the more stable advanced designs.

MONOHULL – The monohull is a compromise between what was the existing fleet of weapon patrol boats and the planing hull. The use of aluminum is minimized, the hull is given a sharper rise, and the engines are less powerful than those used in the planing hull. However, the monohull is still evolutionary. The main advantage of the monohull is its cost. Its primary disadvantage is its generally reduced capabilities.

WPB 95 – The current patrol boat configuration was included in the analysis in order to serve as a baseline.

Objectives

The problem was to determine which of the above vessels "best" met the coast guard's objectives. Based on the authors' knowledge and experience with small patrol craft and the characteristics of the alternatives under consideration, five main objectives were identified:

1. RMA – Reliability, Maintainability, and Availability;
2. Performance;
3. Cost;
4. Human Factors;
5. Basing.

Sub-objectives

Sub-objectives were identified for each of these objectives. These are shown in Figure 19 and will be explained below. The AHP analysis consists of making pairwise comparisons between pairs of factors at one level of the model with respect to the immediately preceding level. Local priorities are derived from each set of pairwise comparisons. Global priorities, relative of the goal, are then calculated and used to determine the ratio scale priorities for the alternatives.

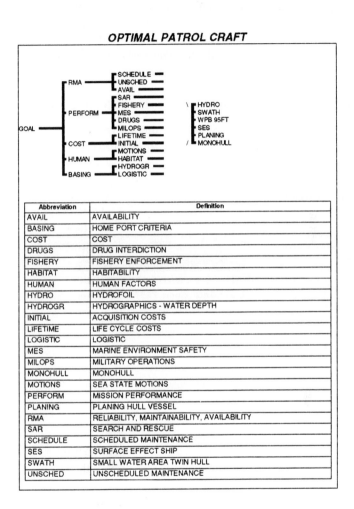

Figure 19 – AHP Model for Evaluating Coast Guard Patrol Vessels

Reliability, Maintainability, and Availability

The vessels being considered must be reliable, maintainable, and available (RMA).   Three sub-sub-objectives were identified for RMA: scheduled maintenance, unscheduled maintenance, and availability.

Derivation of preferences with respect to lowest level sub-objectives

Relative PREFERENCES for the alternatives relative to the each of these sub-sub-objectives were derived from pairwise verbal comparisons, based on data obtained from computer simulations and empirical evidence.

Pairwise verbal judgments

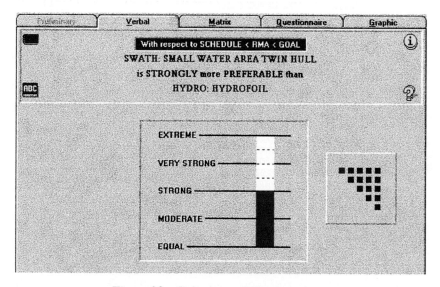

Figure 20 – Pairwise verbal comparison

Figure 20 shows a verbal pairwise judgment in which the small water area twin hull vessel was judged to be strongly more preferable than the hydrofoil with respect to the scheduled maintenance sub-objective. Even when data for comparing the alternatives is available, as is the case for scheduled maintenance, the relative preference is not necessarily linearly related to the data. Another way of saying this, is that the decision maker's "utility curve" for scheduled maintenance is not necessarily linear. Verbal judgments are a natural way of expressing this utility.

Verbal judgments can be represented numerically

Similarly, judgments were made about the relative preference between each pair of alternatives, with respect to the scheduled maintenance sub-objective. These are represented numerically in Figure 21. There is a subtle but important difference between representing verbal judgments numerically and numerical judgments. When representing verbal judgments numerically, a judgment of 'STRONG' is shown as a 5. The decision maker(s) did *not* judge factor A to be five times factor B! *Provided there is suitable redundancy* and that the judgments are reasonably consistent, the eigenvector calculation of priorities based on the full set of pairwise verbal comparisons may result in factor A being only 3 times factor B even though the word 'STRONG' had a numerical representation of 5 (see discussion on page70). Were numerical judgments to be made under similar circumstances, a judgment that factor A is 5 times factor B will, with reasonable consistency of judgments, result in priorities where factor A is indeed about five times factor B.

Priorities for the alternatives with respect to scheduled maintenance are derived by calculating the principal eigenvectors of the reciprocal matrix associated with these judgments as discussed earlier. These priorities are shown in Figure 22. Because more comparisons are made (and entered into the matrix of comparisons) than are actually required to calculate the priorities, the comparison matrix is said to contain some redundancy. This redundancy is, in a sense, used to "average" errors of judgment in a manner analogous to averaging errors when estimating a population mean. The errors of judgment include errors in translating from imprecise words to the numbers that are used to represent these words in the algorithm.

OPTIMAL PATROL CRAFT

Node: 11000

Compare the relative PREFERENCE with respect to: SCHEDULE < RMA < GOAL

1=EQUAL 3=MODERATE 5=STRONG 7=VERY STRONG 9=EXTREME

#	Left	9 8 7 6 5 4 3 2	1	2 3 4 5 6 7 8 9	Right
1	HYDRO	9 8 7 6 5 4 3 2	1	2 3 4 ⑤ 6 7 8 9	SWATH
2	HYDRO	9 8 7 6 5 4 3 2	1	2 3 4 5 6 7 ⑧ 9	WPB 95FT
3	HYDRO	9 8 7 6 5 4 3 2	1	2 3 ④ 5 6 7 8 9	SES
4	HYDRO	9 8 7 6 5 4 3 2	1	2 3 4 ⑤ 6 7 8 9	PLANING
5	HYDRO	9 8 7 6 5 4 3 2	1	2 3 4 5 ⑥ 7 8 9	MONOHULL
6	SWATH	9 8 7 6 5 4 3 2	1	2 3 4 5 ⑥ 7 8 9	WPB 95FT
7	SWATH	9 8 7 6 5 ④ 3 2	1	2 3 4 5 6 7 8 9	SES
8	SWATH	9 8 7 6 5 4 3 2	1	2 3 4 5 ⑥ 7 8 9	PLANING
9	SWATH	9 8 7 6 5 4 3 2	1	2 3 4 ⑤ 6 7 8 9	MONOHULL
10	WPB 95FT	9 8 ⑦ 6 5 4 3 2	1	2 3 4 5 6 7 8 9	SES
11	WPB 95FT	9 8 7 6 5 ④ 3 ②	1	2 3 4 5 6 7 8 9	PLANING
12	WPB 95FT	9 8 7 6 5 4 3 ②	1	2 3 4 5 6 7 8 9	MONOHULL
13	SES	9 8 7 6 5 4 3 2	1	2 ③ 4 5 6 7 8 9	PLANING
14	SES	9 8 7 6 5 4 3 2	1	2 3 4 ⑤ 6 7 8 9	MONOHULL
15	PLANING	9 8 7 6 5 4 3 2	1	2 ③ 4 5 6 7 8 9	MONOHULL

Abbreviation	Definition
Goal	OPTIMAL PATROL CRAFT
RMA	RELIABILITY, MAINTAINABILITY, AVAILABILITY
SCHEDULE	SCHEDULED MAINTENANCE
HYDRO	HYDROFOIL
SWATH	SMALL WATER AREA TWIN HULL
WPB 95FT	WPB 95FT
SES	SURFACE EFFECT SHIP
PLANING	PLANING HULL VESSEL
MONOHULL	MONOHULL

Figure 21 – Matrix of Pairwise Comparisons

The relative preferences for the alternatives with respect to the unscheduled maintenance sub-sub-objective and the availability sub-sub-objective are

Shown in Figure 23 and Figure 24. Although the ranking of the alternatives is the same with respect to each of the three RMA sub-objectives (the 95-foot weapon patrol boat being most preferred followed by the monohull and then the planing vessel), the priorities are slightly different.

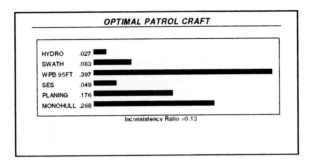

Figure 22 – Priorities with respect to Scheduled Maintenance

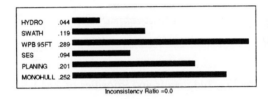

Figure 23 – Priorities with respect to Unscheduled Maintenance

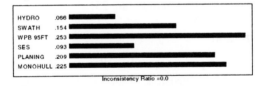

Figure 24 – Priorities with respect to availability

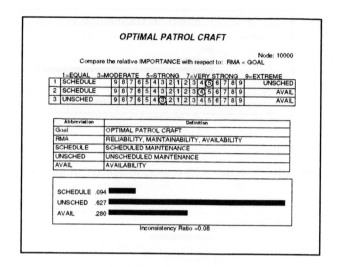

Figure 25 – Judgments and Priorities of RMA Sub-objectives

Next, the relative IMPORTANCE of the three RMA sub-objectives were determined using pairwise verbal comparisons. The judgments and resulting priorities are shown in Figure 25.

Inconsistency Ratio

The AHP comparison mode allows for inconsistent transitivity relationships and the inconsistency ratio (.08 for this last set of judgments) is an AHP measure of the lack of consistency in a set of judgments. One of the strengths of AHP is that is *does* allow for inconsistent and intransitive relationships, while, at the same time, providing a measure of the inconsistency. This strength of AHP has been criticized by multi-attribute utility theory (MAUT) and expected utility theory researchers because it does not conform to their axioms, one of which is the transitivity of preferences. Expected utility theory is grounded on the axiom of transitivity, that is, if A is preferred to B, and B is preferred to C, then A is preferred to C (or if A is three times more preferable than B and B is twice as preferable than C, then A is six times more preferable as C). For numerous reasons (discussed on page 46), the requirement that judgments be transitive and completely consistent is unrealistic. Fishburn[33] (1991, p. 130) concludes a discussion on non-transitive preferences with the following:

> Transitivity has been the cornerstone of traditional notions about order and rationality in decision theory. Three lines of research during the past few decades have tended to challenge its status. First, a variety of experiments and examples that are most often based on binary comparisons between multiple-factor alternatives suggest that reasonable people sometimes violate transitivity, and may have good reasons for doing this. Second, theoretical results show that transitivity is not essential to the existence of maximally preferred alternatives in many situations. Third, fairly elegant new models that do not presume transitivity have been developed, and sometimes axiomated, as alternatives to the less flexible traditional methods.

Luce and Raiffa[34] (1957, p. 25) discuss the transitivity axiom of expected utility theory as follows:

> No matter how intransitivities exist, we must recognize that they exist, and we can take only little comfort in the thought that they are an anathema to most of what constitutes theory in the behavioral sciences today.

They also observe:

> We may say that we are only concerned with behavior which is transitive, adding hopefully that we believe this need not always be a vacuous study. Or we may contend that the transitive description is often a 'close' approximation to reality. Or we may limit our interest to 'normative' or 'idealized' behavior in the hope that such studies will have a metatheoretic impact on more realistic studies. In order to get on, we shall be flexible and accept all of these as possible defenses, and to them add the traditional mathematician's hedge: transitive relations are far more mathematically tractable than intransitive ones.

Although one might first think that being consistent is of utmost importance, allowing for some inconsistency is reasonable. Saaty reasons that:

---

[33] Fishburn, P. C. 1991. Nontransitive Preferences in Decision Theory, Journal of Risk and Uncertainty, 4, 113-134.

[34] Luce, R.D. and H. Raiffa, 1957, *Games and Decisions*. John Wiley and Sons, Inc., New York.

The conscious mind absorbs new ideas by contrasting them through scanning or through concentration and analysis to understand how they are similar to familiar ideas. Ideas are also related to current or future activities and applied to concrete situations to test their compatibility with what is already believed to be workable. The ideas may be accepted as a consistent part of the existing understanding or they may be inconsistent with what is already known or accepted. In that case the system of understanding and practice is extended and adjusted to include the new ideas. Growth implies such expansion. If the adjustment of old ideas to accommodate a new one is drastic, then the inconsistency caused by the new idea is great. This may require considerable adjustments in the old ideas and beliefs whose old relations may no longer be intuitively recognizable and may call for a new theory or interpretation if at all possible. But such major changes cannot be made every hour, every day or even every week because it takes time to interpret and assimilate relations. Thus inconsistency arising from exposure to new ideas or situations can be threatening, unsettling and painful.

Our biology has recognized this and has developed ways to filter information in such a way that we usually make minor adjustments in what we already know when we are exposed to a new or better idea—absorbing new ideas by interpreting them from the vantage point of already established relations. Thus our emphasis on consistency exceeds our desire for exposure and readjustment. As a result, maintaining consistency is considered to be a higher priority of importance than changing. Yet the latter is also considered to be an important concern. One conclusion is that our preoccupation with consistency differs by one order of magnitude from our preoccupation with inconsistency - a split of 90% and 10%.

As discussed on page 65, perfectly consistent judgments would result in an inconsistency ratio of 0 while random judgments would, on the average, result in an inconsistency ratio of 1.0. It is possible to have an inconsistency ratio greater than 1.0, if for example, one or two judgments are accidentally inverted in what would otherwise be a very consistent set of judgments. As discussed on page 65, an inconsistency ratio of more than about 10% should alert us to the need to (1) look for and correct any clerical errors that may have caused the high inconsistency, (2) gather more information, (3) look for erroneous judgments that my have resulted from a lack of concentration, or (4) conclude that this particular aspect of the problem contains more than an average amount of inconsistency. The 10% is not an absolute rule, but rather a guideline. The more non-homogenous the factors in a cluster, the higher the inconsistency ratio is likely to be. If verbal judgments are applied to a cluster of elements that differ by more than an order of magnitude, a higher than normal inconsistency ratio can be expected (and tolerated) since the verbal scale extends only to an order of magnitude. The Numerical Matrix mode can be expanded to two orders of magnitude and the Graphical mode can accommodate two orders of magnitude.

Reducing Inconsistency

It is important that a low inconsistency <u>not</u> become the goal of the decision-making process. A low inconsistency is necessary but not sufficient for a good decision. It is possible to be perfectly consistent but consistently wrong. It is more important to be accurate than consistent. However, if the inconsistency ratio is higher than expected, the Expert Choice numerical matrix assessment mode menu commands can be used to locate the most inconsistent judgment, (as well as the 2nd or 3rd, or 9th most inconsistent judgment). After locating the most inconsistent judgment in the matrix[35], the 'best fit' command will display the direction and intensity of the judgment that would be most consistent with the other judgments in the matrix. One should *not* change their judgment to this value however – but use this value to consider what might be wrong, if anything, with the judgment as it was entered – changing the judgment only if appropriate. If the judgment appears reasonable, then one should examine the 2nd most inconsistent judgment and so on.

A less automated but perhaps more expedient way to examine possible inconsistencies in judgments is to use the Reorder command after calculating the priorities and then display the judgments in the numerical matrix mode[36]. Reorder changes the order of the elements in the comparison matrix according to priority (from highest to lowest). If this ranking is in fact the 'actual' ranking (assuming any erroneous judgments haven't

---

[35] This is only applicable to matrices consisting of four or more elements since when comparing only two factors, there can be no inconsistency. When comparing three factors, any judgment can be the most inconsistent with respect to the two remaining two judgments.

[36] If judgments were entered in the verbal or graphical mode, remember to switch back to that mode so that judgments can latter be explained and justified in the mode in which they were made.

affected the order of the elements) then there should be no inverted judgments and the judgments should be non decreasing going from left to right in each row, as well as going from bottom to top in each column.

Performance

The missions (sub-objectives), which these vessels would be required to perform, are defined by the Coast Guard Operational Program Plan and represented in the model as:

    1) Search and Rescue (SAR),

    2) Fisheries Conservation,

    3) Drug Interdiction,

    4) Marine Environmental Safety, and

    5) Military Operations.

SAR – Search and rescue is an historic and extremely important mission for the Coast Guard. The service proudly proclaims itself as "The Lifesavers" and has a long tradition of protecting life and property at sea. Thus, any Coast Guard vessel must be capable of responding quickly to the reported position of a vessel in distress, often under hazardous sea conditions. The SAR capabilities of the vessel candidates in the model were judged based on a Monte Carlo simulation developed for the SAR performance evaluation.

FISHERY – Fisheries conservation is an important mission for WPBs in some operational areas. The basic function of the program is to conduct boardings of U.S. and foreign fishing fleets to ensure that their catch complies with the Coastal Fisheries Management Act. There is little requirement for speed in performing this mission but more emphasis on habitability and seakeeping. There are major fishing areas on all coasts. However, the model was developed and the comparisons made from the viewpoint of the needs of the Seventh Coast Guard District (Miami, FL) where the fisheries mission is not very important but drug interdiction is. Thus, Fisheries received a very low priority.

MARINE ENVIRONMENTAL SAFETY – MES is a mission that the Coast Guard assumed during the 1960's with the rise of national concerns for the environment and quality of life. In general, the mission requires that virtually any available platform be prepared to respond to emergencies such as major oil or chemical spills and assist with damage control and cleanup operations. The mission is usually performed in sheltered waters near the coast where oil barges and tankers are most likely to run aground. There is some need for speed in reacting promptly to prevent the unchecked spread of an oil or chemical spill.

DRUG LAW ENFORCEMENT – Drug interdiction consumes almost 60% of the Coast Guard mission hours in the Caribbean and the Seventh Coast Guard District. There has been an enormous growth in this mission area since the escalation of the war on drugs. The performance of the candidate hull forms in the drug enforcement mission was estimated with the assistance of computer based simulations. High speed is a primary consideration in this mission area as drug smugglers turn to high performance craft to avoid coastal patrols by the U.S. Coast Guard, Navy, Customs and Drug Enforcement Agency.

MILITARY OPERATIONS – The U.S. Coast Guard, in addition to its traditional peace time duties, also constitutes a military force. In the event of a national emergency the service will be responsible for protecting the coastal waters and shores of the United States. In time of war the service becomes an operational group under the U.S. Navy and provides port security for American coastal establishments. While not a primary mission area in ordinary times, it must be considered as part of the Coast Guard's area of mission responsibilities. Priorities of the alternatives with respect to each of the performance sub-objectives and priorities for the performance sub-objectives with respect to the goal were determined using pairwise comparisons in a manner similar to that described above.

COST

Cost sub-objectives, vessel acquisition and life cycle cost were estimated by the Naval Sea System's Advanced Surface Ship Evaluation Tool (ASSET). ASSET uses a database of historical cost information to establish relationships upon which estimates for the candidate hulls are based.

LIFE CYCLE COST – Life cycle cost is the discounted cash flow of the total system over its projected life. This figure includes acquisition, personnel, maintenance, fuel and related costs.

ACQUISITION COST – Acquisition cost includes the construction cost, general and administrative (G&A), profit, spare parts inventory cost and delivery charges.

HUMAN FACTORS

HABITABILITY – The Coast Guard has long recognized that alert, comfortable personnel are far more effective in the performance of their mission duties. In some mission areas the crew is required to remain at sea for extended periods. The habitability of the vessel affects the retention and morale of skilled Coast Guard officers and crews. The habitability of the different craft can be determined subjectively by comparing the arrangement of berthing, messing, and recreational facilities.

MOTION – The ride quality of the vessel and quality of life on board are extremely important. The performance of the crew is affected by the ride of the vessel since moderate ship motion can induce seasickness and violent motion can cause injury to persons on board. Motions are defined for our model as the vessel's movements in response to the wave motion in a seaway. Motions can be empirically tested by either model or full scale testing. Motions can also be predicted by computer programs. The motions found to be most debilitating to human performance are accelerations in the vertical plane (heave) caused by the longitudinal pitching of the vessel. The judgments entered into the model were those of an expert.

BASING

Some of the advance vessels are not capable of utilizing existing Coast Guard port facilities because of draft or because they require special support services. Basing consists of hydrographic limitations and logistical concerns.

HYDROGRAPHIC LIMITATIONS – The draft and beam of candidate craft may exclude them from some locations. Dredging might not be a practical solution in some cases.

LOGISTICAL CONCERNS – If a vessel uses aluminum as a hull material it should have access in its home port area to a high strength aluminum repair facility. SWATH vessels must be located near a facility capable of dry docking such an unusual hull form.

Judgments for alternative preference with respect to sub-objectives below each of the other major objectives and for the relative importance of the sub-objectives were performed in a similar manner as that descried for the RMA objective above. Finally, verbal judgments were made about the relative importance of the major objectives. These judgments and the resulting priorities are shown in Figure 26 & Figure 27.

OPTIMAL PATROL CRAFT

Node: 0

Compare the relative IMPORTANCE with respect to: GOAL

1=EQUAL 3=MODERATE 5=STRONG 7=VERY STRONG 9=EXTREME

#		9	8	7	6	5	4	3	2	1	2	3	4	5	6	7	8	9	
1	RMA	9	8	7	6	5	4	3	2	1	2	3	4	(5)	6	7	8	9	PERFORM
2	RMA	9	8	7	6	5	4	3	2	1	2	3	4	(5)	6	7	8	9	COST
3	RMA	9	8	7	6	5	4	(3)	2	1	2	3	4	5	6	7	8	9	HUMAN
4	RMA	9	8	7	6	5	4	3	2	(1)	2	3	4	5	6	7	8	9	BASING
5	PERFORM	9	8	7	6	5	4	3	2	(1)	2	3	4	5	6	7	8	9	COST
6	PERFORM	9	8	7	6	(5)	4	3	2	1	2	3	4	5	6	7	8	9	HUMAN
7	PERFORM	9	8	7	6	5	(4)	3	2	1	2	3	4	5	6	7	8	9	BASING
8	COST	9	8	7	6	5	4	(3)	2	1	2	3	4	5	6	7	8	9	HUMAN
9	COST	9	8	7	6	5	4	(3)	2	1	2	3	4	5	6	7	8	9	BASING
10	HUMAN	9	8	7	6	5	4	3	2	(1)	2	3	4	5	6	7	8	9	BASING

Abbreviation	Definition
Goal	OPTIMAL PATROL CRAFT
RMA	RELIABILITY, MAINTAINABILITY, AVAILABILITY
PERFORM	MISSION PERFORMANCE
COST	COST
HUMAN	HUMAN FACTORS
BASING	HOME PORT CRITERIA

RMA	.109
PERFORM	.385
COST	.338
HUMAN	.075
BASING	.093

Inconsistency Ratio =0.05

Figure 26 – Judgments and Priorities for Major Objectives

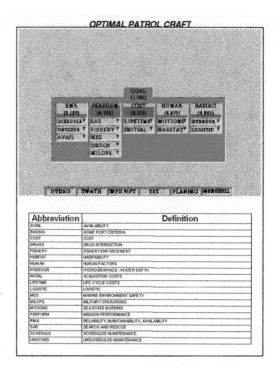

Figure 27 – Priorities from Goal node

Having decomposed the complex problem into its constituent parts, and having derived priorities, a synthesis was performed. The synthesis details are shown in Figure 28, and Figure 29. The results are shown in Figure 30.

OPTIMAL PATROL CRAFT

Synthesis of Leaf Nodes with respect to GOAL
Ideal Mode
OVERALL INCONSISTENCY INDEX= 0.03

LEVEL 1	LEVEL 2	LEVEL 3	LEVEL 4	LEVEL 5
RMA =.109				
	SCHEDULE=.010			
		HYDRO =.001		
		SWATH =.002		
		WPB 95FT=.010		
		SES =.001		
		PLANING=.005		
		MONOHULL=.007		
	UNSCHED=.068			
		HYDRO =.010		
		SWATH =.028		
		WPB 95FT=.068		
		SES =.022		
		PLANING=.048		
		MONOHULL=.060		
	AVAL =.031			
		HYDRO =.008		
		SWATH =.019		
		WPB 95FT=.031		
		SES =.011		
		PLANING=.025		
		MONOHULL=.027		
PERFORM=.385				
	SAR =.114			
		HYDRO =.080		
		SWATH =.019		
		WPB 95FT=.025		
		SES =.018		
		PLANING=.114		
		MONOHULL=.019		
	FISHERY =.000			
		HYDRO =.000		
		SWATH =.000		
		WPB 95FT=.000		
		SES =.000		
		PLANING=.000		
		MONOHULL=.000		
	MES =.023			
		HYDRO =.023		

Figure 28 – Synthesis details

OPTIMAL PATROL CRAFT

		SWATH =.025		
		WPB 95FT=.025		
		SES =.025		
		PLANING =.025		
		MONOHULL=.025		
	DRUGS =.170			
		HYDRO =.096		
		SWATH =.036		
		WPB 95FT=.046		
		SES =.069		
		PLANING =.170		
		MONOHULL=.101		
	MILOPS =.077			
		HYDRO =.077		
		SWATH =.070		
		WPB 95FT=.015		
		SES =.042		
		PLANING =.055		
		MONOHULL=.048		
COST =.338				
	LIFETIME=.281			
		HYDRO =.114		
		SWATH =.157		
		WPB 95FT=.281		
		SES =.161		
		PLANING =.167		
		MONOHULL=.185		
	INITIAL =.058			
		HYDRO =.011		
		SWATH =.026		
		WPB 95FT=.058		
		SES =.028		
		PLANING =.031		
		MONOHULL=.037		
HUMAN =.075				
	MOTIONS =.044			
		HYDRO =.043		
		SWATH =.044		
		WPB 95FT=.004		
		SES =.014		
		PLANING =.009		
		MONOHULL=.006		
	HABITAT =.031			
		HYDRO =.031		

Figure 29 – Synthesis details continued

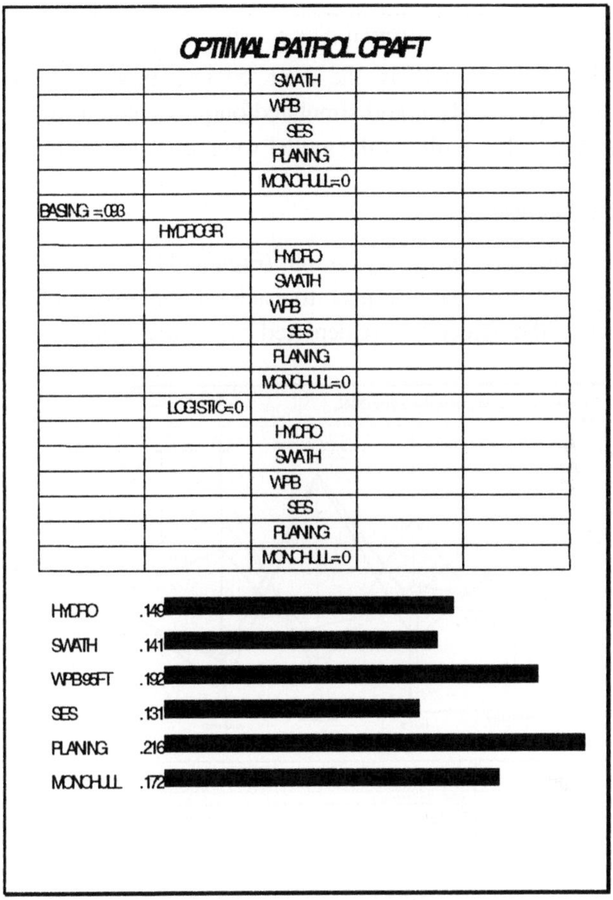

OPTIMAL PATROL CRAFT

		SWATH		
		WPB		
		SES		
		PLANING		
		MONOHULL=0		
BASING =.098				
	HYDROGR			
		HYDRO		
		SWATH		
		WPB		
		SES		
		PLANING		
		MONOHULL=0		
	LOGISTIC=0			
		HYDRO		
		SWATH		
		WPB		
		SES		
		PLANING		
		MONOHULL=0		

HYDRO	.149
SWATH	.141
WPB95FT	.192
SES	.131
PLANING	.216
MONOHULL	.172

Figure 30 – Synthesis Results

RESULT

The planing hull is the best choice, based on the subjective judgments, empirical data, and simulated outputs entered for the designated operating area. The results of the model were also intuitively appealing[37]

Sensitivity Analysis

A performance sensitivity graph (Figure 31) shows how well each alternative performs with respect to each of the major objectives. The importance of the objectives are depicted by vertical bars[38].

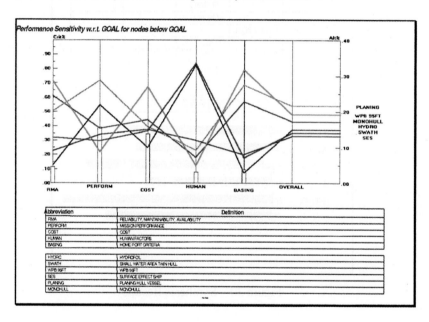

Figure 31 – Performance Sensitivity

---

[37] If the results were not intuitive, then asking *why not* would lead to a modification of the model, and/or judgments and/or a change in intuition.

[38] Priorities for the objectives can be read from the left-hand axis.

The performance of each alternative with respect to each of the objectives is depicted by the intersection[39] of a colored sequence of line segments with the vertical line at each of the objectives. The overall performance of an alternative is depicted by the intersection of the alternative's line segments with the "overall" vertical line at the right of the graph[40].

Ordinal, interval *and* ratio information is conveyed in all of the priorities. For example, the planing hull vessel, depicted by the blue sequence of line segments, is third best for RMA, best for performance, third best for cost, fourth best for human factors, second best for basing, and best overall. But in addition to knowing the order of performance for each alternative with respect to each objective as well as overall, we also know and can see the intervals and ratios between alternatives. Looking at the human factors objective, for example, the interval between the first and second alternatives (SWATH and HYDRO) is insignificant, whereas the interval between the second and third alternatives (HYDRO and SES) is very large. The interval between the best and second best overall alternatives (planing hull and WBP) is much larger with respect to performance than with respect to basing. This is useful information. (Measurement to at least an interval level is necessary in order to determine which alternative is best overall. It would be incorrect to conclude that the WPB was best overall because it was best on three of the five objectives).

---

[39] Performance of the alternatives can be read from the right hand axis.

[40] Alternative line segments between the objectives are drawn for visual clarity only and do not convey any information.

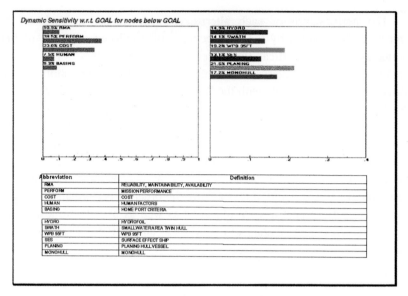

Figure 32 – Dynamic Sensitivity

Ratio interpretations are also meaningful. For example, with respect to RMA, WPB is about six times more preferable than the hydrofoil. Or, for example, the overall priority of the most preferred alternative, the planing hull vessel (about 22%), is not even twice that of the least preferred alternative, the SES (about 13%). A dynamic sensitivity graph is shown in Figure 32.

Suppose we thought that the importance of RMA might be, or become, more important than the 10.9% shown. By 'pulling' the RMA bar to the right, each of the other bars decrease (in proportion to their original priorities) and the overall priorities of the alternatives change as well. The dynamic sensitivity graph with RMA increased to about double its original value is shown in Figure 33. The overall priority of the planning vessel has decreased while priority of the weapon patron boat has increased – however the planing hull vessel is still slightly preferred. Thus, the current result is relatively insensitive to even a doubling in priority of the RMA objective.

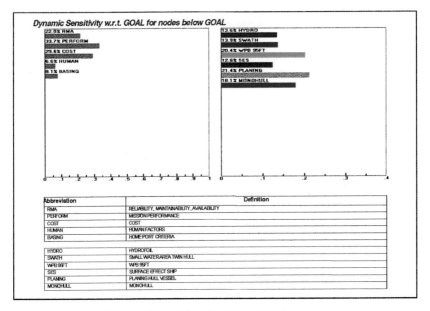

Figure 33 – After doubling RMA

A gradient sensitivity graph for the RMA objective is shown in Figure 34. The red vertical line shows that the original priority of RMA was about 11%. The gradient (slope) of each of the alternative lines (blue for RMA, red for WPB, etc.,) represents the rate of change in priority for the alternative as the priority of RMA is changed. Thus, for example, the priority of the planing hull vessel would decrease while that of the weapon patrol boat would increase if the priority of the RMA objective is increased (red bar is moved to the right.) A change in one sensitivity plot causes changes to each of the other sensitivity plots. The blue dotted vertical line in the gradient sensitivity plot (Figure 34) corresponds to the doubling of the importance of the RMA objective on the dynamic sensitivity graph (Figure 33). The planing hull vessel is still preferred to the weapon patrol boat at this RMA priority. However, if RMA were increased to beyond about 30.3%, the weapon patrol boat would become the preferred alternative. If the priority of RMA were increased to 100% (the vertical bar moved all the way to the right, the priorities would correspond to the intersection of each alternative's line segment with the vertical line for the RMA objective on the performance sensitivity graph (Figure 31). That is, if RMA were the only objective then the planing hull vessel would drop to the third most preferred alternative.

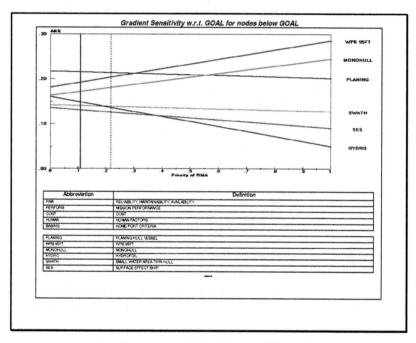

Figure 34 – Gradient Sensitivity

A graph of the differences between the top two alternatives is shown in Figure 35. The planing hull vessel is preferred to the weapon patrol boat on performance by quite a margin, and only slightly on human factors, while the weapon patrol boat is preferred to the planing null vessel on cost, less so on RMA and even less on basing.

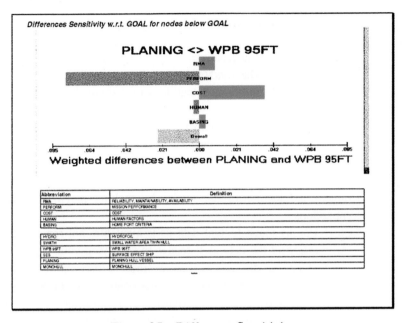

Figure 35 – Difference Sensitivity

Seven Step Process for Choice

We have now looked at four steps in applying AHP and Expert Choice to a choice problem: (1) decompose the problem – develop a hierarchy; (2) establish priorities; (3) synthesis; and (4) sensitivity analysis. These steps can be elaborated by imbedding them in a more encompassing seven step process as follows:

Step 1: Problem definition and research

    1a: Problem *identification*

    1b: Identify *objectives*[41] and *alternatives*. A listing of the *pros and cons* of each alternative is often helpful in identifying the objectives.

---

[41]A rational decision is one made on the basis of *objectives*. *Criteria* are used to measure how well we achieve our objectives. The words objectives and criteria, although having different definitions, are commonly used interchangeably in analyzing a decision. The word *objective* is preferred because it helps us

      1c: Research the alternatives

Step 2: Eliminate infeasible alternatives
      2a: Determine the *"musts"*
      2b: Eliminate alternatives that do not satisfy the "musts"

Step 3: Structure a decision model in the form of a hierarchy to include goal, objectives (and sub objectives), and alternatives. Add other factors (such as actors and scenarios) as required

Step 4: Evaluate the factors in the model by making pairwise relative comparisons
      4a: Use as much factual data as is available, but remember to *interpret* the data as it relates to satisfying your objectives. (That is, do not assume a linear *utility curve* without thinking about whether it is a reasonable assumption).
      4b: Use knowledge, experience, and intuition for those qualitative aspects of the problem or when hard data is available.

Step 5: Synthesize to identify the "best" alternative

Step 6: Examine and verify decision, iterate as required
      6a: Examine the solution and perform sensitivity analyses. If the solution is sensitive to factors in the model for which you do not have the best data available, consider spending the time and money to collect the necessary data and iterate back to step 4.
      6b: Check the decision against your *intuition*. If they don't agree, ask yourself why your intuition tells you a different alternative is best. See if the reason(s) are already in the model. If not, revise the model (and or judgments). Iterate as required. In general you will find that both your model

---

focus on what we are trying to achieve as we perform the evaluation. However, the word criterion is commonly used in practice.

and intuition may change (i.e. you are learning). When your intuition (possibly different now than it was before) and the model agree, continue on to step 7.

Step 7: Document the decision for justification and control

Other decision-making 'recipes'

Numerous other recipes for decision-making have been published over the years. Most have similar components. One of the most widely disseminated recipes is the following seven steps from Kepner &Trego[42]

1) establish objectives
2) classify importance of objectives
3) develop alternative actions
4) evaluate alternatives against established objectives
    determine musts
    determine wants
5) choose the alternative that is best able to achieve the objectives as tentative decision
6) explore the tentative decision for future possible   adverse consequences
7) control the effects of the final decision by taking other actions to prevent possible adverse consequences from becoming problems, and by making sure the actions are carried out.

Musts and Wants

Each of the above 'recipes includes the considerations of 'musts'. Kepner &Trego advised using 'musts and wants' in their step 4. 'Musts' are used to eliminate infeasible alternatives in step 2 of our 'recipe.'   An alternative that does not satisfy any one (or more) of the musts is said to be 'infeasible' and is eliminated from consideration.   The remaining

---

[42] C. H. Kepner and B. B. Tregoe, B.B. *The Rational Manager: A Systematic Approach to Problem Solving and Decision Making*, McGraw Hill, New York, NY, 1965.

alternatives are then evaluated based on how well they meet the 'wants'. We can look at 'musts' in terms of Simon's bounded rationality and Janis' common simplistic strategies discussed earlier. Musts represent aspiration levels that are used in a satisficing mode of decision-making. However, instead of selecting the first alternative that meets all of our 'musts' as is done as a common simplistic strategy when satisficing, we continue to identify additional alternatives that also satisfy our musts and then make a selection based on how well the 'feasible' alternatives satisfy our 'wants'. The 'wants' are the *objectives* that form the basis of our definition of what is a rational choice.

Attributes, such as the cost of an automobile, or the price to earnings ratio of a stock, can be *both* musts and a wants. For example, in selecting an automobile, we might require that the automobile must cost less than $40,000 (eliminating all those that cost more than that) and then use (low) cost as a want (one of our objectives) in evaluating the remaining, feasible, alternatives. We make the following recommendations when considering 'musts':

Do not use 'musts' alone as a way of making any important decision. For example, don't offer to buy the first house that you find that meets your 'musts'.

It is often to use 'musts' to narrow down the alternatives before making a compensatory evaluation. The advantage of doing this is that it is relatively easy to do and it reduces the complexity of the compensatory evaluation. The disadvantage is that it is possible to be shortsighted and eliminate one or more alternatives that, in the compensatory evaluation, might have been preferred because of the degree to which one or more of its other attributes contribute to other objectives.

If there are too many alternatives to evaluate in a practical sense, (such as stocks on the major exchanges), uses musts (such as stocks must have a price to earnings ratio of not more than 40 to 1 and a capitalization of at lease $1 Billion) to reduce the alternatives to a reasonable number. However, try to be conservative in specifying the aspiration levels for the musts.

Summary of the benefits of AHP

In summary, AHP makes it possible for executives to assimilate all the facts, weigh the pluses and minuses, reach, re-evaluate, and communicate their decision. Once an initial decision is made, it is not final; even a strong willed decision maker is subject to external pressures from special interest groups such as, suppliers, customers, employees, trade unions or politicians. Objectives that were thought to be central to a decision, may, under these outside influences, become less central or dominant and a re-evaluation becomes necessary. Gradually, priorities are changed until a new, re-shaped, decision emerges. Without a decision model audit-trails are lost and executives find it impossible to systematically review or retrace the steps and sub-decisions made in the decision process. The difficulty of conducting a proper review increases exponentially with the number of objectives.

Incremental Improvement

Now that we have seen some of how AHP works, we address the question of how you might begin using AHP in your organization. There are two basic approaches corresponding to two important business processes that have been widely publicized: (1) business process re-engineering, and (2) incremental improvement. Re-engineering is typically more costly and risky and requires commitment and freedom from constraints that are more the exception than the rule. Continuous improvement is often an easier starting path. By examining how your organization currently makes decisions or performs evaluations, and asking how the details of the current process(es) fair relative to the decision-making concepts embodied in AHP, you will see many opportunities for easy, yet significant improvements. After a few such improvements, people in your organization should become 'comfortable' with the changes and perhaps willing to make a commitment to a re-engineering of the organizations basic decision processes.

Retirement Places Rated

We will illustrate how an existing 'successful' evaluation methodology, rating retirement places, can be examined, found 'lacking' in one or more aspects, and 'improved' using some of the concepts on which AHP is based.

Background

There are many kinds of location decisions. One such decision that is becoming more widespread is selecting a location for retirement. The best reference we found on this topic is a book by David Savageau called *Retirement Places Rated*[43]. Although the former head of the National Institute on Aging, Dr. Robert Butler, advised that the best place to retire for most people "is the neighborhood where [they] spent [their lives]", Savageau says "possibly,— just possibly—there is someplace in this country where you might prosper more than the place where you now live". Perhaps Savageau recognized that as our society has become more mobile, fewer and fewer people spend the majority of their lives in any one place, so perhaps the need to select a retirement place has become more important than in the past. To take advantage of this 'opportunity', Savageau collected interesting and useful information about more than one hundred fifty retirement places throughout the United States. Realizing that just presenting this information in a book was not enough, Savageau graded the places on the basis of seven[44] factors that he felt influences the quality of retirement life: money matters, climate, job outlook, available services, housing, leisure, and personal safety.

Savageau recognized the difficulty in rating retirement places. Early in his book he states:

> "There are three points of view on rating places. The first says that defining what's good for all people at all times is not only unfair, it's impossible and shouldn't be tried at all. Another view says you can but shouldn't because measuring a touchy thing like "livability" pits cities and towns against each other and leads to wrong conclusions. The third point of view says do it as long as you make clear what

---

[43] Savageau, David, *Retirement Places Rated*, Macmillan, New York, N.Y., 1995
[44] Notice the 'magic number seven' appearing again.

your statistical yardsticks are and go on to use them consistently. Although the first and second positions may be valid, Retirement Places Rated sides with the third.

Even though *Retirement Places Rated* is the best book we found on the subject, and we agree that there is a need to rate, score, evaluate – call it what you will – in order to make a decision, there is considerable room for improvement in the concepts and methods contained in *Retirement Places Rated.* Just making your statistical yardsticks clear and using them consistently is not enough! In all fairness to Savageau, much of what we address below as inadequacies (opportunities for improvement) in *Retirement Places Rated* and its methodology are difficult to circumvent given the constraints of a static book. However, these constraints are easy to circumvent in today's world of personal computer availability. People making the important decision about where to retire need not settle for what we can best describe as 'inferior' decision-making. We next look at the following opportunities for incremental improvement:

- measuring and synthesizing from ratio rather than ordinal scales
- structuring hierarchically to better understand relationships and avoid double counting
- deriving meaningful priorities of objectives

Change in methodology – from adding ranks to averaging scores

Retirement Places Rated has more data than most people would ever care to peruse[45]. Savageau had to find ways to help interpret and synthesize this data because its impossible to synthesize it all mentally[46]. Savageau did this with the best tools he knew how to use, creatively "inventing" and refining formulas and methodologies as he progressed. In the 1990 edition of his book, Savageau ranked 151 retirement places on each of seven criteria and then added the ranks[47] to determine an overall ranking. Using this methodology, Las Vegas Nevada came in 105th. If we review the decision-

---

[45] Although our Murphy's axiom of data "the data you have you don't need and the data you need you don't have" is sure to apply in part.

[46] See page 6.

[47] Adding ranks, is as we now know, a mathematically meaningless operation since ranks are 'ordinal' level data and cannot be meaningfully added.

making concepts presented in an earlier section of this book, we will observe that the addition of ranks is mathematically meaningless! Perhaps Savageau recognized this himself, even though his book was commercially successful.

In the next (1994) edition of *Retirement Places Rated* Savageau improved his methodology by 'scoring' (instead of ranking) 183 cities on the seven criteria and then averaging the scores to determine an overall score. If the scores possess interval or ratio meaning (and presumably they do), then this is an obvious improvement. This time, Las Vegas came in first! A casual observer might conclude that Las Vegas must have improved remarkably in those five years. But the change in the result is due much more to the change in methodology than any changes in Las Vegas. Looking at Table 4 we see that Las Vegas' ranks improved in some categories, but actually got worse in others. The total of the ranks for Las Vegas did improve from 521 to 504 between the two editions of the book. But how could this small change in the rank total cause Las Vegas's overall standing to change from 105th to 1st? The answer is that adding ranks was (and is) mathematically meaningless so it is not too surprising when we see things like this happen.[48] We will now look more closely at Savageau's methodology and how it can be further improved.

Table 4 – Ranks of Las Vegas

Year Rated	1990	1995
Money Matters	128	117
Housing	128	86
Climate	63	38
Personal Safety	154	140
Services	30	105
Working	5	8
Leisure Living	13	10
Total Ranks	521	504

---

[48] We often wonder how often misleading results due to the adding of ranks are produced but go unrecognized!

An Expert Choice representation of Savageau's 'model', along with subcriteria he included under some of the criteria, is shown in Figure 36

Creating 'magic' formulas

To avoid adding ranks, Savageau needed a way to 'score' the cities on each of his lowest level 'criteria'[49] or subcriteria. To do this, he creatively invented ways to translate data into 'scores'. For example,. when evaluating the cities with respect to the Housing criterion, Savageau reasoned that the sum of mortgage payments and property taxes, as a percentage of local household income, was a reasonable measure to use. Lacking a scale on which to place these measurements (as well comparable scales for measurements for the other criteria and sub-criteria), he did what he could – he 'made up' formulas for constructing scales[50]. His housing scale, for example, is constructed using the following formula:

Mortgage payments and property taxes are added together and expressed as a percent of local household income. This percent figure is then graded against a standard where half the typical 25% mortgage lending requirement gets 100 and three times the 25% lending requirement gets a 0.

---

[49] We will call these 'objectives' to make the evaluation more meaningful.

[50] A common misconception and one made in *Retirement Places Rated*, is that if each of several separate scales have the same 'range', in this case 0 to 100, then they are 'comparable' and can be added. This is not necessarily true!

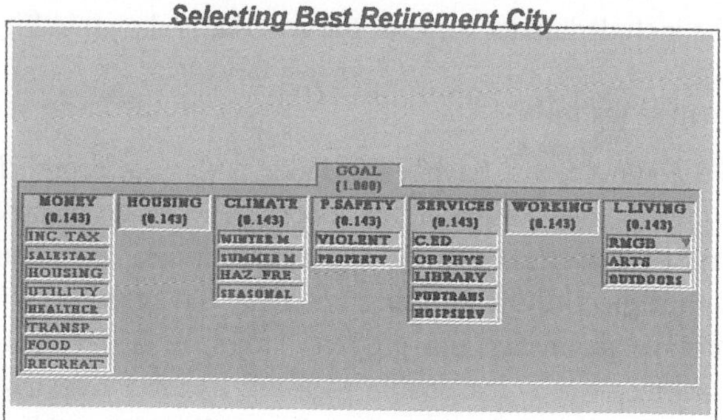

Abbreviation	Definition
ARTS	Lively arts
C.ED	Continuing Education
CLIMATE	Climate
FOOD	Cost of Food
HAZ. FRE	Hazard free
HEALTHCR	Health Care Costs
HOSPSERV	Short-term Hospital Services
HOUSING	Home mortgage payments and property taxes
INC. TAX	State Income Taxes
L.LIVING	Leisure Living
LIBRARY	Public libraries
MONEY	Money matters
OB PHYS	Office based Physicians
OUTDOORS	Outdoor Assets
P.SAFETY	Personal Safety
PROPERTY	Property Crimes
PUBTRANS	Public transportation
RECREAT	Recreation Costs
RMGB	Restaurants, Movies, Golf, Bowling
SALESTAX	State and local sales taxes
SEASONAL	Seasonal affect
SERVICES	Services
SUMMER M	Summer mildness

Figure 36 – Criteria and subcriteria

This formula, although perhaps as good as any other, is rather arbitrary! Why does a location with a percent equal to 'half' the typical 25% get a score of 100? Why not score it 100 if the percent is 1/10th the typical 25% instead? Even if we assume that those using the Savageau's book agree with basing the score on a percentage of local income, by using Savageau's formula, a location with a (mortgage payment plus property tax percent of local household income) value of 2.5% would get the same score as another location with a value of 12.5%. Obviously, they should not be equal! But is the former five times more preferable? Perhaps not, since the 'utility' of lower payments may not be linear for any individual or couple. The point is, there is no magic formula that will fit everyone. All we can say that in general, the scale is subjective, and probably non-linear at that.

The Climate criterion has four subcriteria, as seen in Figure 36 Savageau's formula for Winter Mildness is:

Winter Mildness: Equal weights to:

(a) Winter severity –average apparent (influenced by wind chill) temperature from November through April

    scale: 0 = 0; 55=100

(b) Winter length – # of days when temperature falls below freezing

    scale: 0 = 100; 365=0

While this 'formula' might, on the surface, seem reasonable, a look at some of the resulting values shows that it does not convey what most people looking for a retirement location would feel. The ratio of preferences for Florida over Maine for winter mildness (see Table 7) using Savageau's data and formula is *less* than two to one! Preferences can be estimated in many ways[51]. Whatever the way, common sense tells us that the ratio of values for the preference of Florida over Maine (for winter mildness) should be *much more* than two to one and thus Savageau's formula does *not* provide a good measure! It's possible, although not practical in the context of a hard copy book like *Retirement Places Rated,* to improve on such 'magic' formulas based on 'objective' data. Fortunately, we are no longer limited to hard copy books alone. Using the Analytic Hierarchy Process and readily available computer technology, we can elicit judgments from decision maker(s) about how many times more preferable Florida is than Maine for winter mildness. Pairwise comparisons can be made verbally, numerically or graphically. A sequence of pairwise comparisons, can, as we have seen above with Expert Choice, derive accurate ratio scale measures of

---

[51] Economists often take the approach, which we don't fully subscribe to -- to convert everything to 'dollars'. In this context, an economist might compute the ratio of the average winter hotel room rental rates in Bar Harber Maine vs. Lakeland Florida (adjusting, as Economists try to do) for other factors such as differences in economic conditions of the two areas. Another approach an economist might use would be to estimate the ratio of the number of retired people going 'South' for the winter rather than 'North' for the winter. But this measure too would have to somehow be adjusted for other related factors, not indicative of 'winter mildness' such as those who go to Maine in the winter in order to Ski.

preference for the alternatives for each objective (criterion), which in turn, can be meaningfully synthesized.

Savageau justifies his methodology by saying "do it as long as you make clear what your statistical yardsticks are and go on to use them consistently." Assuming things are correct because they are consistent is a common misconception. Can we conclude that since Savageau's Summer Mildness formula (see Table 5) produces substantially the same results (although in the opposite direction) as the winter formula, then together they form a consistent approach? The answer is obviously No. Two wrongs do not make a right. Consistency[52] is a necessary but not sufficient condition for correctness.

Table 5 – Savageau's Summer Mildness formula

Location	Winter Mildness	Summer Mildness
Bar Harbor ME	56	94
Lakeland-Winter Haven FL	100	53

Double Counting

Notice that 'Housing' appears in two places in Figure 36: both as a subcriterion of money matters, and as a criterion on its own. True, it does 'fit' both places, but we may be counting the same thing twice. If we focus on 'objectives', rather than 'criteria' we can more easily see whether this is or is not the case. What do we mean when we say housing is a criterion? The answer is not clear – only that we will use housing somehow in evaluating the alternatives. However, when we say that housing is an *objective*, and ask ourselves what we would *want* in terms of housing, several things come clearly to mind – cost of housing, availability of housing, age of housing, style of housing, etc. By including housing as both a subcriterion below money matters and as a criterion on its own, and by using formulas that score alternative locations based on the cost of housing

---

[52] A reasonable amount of consistency is necessary, but perfect consistency is not necessary.

in each instance[53], this model counts the same *objective* twice! The severity of the double counting depends on how much 'weight' is 'given' to the main housing criterion and the housing criterion below money matters. In the 'Putting it All Together' chapter of his book, Savageau uses equal weights for all the major criteria[54], with about 45% of the money matters weight going again to the housing sub-criterion! This is a considerable amount of double counting.

A better 'model' would be to have 'cost of housing' as a sub-objective under money matters as it now stands, and eliminate the stand alone housing criterion. Still better would be to include a major criterion representing the non-monetary housing factors, such as availability of housing styles[55]. Structuring the evaluation as a hierarchy and focusing on objectives rather than criteria will give us a much better idea of what we are evaluating in our 'model'. The model can help us to synthesize the multitude of factors involved in the evaluation by enabling us to determine how well the alternatives perform relative to our objectives!

Equal Weighting

As mentioned above, Savageau used equal weights for each of the seven criteria in calculating an overall score for the alternative retirement locations. However, he recognized that this wasn't necessarily the best thing to do. Savageau explained:

> "At the end of [this] book, in the chapter entitled "Putting It All Together", money matters, housing, climate, personal safety, community services, working and leisure living get equal weight to identify retirement places with across-the-board strengths.

---

[53] Savageau's formula for scoring locations based on housing costs under money matters is based on the cost of housing index for each location: housing costs that are 25 percent below the national average get a 100 and housing costs double the national average get a 0. This formula, while different from the one used for the criterion housing under the goal, not only uses information based on the same costs, but obviously points to the same objective -- lower housing costs.

[54] What else could he do? The weights are subjective and will depend on who is deciding where to retire.

[55] Savageau does indeed include information about historic neighborhoods, but these are not considered in deriving the scores for the alternative locations.

You may not agree with this system. To identify which factors are more important and which factors are less, you might want to take stock of your own preferences."

Toward that end, Savageau provides a "Preference Inventory" consisting of sixty three pairwise comparisons of the following form:
For each numbered item, decide which of the two statements is more important to you when choosing a place to retire.

A) The cost of living, or
B) Historic homes in an area
C) The duration of the winter, or
D) The odds of being a crime victim., etc.

Savageau then says to "count all the marks you've made in the boxes next to the letter A, and write that down next to money-matters; similarly items with the letter B correspond to housing, etc."

This is a valiant attempt to move away from equal weighting, which most people agree is not appropriate. However Peter Drucker emphasized (see page 45) we must 'measure', not count. Let's see why counting is not very accurate. There are 21 possible pairs of the seven criteria (or the letters A through G). Savageau provided three questions for every possible pair (63 questions in all), with each question containing a different aspect of the respective criterion. Lets consider just 21 of the questions[56] and a question representing each criterion will appear in six of these questions. Suppose someone's 'true' weights as determined from the principle eigenvector of a matrix of pairwise comparisons are as shown in the second column of the following table[57]:

---

[56] The following results will be the same if we consider all 63 questions.
[57] The following arguments hold regardless of whether the true order is A, B, C, D, E, F, G or any other order.

Table 6 – True Weights

	True Weights	Count	Calculated
A	45	6	28.6
B	16	5	23.8
C	14	4	19.0
D	10	3	14.3
E	8	2	9.5
F	5	1	4.8
G	2	0	0

Thus A is preferred to B, B to C and so on. If we assume assessments of the 21 questions that are consistent with the order of priorities in column 1, A will be preferred in each of the six questions in which it appears. That is A will be preferred in the question in which it is paired with B, and in the question in which it is paired with C, and so on. A will be preferred 6 times. B will be preferred in questions in which it is paired with C, D, E, F and G, or five times. C will be preferred in questions in which it is paired with D, E, F, and G, or four times. And so on. The count of the number of times each criterion is chosen and the resulting weights are shown in columns three and four of the table. Assuming accurate and consistent judgments, a counting technique like this would produce the same calculated weights *regardless* of the 'true' weights. Thus, for this example, the weight for criterion A, money matters, is much less than the 'true' weight. Generalizing, we can say that this counting technique will produce incorrect results in *all* cases except when the 'true' weights happen to be proportional with ratios of 6:5:4:3:2:1.

Another difficulty with this technique is the use, in the pairwise comparison questions, of different dimensions of a criterion as surrogates for the criterion. A criterion with five subcriteria, one of which is much more important than the others, would receive far less weight than it deserves because it would 'win' the comparison in the question containing an aspect of the most important sub-criterion, but might 'lose' the comparisons in questions involving the less important sub-criteria.[58]

Incremental improvement using AHP

After seeing how AHP can be used to measure and synthesize, how could you incrementally improve on the methodology used in *Retirement Places Rated*? Some of the possibilities include:

- Focus on objectives rather than criteria. This will make clear when double counting is inappropriate (and, in some cases, when it is appropriate).

- Have the decision maker(s) derive priorities for the relative importance of the major objectives by making pairwise comparisons.

- Have the decision maker(s) derive priorities for the relative importance of the sub-objectives by making pairwise comparisons.

- Improve and/or replace the formulas. It is difficult, if not impossible, to measure preferences with 'data based' formulas. Some of the formulas used in the book might be reasonable as crude approximations, but many are not. Some provide too much spread, some not enough. None include non-linearities, which might be very important. In general, formulas do not measure utility with respect to meeting objectives.

- Extract the most attractive (seven or so) alternatives from the initial ratings, and perform sensitivity analyses. Revise judgments and/or model structure as necessary. Refine alternative priorities derived from ratings with more accurate priorities derived from pairwise comparisons. The extracted set of alternatives could influence the judgments or model structure.

---

[58] Another problem with Savageau's approach is that many of the questions used subcriteria to generate the counts, but values for these subcriteria were not used in the scoring process. For example, one question asked if the cost of living was more important than historic homes in an area, the latter supposedly being used to determine the importance of housing. Yet the formula for housing did not consider historic homes at all.

For example, if each of the alternatives being considered is relatively safe, then safety might not be as important. Similarly, if one assumes that only safe neighborhoods will be considered then crime data for the entire area might not be appropriate.

Incremental improvements such as these are very general and can be applied to *any* decision-making or evaluation methodology in *any* organization. However, decision-making and evaluation processes have significant impact on the power structure of most organizations. Thus, they are difficult to change. A sequence of incremental improvements is often wiser than trying to re-engineer or develop a 'perfect' evaluation process because such improvements will, one small step at a time, add competitiveness, demonstrate credibility, and make people feel more comfortable with the resulting power shifts.

Chapter 5

From Brainstorming to Structuring to Evaluation and Choice

Brainstorming

Abandoning the bogsat[1] for compensatory decision-making with AHP is sometimes too big a first step for some organizations. Instead, a series of small steps might be easier to implement. An easy and productive first step is to encourage the seeking out of several alternative solutions to a problem or opportunity rather than settling on the first one that seems feasible. Since most people don't like problems, they usually react by taking the first way out they can find. Having only one idea or course of action open to you is quite risky in a world where flexibility is a requirement for survival. If you have only one idea, you have nothing to compare it to. The French philosopher Emile Chartier said "Nothing is more dangerous than an idea when it's the only one you have." Nobel Prize winning chemist Linus Pauling expressed a similar thought – "The best way to get a good idea is to get a lot of ideas."[2]

Brainstorming is a technique that is useful in identifying alternative solutions to a problem. The main point of the initial phase of brainstorming is to generate as many alternatives as possible. Criticism of people's contributions must be avoided, as should intimidation of some group members by the more competitive, verbal members of the group. The following are some typical brainstorming 'rules' and techniques:

- Everyone can (must) contribute.
- Let imaginations run wild. Quantity not quality of ideas is sought during the initial phase of brainstorming.

---

[1] See page 5.
[2] Von Oech, Roger A., *Whack on the Side of the Head: How You Can Be More Creative*, Warner Books, Inc., New York, N.Y., 1990, p 24.

- There is no such thing as a bad idea. Do not be judgmental at the beginning. Make absolutely no judgments about your own or anyone else's ideas or suggestions.
- Think about the ideal or the perfect situation. Push extremes. Look for opposites. Think about unlikely as well as likely situations. Utilize free-form word associations. Go off on tangents. Look for combinations of words or ideas.

Creativity

Creativity is an important part of brainstorming. Doug Hall, after reading many insightful books on creativity and thinking from numerous authors[3], provides an interesting perspective on how to increase creativity in brainstorming[4]. Hall found that providing stimuli is the key to increasing creativity. In the vast majority of brainstorming sessions people use their brains primarily as encyclopedias, digging deep-down into memory to root out ideas. As the ideas are extracted, the well begins to go dry – a process he calls brain-draining. In contrast, if provided with adequate stimuli, people can use their brains not just to withdraw ideas from their brains, like encyclopedias, but more like computers to generate ideas as combination of other ideas. Stimuli are anything takes you out of your normal frame of reference that spurs the brain to make new connections, new associations. Stimuli can be anything you see, hear, smell, taste, or touch. The ideas you hear from others in a brainstorming session are, in fact, one form of stimuli. The use of Hall's multidimensional stimuli approach to excite and agitate original thoughts has led to some impressive results – Dr. Arthur VanGundy of the University of Oklahoma experimented with groups of four college students to see how many ideas for snack food they could think of in 45 minutes. The average was 29.7 ideas per group without stimuli and 310.8 with stimuli such as product samples, magazine photos, and a spontaneous environment with loud music, good food, and Nerf guns.

---

[3] From authors including Tony Buzan, Edward de Bono, Betty Edwards, Benjamin Franklin, Guy Kawasaki, Alex Osborn, Arthur VanGundy, Joyce Wycoff.
[4] Hall, Doug, *Jump Start Your Brain*, Warner Books, Inc., New York, N.Y., 1995.

Narrowing Down

During the initial phase of brainstorming criticism is ruled out, but after the initial phase it's time to narrow down the ideas. Doug Hall puts it this way:

> ...you were sworn to respect the newborns. Now it's time for mercy killing. It's time to be tough on yourself. Time to weigh your musings against reality. Time to pick nits.

Consideration of practicalities, feasibilities, and costs will help in eliminating a few, or perhaps many of the ideas that were generated. Those that are left can be evaluated using techniques ranging from simple voting methods to a full blown AHP compensatory tradeoff analysis. There is a delicate balance between eliminating too many or too few alternatives at this stage as opposed to a later stage. Being ruthless and eliminating all but the seemingly best alternatives will make subsequent evaluations easier and faster, but also increases the chance of eliminating an alternative that, when all factors are considered, might have turned out to be the best choice.

Categorizing and Combining

Following the weeding out of impractical alternatives, it is often helpful to categorize the remaining ideas. Some ideas might pertain to problems other than the one under consideration, in which case they can be set aside and saved for future consideration. Some ideas might pertain to only one aspect of the problem under consideration in which case they must be combined with other ideas to form holistic alternatives, or alternatives that provide a total solution. For example, some ideas might pertain to products, others to marketing, others to an intended market segment, and so on. One alternative solution could be a combination of a product idea with an idea for a market segment with an idea for a marketing channel. Several alternative solutions should be designed for subsequent evaluation. This can be done quickly, without much detail, or carefully, considering all important tradeoffs. The quality of the evaluation should be commensurate with the importance of the problem or decision.

We will now illustrate a range of evaluation techniques, starting with simple voting and progressing to a full-scale compensatory evaluation using AHP.

Voting

Voting is a popular and relatively easy procedure. Voting can take many forms, including yes/no, multiple choice and rating.

Multiple Choice

Two of the simpler forms are voting yes or no on an issue or for a candidate and selecting one from a set of choices (multiple choice).

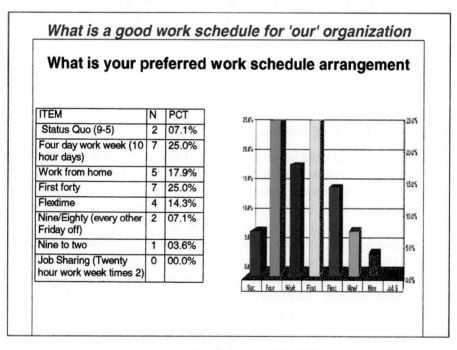

Figure 1– Multiple Choice Voting

Suppose an organization is considering the adoption of a work schedule alternative to the typical nine to five arrangement. During a brainstorming session with Team Expert Choice, the alternatives in Figure were proposed and voted on in a multiple choice (forced choice) format.

The quality of the information from such voting is minimal at best. Participants are allowed to vote for only one of the alternatives and are unable to express how strongly they feel about their choice.

Rating

We can improve the quality of the results by allowing participants to rate each of the alternatives, say on a scale from 1 to 10. We can then calculate the average rating for each of the alternatives. In order for this to be a meaningful average, however, the participants' ratings must be at least an interval measure[5]. This is not always the case. When rating gymnasts in an Olympic event, for example, judges may view the interval between 9.9 and 10.0 as being (much) greater than the interval between 9.0 and 9.1. We cannot guarantee that each participant will provide interval judgments, but we can increase the likelihood that they will do so by providing instructions such as the following:

> Please rate the alternatives such that, according to your understanding, corresponding intervals are equivalent. For example, the interval between 1 and 2 is equal to the interval between 4 and 5 or the interval between 9 and 10.

Although not necessary for calculating a meaningful average, it may be desirable to ask participants to try to provide ratio level judgments as well as interval judgments. Ratio judgments are necessary if we want to be able to interpret the ratios of the resulting averages as representing ratios of the average participant preference. For example, if the average rating of one alternative is 7, and another is 3.5, then we could say that on average, the participants preferred the former twice as much as the latter. We can increase the likelihood that participants will provide ratio judgments by providing instructions such as the following:

Please rate the alternatives such that, according to your understanding, the ratios of your ratings correspond to the ratios of your preferences. For example, a rating of 10 for one alternative and a 5 for another means that

---

[5] See page 32.

you prefer the former twice as much as the latter; similarly, a rating of 8 for one alternative and two for another means that you prefer the former four times as much as the latter.

Figure 2 contains a plot of the average ratings of a group of participants for the same alternatives shown in Figure .

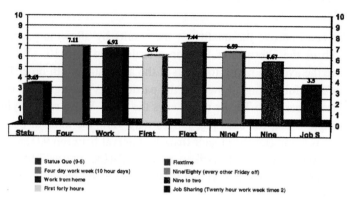

Figure 2 – Average Ratings

Comparing the multiple choice and rating results, we can see significant differences. For multiple choice voting, Flextime ranked fourth (receiving just a bit more than half the number of votes as the top two alternatives). But when participants were given the opportunity to rate each of the alternatives, Flextime was the most highly rated alternative! The differences (intervals) between Flextime and some of the alternatives in Figure 2 are rather small so we cannot say that Flextime is clearly preferred. More importantly, we haven't yet considered objectives or specific pros and cons of the alternatives.

Considering Multiple Objectives

To summarize, we increased the quality of information by going from a multiple-choice question to rating each of the alternatives. This, however, is still not adequate when considering important, or 'crucial' decisions. We should ascertain *reasons* by asking 'why is one alternative preferred to another?' What are the pros and cons of each of the alternatives. What are the objectives in making the decision? How important are the objectives, and how well does each alternative help to achieve each of the objectives? We are now in a position to answer these questions using AHP. As previously discussed, AHP is a compensatory evaluation methodology in which alternatives that are deficient with respect to one or more objectives can compensate by their performance with respect to other objectives. In other words, we can evaluate the alternatives using a reasoned approach entailing an evaluation of the relative importance of objectives, as well as an evaluation of the relative preference for the alternatives with respect to each of the objectives.

Our work schedule evaluation example has only eight alternatives, although in general we may have tens or hundreds of alternatives. We can begin structuring a decision hierarchy by sorting the alternatives rated and considering only those with the highest average ratings. Looking at the intervals between the average ratings in Figure 2, we might consider extracting the top six for a more detailed evaluation. However, it is usually advisable to include the status quo as one of the alternatives under consideration for a baseline. We will extract the top seven alternatives for subsequent evaluation in a decision hierarchy of objectives.[6]

Structuring

We can construct a decision hierarchy using either a top down (strategic) or bottom up (tactical) approach. Both strategy and tactics are instrumental to a well conceived business plan or military plan. It is difficult to plan good strategy without a fairly good knowledge of tactics – the design of a strategy that is tactically impossible to implement is useless. Similarly, brilliant tactics that do not achieve strategic objectives are misguided and perhaps useless.

A top down construction of a decision hierarchy focuses first on the identification and organization of objectives. A bottom-up approach focuses first on the alternatives – identifying pros and cons each alternative. These

---

[6] The Brainstorming module of TeamEC has a command for extracting alternatives from a Brainstorming file and automatically entering them in a Structuring file.

pros and cons will be of help in identifying objectives. If the decision maker(s) have a good understanding of their objectives then a top down approach is recommended. Otherwise a bottom up approach should be used. In practice a little top down structuring can be followed by some bottom up structuring, followed by more top down, and so on.

Top Down Structuring

Top down structuring begins with members of the group identifying objectives, such as those shown in Figure 3. As additional objectives are identified, they can be clustered (for example by using the 'Clusterview of Objectives' window in the Structuring module of Expert Choice and TeamEC) into major objectives, sub-objectives, sub-sub-objectives and so on. Instead of following this path, we will, for illustrative purposes, switch to a 'bottom up' approach.

Figure 3 – Top down identification of objectives

Bottom Up Structuring

A 'bottom up' approach focuses on the alternatives and their pros and cons. For example, pros for the Flextime alternative (see Figure 4) include flexibility for employees to schedule outside appointments and reduced commute time. Office coverage was a con for the Flextime Alternative. The Nine to Two alternative (Figure 5) would help attract better people (for example some very qualified professional women who were leaving the workforce to attend to their families), but had cons of decreased office coverage, increased overhead cost per person, and less pay for some employees.

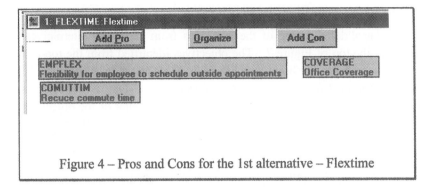

Figure 4 – Pros and Cons for the 1st alternative – Flextime

A pro for one alternative can be a con for another alternative. For example, cost might be a pro for an inexpensive alternative and a con for an expensive alternative.

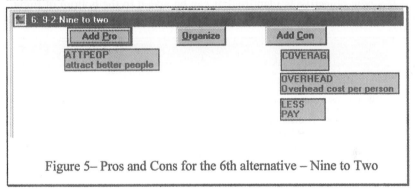

Figure 5– Pros and Cons for the 6th alternative – Nine to Two

It is not necessary to develop an exhaustive pro/con list for each alternative. The pros and cons serve mainly to help identify objectives. (It may be desirable, however, to develop an exhaustive pro/con list for each alternative for documentation purposes and to defend any subsequent recommendation from adversaries who claim that some considerations were omitted from the evaluation.)

From Pros/Cons to Objectives

A consolidated listing of the pros/cons from all of the alternatives is shown at the top of Figure 7. The objectives identified from the top-down approach appear at the bottom of Figure 7. Each of the pros/cons will help identify (point to) one (or more) objectives. This cannot be done automatically[7] because the decision maker(s) must think of the objective(s) pointed to by the pro/con and rephrase it, when necessary in the form of an objective. Rephrasing is usually necessary for cons. For example, the EMPFLEX pro does not require rephrasing, but LESS PAY does. In fact, LESS PAY might 'point' to two objectives: (1) Employee compensation, (which might subsequently be clustered under 'employee objectives') and (2) Reducing business expenses (which might subsequently be clustered under 'business objectives').

If a new objective is identified, it can be added to the bottom of Figure 7. The objectives can also be clustered into levels and additional objectives

	PC Abbrev	Description				
1	EMPFLEX	Flexibility for employee to schedule outside appointments				
2	COVERAGE	Office Coverage				
3	COMUTTIM	Reduce commute time				
4	LESS PAY	Less pay				
5	COVERAGE	Coverage				
6	OVERHEAD	Overhead cost per person				
7	LESS PAY	Less pay				

	Level 1	Level 2	Level 3	Level 4	Level 5	
1	TRAFFIC					Less traffic
2	PRODCTVT					Productivity
3	OFFICE C					office coverage
4	ATTPEOP					attract better people
5						
6						
7						

Figure 6 – From Pros/Cons to Objectives

added directly to the list. A tree view of the resulting objectives hierarchy is shown in Figure 6 and a clusterview is shown in Figure 8. The top level

---

[7] The Structuring module of Expert Choice prompts the decision-maker for the desired phrasing when pros/cons are dragged from the pro/con list and dropped into the objectives hierarchy.

	Level 1	Level 2	Level 3	Level 4	Level 5	
1	EMPMORAL					Emp morale
2		PAY				pay
3		EMPFLEX				Flexibility for employee to schedule outside appointments
4		LESSFRIC				Less friction in operation
5		TRAFFIC				Less traffic
6		COMUTE T				comute time
7	PRODCTVT					Productivity
8		OUTPUT				Output
9		OFFICE C				office coverage
10	ATTPEOP					attract better people
11	FINANCIA					Financial considerations
12		OVERCOST				overhead cost
13		HEADCNT				Minimize head count
14	COMPETIT					Competitiveness
15		CUSTSAT				Customer satisfaction
16		QUALITY				Quality

Figure 7 – Treeview of Objectives Hierarchy

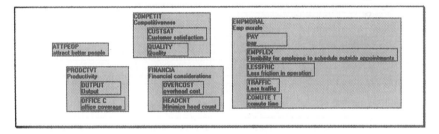

Figure 8 – Clusterview of Objectives Hierarchy

objectives include employee morale, productivity, attracting better employees, financial considerations, and competitiveness. The resulting Expert Choice Evaluation and Choice model[8] is shown in Figure 9.

Evaluation and Choice

From this point on, a full compensatory evaluation can be performed including making pairwise comparisons to derive priorities (see page 78), synthesizing priorities (see page 78), and performing sensitivity analyses (see page 79). With Team Expert Choice, individual decision makers can each enter their judgments using either radio frequency keypads, or remotely

---

[8] The Expert Choice Structuring module command File Build EC model automatically creates the Evaluation and Choice model by appending the alternatives to the bottom of the objectives hierarchy.

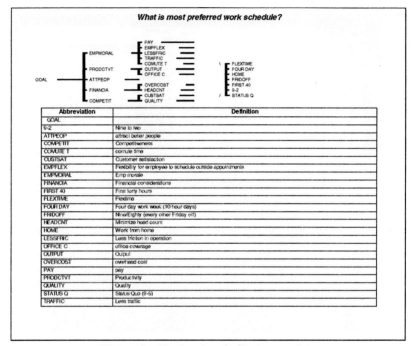

Figure 9 – Evaluation & Choice model

use the Internet. Then individual judgments can be transmitted for aggregation and dissemination.

Chapter 6

Other Topics / Refinements

Missing Judgments

The pairwise comparison matrices each contain redundant judgments in the sense that there are N x (N-1)/2 judgments in a matrix of size N, when in fact, only N-1 judgments are required to solve for priorities using simple algebra. The redundancy is very useful, however, as it improves accuracy in a manner somewhat analogous to estimating a quantity by taking the average of repeated (and hence redundant) observations. The increased accuracy permits priorities to be calculated even for less accurate or fuzzy judgments, such as when words are used instead of numbers.

An additional property related to the redundancy of judgments is the measure of consistency. Saaty[1] defined a measure of deviation from consistency, called a consistency index, as:

$$C.I. = (\lambda_{max} - N)/(N-1)$$

Saaty calculated a consistency ratio (C.R.) as the ratio of the C.I. to a random index (R.I.) which is the average C.I. of sets of judgments (from a 1 to 9 scale) for randomly generated reciprocal matrices. Harker[2] discussed three reasons why one would want to make fewer than the full set of N(N-1) judgments for each of one or more sets of factors in an AHP model:

- to reduce the time to make the judgments
- because of an unwillingness to make a direct comparison between two particular elements
- because of being unsure about some comparisons

Harker also proposed a method of dealing with missing entries. This method, which is also very useful in helping to reduce inconsistency has been programmed into Expert Choice. If one identifies a judgment possibly in

---

[1] T. L. Saaty, The Analytic Hierarchy Process, McGraw-Hill, New York (1980).
[2] P. T. Harker, "Alternative Modes of Questioning in the Analytic Hierarchy Process", Math Modeling, Vol. 9, No. 3-5, pp. 353-360, 1987, Pergamon Journals.

error, either by manual inspection or with the help of a computerized
algorithm, then it is useful to be able to treat the judgment in question as
missing, and calculate what it should be in order to be as consistent as possible
with the other judgments.

Using Hard Data

Priorities can be derived from data as well as from pairwise
comparisons – provided a linear or inverse linear relationship is deemed to
be reasonable. For example, the relative preference for a set of alternatives
with respect to longevity can be derived directly from expected time to
failure data for each of the alternatives. Assuming a linear relationship, an
alternative with an expected time to failure of 4 years would be twice as
preferable as one with an expected time to failure of 2 years. Simple
arithmetic (usually carried out by a computer) is adequate to derive the
priorities by adding up the expected time to failures, and dividing by the
total to normalize such that the priorities add up to one. The relative
preferences for three alternatives with time to failure of 2, 4 and 6 years
would be approximately .167, .333 and .500 respectively. Inverse
relationships, appropriate when a higher data value is less desirable, can be
calculated in a similar fashion. For example, the relative preference with
respect to cost for three alternatives costing $2, $4, and $5 respectively
would be .545, .273, .182 since the first is twice as preferable as the second
and three times as preferable as the third.

The temptation to derive priorities from hard data is difficult to resist.
For one thing, the data might have been costly and time consuming to
gather, so why contaminate it with human judgment? Secondly, an
evaluation that uses as much 'hard data' as possible gives the appearance of
being more 'objective'. But it is often advisable to resist deriving priorities
directly from hard data, and use the hard data as the basis and substantiation
for judgments instead. Preferences are often not linearly related to data. A
vehicle with a top speed of 240 mph is not twice as preferable as a vehicle
with a top speed of 120 mph for ordinary drivers. A vehicle with a top
speed of 240 mph might, however, be twice as preferable as one with a top
speed of 200 mph for a racing car driver. The human judgment that is

required to translate the data into ratio scale priorities (using pairwise comparisons) adds to the accuracy of the evaluation – provided the human is knowledgeable! This judgment can be applied using verbal, numerical or graphical comparisons.

Converting to Pairwise

It is sometimes desirable to convert data to pairwise ratios and then adjust the ratios using human judgment. Expert Choice has a command to convert data to pairwise comparisons after which the pairwise comparisons can then be modified to reflect any non-linearities in utility appropriate to the evaluation.

Transformation of data

AHP is not intended to replace calculators or spreadsheet programs but to help synthesize the results from many analyses and perspectives. Financial calculations, in particular, are best made with a spreadsheet program, the results of which can be applied in an AHP model. Year by year income and expenses can be entered, totaled, and discounted if desired, to produce a net present value for each alternative under consideration. The financial objective might be evaluated only in terms of net present value, but more typically, other objectives such as initial investment, financing arrangements, and cash flow are important as well.

Although financial calculations are not normally done in an AHP model, Expert Choice does have a feature to transform financial data (or other hard data) to produce results that are comparable to what one would do in a spreadsheet. Consider the following example involving two financial objectives – interest income and capital appreciation:

Table 1 – Interest and Capital Appreciation

Alternative	Interest	Capital Appreciation	Total
Alternative A	$120	$1500	$1620
Alternative B	$160	$1200	$1360
Alternative C	$250	$ 900	$1150
Total	$530	$3600	$4130

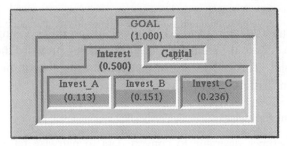

Figure 1 – Priorities with respect to Interest Income

Figure 1 and Figure 4 show the priorities of the alternatives with respect to Interest and Capital Appreciation based on the data entered directly into an Expert Choice model. The priorities for the objectives, Interest and Capital, should not, however, be equal, since capital appreciation is so much more than interest income.

Rather than making pairwise comparisons as to the relative importance of interest and capital appreciation, the priorities can be derived from the data entered for the alternatives. The priorities[3], shown in, Figure 2 are precisely the ratio of $530/$3600. A synthesis of this small model (which in

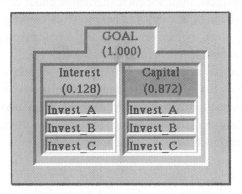

Figure 2 – Data transformed to calculate priorities of objectives

---

[3] From the Expert Choice Transformation option at the goal to determine the priorities of the children based on use the data in the grandchildren.

Figure 3 – Alternative priorities

reality would be part of a larger model) results in the alternative priorities shown in Figure 3. The ratio of these priorities is the same as the ratio of the total incomes of the three alternatives: $1620: $1360: $1150.

Artificial Clustering of Elements – Linking Clusters

Earlier we talked about how the decomposition principle of AHP is applied to structure a complex problem into a hierarchy of clusters, sub-clusters, sub-sub clusters and so on. The main reason for clustering elements is to better cope with complexity. A second reason is to reduce the number of pairwise comparisons required. Pairwise comparison of 24 nodes would require 24 x 23 / 2, or 276 comparisons. Pairwise comparing three clusters of 8 nodes each would require 3 x 8x 7/2 +3 (to compare the three clusters) = 87 comparisons in all. Still another reason to organize elements into subclusters is accommodate situations where the disparity between elements in a group is so great that they are not of the same "order of magnitude". We also discussed why each cluster should have no more than seven, plus or minus two elements.

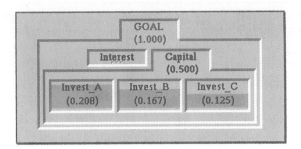

Figure 4 – Priorities with respect to Capital Appreciation

Occasionally, a decision-maker may have more than nine nodes in a cluster and will not want to, or cannot cluster them into meaningful sub-clusters·

It is possible to organize the elements into artificial clusters of up to nine elements each and perform pairwise comparisons of the elements within each of the clusters. When deriving the priorities for the artificial clusters, the Expert Choice "link elements" option will select the first element from each of the artificial clusters for pairwise comparisons. The priorities for the artificial clusters that result from these pairwise comparisons are then calculated such that the ratios of the *first elements* within each of the clusters correspond to the pairwise comparisons of these elements.

Ratings Approach

Absolute vs. Relative Measurement

The two ways to prioritize alternatives are known as relative measurement and absolute measurement. When you create a model using all *relative measurement* the priorities of the objectives, sub-objectives *and alternatives* are computed by comparing the elements one to another. In contrast, an absolute measurement model is used to gauge the *alternatives* against an established scale and not against each other. In everyday life we often use absolute measurement – for example, when measuring distance (e.g. miles), volume (e.g. liters), and temperature (e.g. degrees Celsius). In Expert Choice we can derive new scales even where none exist. For example we can establish categories (which we call intensities) into which letters of recommendation for students fall: Excellent, Above Average, Average, Below Average, and Poor; and then prioritize them. After prioritizing the categories, they become the standards or scale for measuring letters of recommendation. Absolute measurement is performed in the Expert Choice Ratings spreadsheet. In a Ratings approach the objectives are pairwise compared against one another as usual, but the alternatives are evaluated using a pre-established scale instead of compared to one another. While some scales such as miles or liters are well established and widely recognized[4], you will often create your own scales that can be customized for your particular evaluation.

The ratings approach combines the power of the hierarchy and the pairwise comparison process with the capability to rate hundreds or thousands of alternatives. Ratings models are used in a wide variety of applications such as college admission decisions, personnel evaluation, and resource allocation (see page 235). The ratings approach looks more like the traditional weights and scores approach for evaluating alternatives in that alternatives, arranged in rows, are rated against the lowest level sub-objectives of the hierarchy, arranged in columns. The priorities of the columns are derived with pairwise comparisons, but pairwise comparisons are *not* used for evaluating the alternatives. Instead, each alternative is rated in each column (representing a lowest level sub-objective) on a scale of intensities specific to that column (lowest level sub-objective).

The hierarchy for a RATINGS model differs from that of a traditional AHP model in that intensities appear at the lowest level of the hierarchy instead of the alternatives.[5] The intensities, in a sense, serve as surrogates for the alternatives. Instead of deriving priorities for the alternatives with respect to each of the lowest level sub-objectives, we derive priorities for the intensities through a pairwise comparison process. For example, instead of

---

[4] Even when working with well defined scales it may desirable to derive a new scale based on the defined scale in order to reflect preference which is often non linear and sometimes even non-monotonic.
[5] A traditional AHP model can be converted to a RATINGS model by deleting the leaves of the Goal plex and then adding intensities below each of the lowest level sub-objectives.

comparing alternatives such as John and Sue with respect to quality of work, we define rating intensities for rating quality of work, such as OUTSTANDING, EXCELLENT, AVERAGE, BELOW AVERAGE, POOR, and make judgments such as: how much more preferable would an employee who produces outstanding quality of work be to one who produces excellent quality of work. Subsequently, the alternatives are entered in as rows of the ratings spreadsheet and rated using the intensity scales specific to each lowest level sub-objective (or column of the spreadsheet).

Do not necessarily reserve the Ratings approach only for models with a large number of alternatives. Sometimes a Ratings model is used even when you have only a few alternatives because it looks more like a traditional evaluation methodology and therefore may be more familiar to those using it, or because there may be rules or regulations that prohibit comparing one alternative against another[6].

An Overview of a Ratings Model

We illustrate the RATINGS approach using an employee evaluation model. Rating intensities must be established for each lowest level sub-objectives. For example, the lowest level sub-objectives in the employee evaluation model are Education, Years of Experience, Quantity of Work, and Quality of Work. We decided that the Education intensity should have the four intensities: High School degree, Bachelor's degree, Masters degree, and Ph.D. There are five intensities for the Years of Experience objective: 1 to 2 years, 3 to 5 years, 5 to 10 years, 10 to 15 years and more than 15 years. The objectives Quantity of Work and Quality of Work have the same intensities: Excellent, Above Average, Average, Below Average, and Poor.

The intensity nodes are inserted into the model under the objectives (or sub-objectives) to which they apply. In the pairwise comparison process you will be asking questions such as: "How much more preferable a worker who is Excellent rather than Above Average with respect to Quality of Work?" When the priorities have been determined, you, the decision

---

[6] Government procurement rules sometimes prohibit comparing one alternative against another.

maker, have derived a new customized scale, a standard with which to consistently measure each alternative with respect to the overall decision goal, based on your experience. Some scales may be widely used by others, while some will be specially derived scales created to measure some objectives or criteria for which no scale previously existed.

Creating the Ratings Model from Evaluation and Choice

Like the relative measurement models, Ratings models can be created directly in EVALUATION AND CHOICE. However, instead of alternatives, you will enter intensity scales at the bottom of the hierarchy. The alternatives are then entered into the Ratings spreadsheet for the final comparisons.

The main steps for creating a Ratings model are:
- Open a new file
- Edit Insert:
  - Goal
  - Objectives
  - Sub-objectives - from one to several levels of sub-objective
  - Intensities
- (Assessment) Pairwise compare all (sub)objectives throughout the model to establish priorities
- (Assessment) Pairwise compare the intensities under the lowest level of (sub)objectives
- (Assessment) RATINGS and enter the alternatives in the RATINGS spreadsheet
- Rate the alternatives in the RATINGS spreadsheet.

A typical ratings model is shown below. The EVALUATION AND CHOICE part of the model includes the goal, objectives, (sub)objectives and has intensities as the leaves of the model.

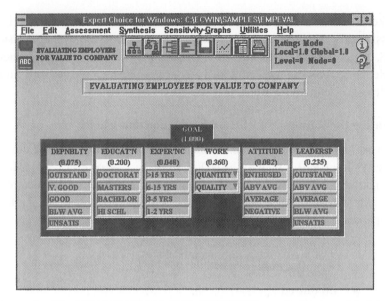

Figure 5 – The EVALUATION AND CHOICE Part of a Ratings Model.

Using Ranges for Intensities

Often people are more comfortable making judgments if the intensity nodes are expressed as a range of values. For example, under the objective, **Years of Experience** in the employee evaluation model there are four intensity nodes: 1-2 YRS, 3-5 YRS, 6-15 YRS, and > 15 YRS (more than 15 years). Note that the ranges do not have to be equal in span.

In constructing intensity scales the intention should be to convey the information about the alternative being rated and to use ranges that are logical to the evaluator. **Years of Experience** conveys something about how useful the employee is to the company and an experienced evaluator knows what it means for an employee to have experience of 1-2 YRS or 6-15 YRS. It would perhaps make no sense to the evaluator to distinguish between 9 years and 10 years of experience. Another option would be to name the intensities with category names such as Novice, Some experience, Solid experience, and Senior person.

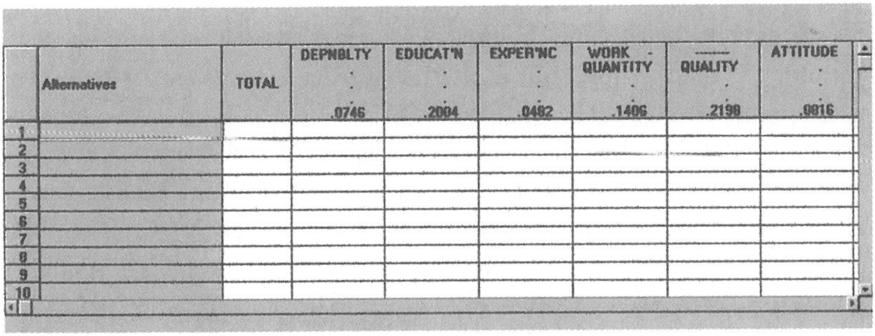

Figure 6 – The Startup Ratings Screen

Using the Same Intensities for all Objectives

Intensities, should be specific to lowest level sub-objective. However a helpful shortcut is to build the first rating set, derive its priorities through the usual pairwise comparison process, and then replicate this set to the leaves, the other bottom level (sub)-objectives in the hierarchy. Then revise the intensities for specific sub-objectives where necessary. For example, an intensity set of Outstanding, Excellent, might be appropriate to the lowest level sub-objectives, but not to all. Furthermore, examine and revise the judgments that are used to derive intensity priorities where necessary. For example, ratio of outstanding to good for appearance of an Air Force Pilot should be different than ratio of outstanding to good for ability to maneuver fighter aircraft in combat.

Note there is a column for each objective or lowest level sub-objective in the ratings spreadsheet. For example, DEPNBLTY, EDUCAT'N, EXPER'NC, and ATTITUDE are objectives and have their own columns. The objective of WORK has two sub-objectives, QUANTITY and QUALITY, so WORK itself does not have a column, but it's sub-objectives do.

From absolute to relative measurement

After prioritizing the alternatives using the ratings approach it is possible to select a subset of the alternatives (up to nine) and extract them to a temporary E&C model (named $$$) in order to: (a) view sensitivity graphs, and/or (b) refine the priorities with pairwise relative comparisons.

The E&C model named $$$ that is created by extracting up to 9 alternatives from a ratings spreadsheet will, down to the lowest level of sub-objectives, be identical to the E&C model on which the ratings spreadsheet is based. The alternatives that were extracted from the ratings spreadsheet will replace the original intensities under each of the lowest level sub-objectives. Data for the alternatives will based on the absolute ratings entered in the ratings spreadsheet. If one of the alternatives extracted is an 'ideal' alternative (received the highest intensity for every lowest level sub-objective), then an ideal mode synthesis will produce priorities for the alternatives in exactly the same ratio as those obtained in the absolute ratings mode.

Sensitivity graphs can be viewed for the alternatives extracted from the ratings spreadsheet. In addition, the priorities of the alternatives with respect to the lowest level sub-objectives can be 'refined' through the pairwise comparison process, by converting the alternative data to pairwise judgments and adjusting the judgments. For example, two alternatives that performed approximately the same might be each rated as Excellent with respect to one of the objectives then their data values will be the same. When these data values are converted to pairwise, the judgment between the two will be equal. However, a decision maker might, when comparing one directly to the other, feel that one is a bit more preferable, and can adjust the pairwise judgment accordingly. If adjustments are made to pairwise comparisons, the $$$ temporary model should be saved under a permanent name.

Ideal and Distributive Synthesis Modes (Preventing or allowing rank reversals)

Researchers in decision analysis fields that developed prior to AHP, (expected utility theory and multiattribute utility theory) based their work on axioms that did not allow rank reversals to occur when "irrelevant alternatives", are introduced for consideration.   More specifically, the axiomatic base of utility theory includes an assumption like the one made by Luce and Raiffa[7]:

"Adding new acts (alternatives) to a decision problem under uncertainty, each of which is weakly dominated (preferred) by or is equivalent to some old act, has no effect on the optimality or non-optimality of an old act."

The above axiom is strengthened into the axiom that states the principle of the *independence of irrelevant alternatives*, Luce and Raiffa (1957, p288):

"If an act is non-optimal for a decision problem under uncertainty, it cannot be made optimal by adding new acts to the problem."

In contrast, AHP can either allow or prevent rank reversals.   AHP, as originally conceived by Saaty (1980), assumes what we will call a "closed" system in allocating priorities to alternatives. By a closed system we mean that the sum of the priority *distributed* to the alternatives from each lowest level (sub)criterion does not increase or decrease if new alternatives are added or existing alternatives are removed from consideration.   Multi-attribute Utility Theory (MAUT) on the other hand, employs what we will refer to as an "open" system because the sum of the priorities allocated to alternatives will increase or decrease as new alternatives are added or existing alternatives are removed.   As will be illustrated below, the ranking of alternatives in a "closed" system can change when a new but dominated (or so called irrelevant) alternative is added to a decision. We will refer to a changing of rank when an irrelevant alternative is added to the decision as a rank reversal.

---

[7] Luce, R.D. and H. Raiffa, 1957, *Games and Decisions*. John Wiley and Sons, Inc., New York., p. 288

Discussion of rank reversal in what follows will always be in the context of the introduction or removal of an irrelevant alternative as there is no debate about the reversal of rank when a relevant alternative, i.e., one that is not dominated on every criterion is added to or removed from a decision. Rank reversal cannot happen in an "open" system. A debate has been ongoing between practitioners of AHP and MAUT about whether the rank of alternatives should be *allowed* to change when an "irrelevant" alternative is added to the decision. AHP practitioners have argued that a change in rank is legitimate. MAUT practitioners have argued that it is not. Each side has presented examples where their argument has appeal. As we will see, both sides are correct, but under different circumstances. We will see that when dealing with a "closed" system, rank adjustment is not only legitimate, but is often desirable. Conversely, when dealing with an "open" system, rank adjustment should be precluded. Rank adjustment, or what MAUT practitioners call rank reversal, occurs when the ranking of a set of alternatives changes upon the introduction of a so called "irrelevant alternative" – an alternative that is dominated by one or more previously existing alternatives. There are two basic misconceptions about this phenomenon. First, the description of such an alternative as "irrelevant" is misleading. Huber, Payne, and Puto[8] (1982) state that "the very presence of [a] dominated alternative results in quite different choice probabilities among the remaining alternatives than in the pristine state, where such items are never considered." This is certainly true when using AHP relative measurement as any alternative is a fortiori relevant since all other alternatives are evaluated in terms of it. We illustrate this with an example on page 156.

The second misconception is about the effect that irrelevant alternatives "should" have in an evaluation. Some MAUT practitioners demand that "irrelevant" alternatives "should" not affect the ranking of other alternatives. This is sometimes referred to as an "independence of irrelevant alternative" assumption. For example, Dyer[9] (1990) cautions about generating "rank

---

[8] Huber, J., Payne, J. W., and Puto, C., 1982. Adding Asymmetrically Dominated Alternatives: Violations of Regularity and the Similarity Hypothesis. Journal of Consumer Research. Vol. 9, June, 90-98.
[9] Dyer, J. S. 1990. Remarks on The Analytic Hierarchy Process, Management Science, Vol. 36, No. 3, 249-258.

orderings that are not meaningful with respect to the underlying preferences of the decision maker" when additional alternative(s) are introduced for consideration. Although it is possible for any algorithm to generate ranks that do not agree with the underlying preferences of a decision maker, there is nothing to have us believe that a rank adjustment is necessarily contrary to the underlying preferences of decision makers. Furthermore, the arbitrary prohibition of rank adjustment may *lead* to flawed results because there are many situations where a rank adjustment (reversal) is desirable. This will be illustrated below.

The Cause of Rank Adjustment

Rank reversal does *not* occur because of eigenvector calculations, because of the nine point scale used in AHP, because of inconsistencies in judgments, nor because "exact" copies are included in an evaluation. Forman (1987) gives an example where there is perfect consistency and where the introduction of new alternatives causes a rank reversal. The example given by Belton and Gear (1982) has an "exact" copy, but a similar example by Dyer (1990) does not. Dyer argues that "The defense of the AHP on the grounds that copies should not be allowed as alternatives is without foundation, and cannot be supported on intuitive or on technical grounds." We agree in part — copies should be allowed. However, the "defense" of AHP, or its strength, is that it can adjust rank when copies are introduced and this in fact can be supported on both intuitive and technical grounds as will be shown later.

Rank reversal can take place with *any* technique that decomposes and synthesizes in a relative fashion, regardless of whether it uses pairwise comparisons, eigenvector calculations, or demands perfect consistency. There is agreement between AHP and MAUT practitioners. Rank reversal occurs because of an *abundance* or *dilution* effect (or what has also been called a *substitution* effect). This is discussed in Saaty[10] (1990), Dyer[11]

---

[10] Saaty, T. L. 1990. An Exposition of the AHP in Reply to the Paper "Remarks on the Analytic Hierarchy Process", Management Science, Vol. 36, No. 3, 259-268.

[11] Dyer, J. S. 1990. Remarks on The Analytic Hierarchy Process, *Management Science*, Vol. 36, No. 3, 249-258.

(1990), and Forman[12] (1987), and illustrated below. Since value or worth is, more times than not, affected by relative abundance or scarcity, the ability for a methodology to adjust rank is often a desirable property.

Saaty[13] (1991b), discusses conditions under which one might justifiably say that rank can and should be preserved and when it should not. While some authors (Belton and Gear[14] (1982), Shoner and Wedley[15] (1989), and Dyer (1990)) have suggested that the choice of a modeling approach be based on rank reversal considerations, we propose that a more fundamental and meaningful consideration is whether scarcity is or is not germane to the decision. If scarcity is germane then a closed system (distributive synthesis) is appropriate and rank reversal should be allowed to occur. If scarcity is not germane, then an open system (ideal synthesis) is appropriate and rank reversal should not be allowed to occur. Consequently, a robust decision methodology should be able to accommodate either situation. An extension to AHP to allow modeling both open and closed systems will be presented below. Other modifications to AHP, such as B-G modified AHP (Belton and Gear 1982) and Referenced AHP (Schoner and Wedley 1989) have been advocated in order to prevent rank reversal. While these modifications hold merit and are in fact the same as, or similar to, the open system (ideal synthesis) of AHP discussed below, the merit does not stem from preventing rank reversal nor should these modifications replace the conventional AHP since rank reversals are sometimes, perhaps even often, desirable.

Closed and Open Systems – Scarcity and Abundance

In a "closed" system with a *fixed amount of resources*, scarcity is germane. The distribution of a country's gold, the allocation of a corporation's R&D budget, and the distribution of votes to political candidates are good examples. Suppose a newly formed country decided to

---

[12] Forman, E. H., 1987. Relative Vs. Absolute Worth, *Mathematical Modeling*, Vol. 9, No. 3-5, 195-202.

[13] Saaty, T. L. 1991b. Rank and the Controversy About the Axioms of Utility Theory -- A Comparison of AHP and MAUT, *Proceedings of the 2nd International Symposium of The Analytic Hierarchy Process*, Pittsburgh, PA, 87-111.

[14] Belton, V. and Gear, T. 1982. On a Shortcoming of Saaty's Method of Analytic Hierarchies. *Omega* Vol. 11 No. 3, 226-230.

[15] Schoner, B. S. & Wedley, B. W, 1989, "Ambiguous Criteria Weights in AHP: Consequences and Solutions", Decision Sciences, 20, 462-475.

distribute its gold reserve to identified segments of society based on evaluation objectives that included population and economic potential. Suppose that after distributing the gold a previously overlooked segment of the society with a small population but great economic potential was identified. In order to make a distribution to this segment, gold would have to be taken back from the existing segments and redistributed. Because the previous distribution was made partly on the basis of population and economic potential, sectors that were highly populated but with relatively low economic potential would lose less than segments with relatively low population and high economic potential and a rank reversal could occur. Similarly, a conservative independent candidate entering the race for the U.S. Presidency in which the Republican candidate had the lead might appeal more to Republican voters than to Democratic voters and a rank reversal might take place between the Republican and Democratic candidates.

In contrast, scarcity is not germane in an "open" system where *resources can be added or removed*. As an example, consider the distribution of a new country's currency. Suppose a new country was deciding how to distribute currency to identified segments of society based on evaluation objectives that included population and economic potential. If after distributing its currency, a new segment appears, more currency can be printed and distributed to the new segment based on its population and economic potential (as well as the other evaluation objectives). There is no need to take back currency from existing segments. While the percentage of wealth (in currency) of the previously existing segments would diminish because more currency was printed, the relative amounts of currency and hence the rank order of the segments would not change.

The assumptions of an open system can be better understood by defining a reference "unit of wealth". Suppose there were an alternative that was best on every objective used in the evaluation – an "ideal" alternative.[16] A reference "unit" of wealth is the amount of wealth that this "ideal" alternative would receive. Each real alternative, or segment of society in this

---

[16] This is in contrast with a utopian alternative which could be defined as having the best conceivable values on each objective.

example, would receive some percentage of the reference "unit". Subsequently, the relative wealth of each alternative can be found by normalizing over all real alternatives.

In the currency distribution example, if a new segment of society is introduced and additional currency is printed for the new segment, the ratios and rank order of wealth for previously existing segments will not change.

Closed and Open Synthesis Modes with AHP.

The treatment of closed and open systems leads us to the following two AHP synthesis modes. We next discuss, in turn, Closed and Open Synthesis modes with AHP.

Closed System (Distributive Synthesis)

When priorities are distributed in an AHP hierarchy of objectives and sub-objectives, the global priority of the goal (standardized to 1.0) is distributed to the objectives, and subsequently to the lowest level sub-objectives. (This also would be true for an MAUT hierarchy of objectives). In the original AHP implementation (which we will henceforth refer to as the closed system or distributive synthesis) the priorities of the lowest level sub-objectives are *distributed* to the alternatives in the same fashion. If, for example, an objective's global priority were .4 (see Figure 7) and the local priorities of the three alternatives under the objective were .5, .3 and .2, the global priority of the objective would be distributed to the three alternatives as global priorities of .2, .12, and .08 respectively; see Figure 8.

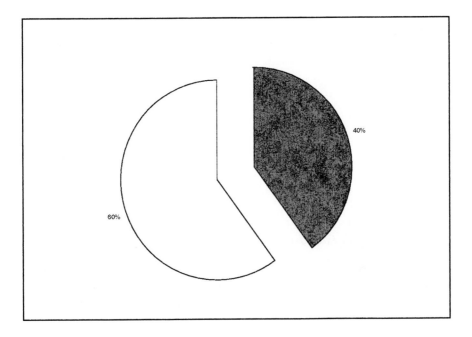

Figure 7 – Evaluation Objective with .4 global priority

If a new alternative were added to (or removed from) the analysis, the existing alternatives would lose (or gain) priority under each objective. For example, if a new alternative D, identical to the second best alternative B, were added under this objective, the local priorities would change to 0.385, 0.231, 0.154, and 0.231. The distribution of the .4 priority of the objective would be 0.154, 0.092, 0.062, and 0.092 as shown in Figure 9. The system is "closed" in that the total priority of the alternatives under each (sub)objective will not change and the total priority for the alternatives under all (sub)objectives will always equal 1.0.

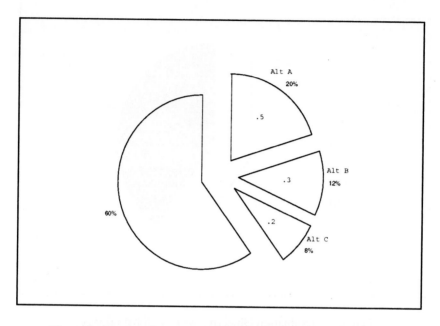

Figure 8 – Evaluation objective priority distributed to the alternatives

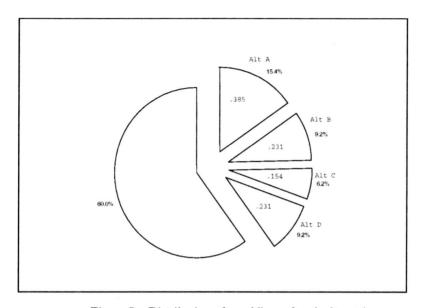

Figure 9 – Distribution after adding a fourth alternative

Open System (Ideal Synthesis)

A simple extension has been made to AHP in order to model open systems. Instead of distributing each (sub)-objective's priority to the alternatives, the priority is allocated to the alternatives such that the most preferred alternative under each (sub)objective receives the full priority of the (sub)objective. This idea was first proposed by Belton and Gear as a replacement for, rather than an extension to, AHP. Each of the other alternatives receives a priority *proportional to its preference relative to the most preferred alternative.* For example, if an objective's priority were .4 (as shown in the right hand segment of the pie chart in Figure 8) and the local priority of three alternatives under the objective were .5, .3 and .2 respectively, the three alternatives would receive global priorities of .4, .24 and .16 respectively as shown in Figure 10.

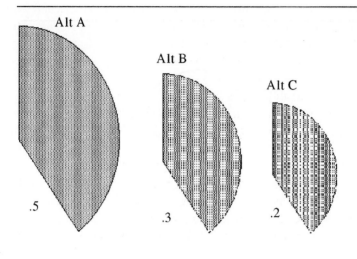

Figure 10 - Three alternatives under the .4 priority objective

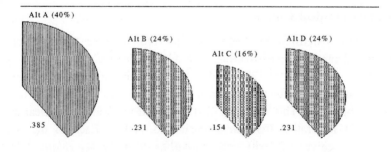

Figure 11 – Ideal mode: Objective with .4 global priority and four alternatives

If, as above, a new alternative that is identical to the second best alternative under this objective were added, the local priorities would again change to 0.385 0.231 0.154 and 0.231. However, the allocation of the .4 priority of the objective using the open system (ideal synthesis) would be .4, .24, .16, and .24 as shown in Figure 11.

The rationale for this approach is that an "ideal" alternative (an alternative having the most preferred attribute value for every objective) would serve as a reference and receive a total priority (before normalization) of 1.0, while each real alternative would have priorities proportionately less. If we think of 1.0 as representing a "standard", each real alternative receives some fraction of the "standard" depending on how well the alternative compares to the ideal on each objective. Although, no alternative can receive a priority from a (sub)-objective greater than the (sub)-objective's priority, the sum of the alternatives' priorities under a (sub)objective is not limited as in the "closed" system. If a new, irrelevant alternative is added (or an existing irrelevant alternative is removed), the priorities allocated to the existing alternatives under each objective do not change because the alternative being added (removed) is, by definition, not better than the ideal under any objective. Therefore, the ideal continues to receive the full priority of the respective objective. Furthermore, the priorities allocated to the other alternatives, being proportional to the ideal, would not change either. However, the alternative being added (removed) would receive (relinquish) a priority in proportion to its preference with respect to the ideal alternative. Thus the total priority allocated increases (decreases) and the system can be said to be "open". After the alternatives receive priority from each of the lowest level (sub)objectives, a subsequent normalization is performed so that the alternative priorities sum to 1.0.

It is important to note that the only operational difference between the open and closed system occurs when a synthesis is performed. There is no difference in model structure or judgment process for closed or open systems. Also of importance is that both closed and open AHP systems produce *ratio scale* priorities. Ratio scale priorities have a higher level of measure than, and are preferred to interval scale priorities. If, in the open system (ideal synthesis), a transformation was made whereby the 'worst' alternative for each objective received 0 priority (in addition to the transformation assigning all of an objective's priority to the 'best' alternative), the mathematics would be analogous to that of MAUT but the resulting priorities would only be on an interval scaled rather than on a ratio scale. Not only are ratio scale priorities more preferable in general, but ratio scale priorities are *required* for many applications (such as resource allocation or systems with feedback) since the product of interval scaled measures is mathematically meaningless.

Illustrative Example

Consider the evaluation and ranking of employees in a small firm with a few employees. Suppose that Susan is as good or slightly better than John with respect all attributes except one – John is the only employee who is proficient in application of personal computers in meeting the needs of the firm's clients. Suppose a multi-objective evaluation is performed and the results indicate that John is the most valuable to the firm, with Susan a close second.

Subsequently, a new employee is hired, who is very knowledgeable about the use of PC's, but not quite as knowledgeable as John. John is superior with respect to the new employee in all other objectives as well. Since John dominates the new employee, the new alternative is "irrelevant", and according to MAUT practitioners, "should" not affect the ranking of the pre-existing employees. Is this necessarily reasonable? Since John's *relative* value to the firm has been diminished "should" John still be more valuable to the firm than Susan? We would conclude no!

To see that a *prohibition* of rank reversal in this evaluation is *not* reasonable, suppose more and more (similar) "irrelevant" alternatives are hired. Surely there would come a point where the value of John's ability with PC's would be diluted to the point where Susan would be considered to be the most valuable employee. This example, typical of many evaluations, leads us to conclude that *value* is *relative* in many evaluations, and that a methodology that allows for rank reversal is desirable in these situations. Conversely, methodologies, such as MAUT, which preclude rank reversal can produce flawed results for situations where worth *is* affected by relative abundance (above and beyond the impact of affecting the relative importance of the objectives.) This conclusion is not new! The need for a methodology to allow for rank reversal has long been recognized.

For example, Huber and Puto[17] (1983), in an article "Market Boundaries and Product Choice: Illustrating Attraction and Substitution Effects", state that:

> "Choice researchers have commonly used two general approaches to account for the way proximity of a new item affects choice. These approaches differ primarily in the way item similarity, as derived from the dimensional structure of the alternatives is assumed to affect the choice process. The first proposition (proportionality) assumes that the new item takes share from existing items in proportion to their original shares (i.e., no similarity effect)."

Proportionality would *preclude* rank reversal. Huber and Puto continue to say:

> "The second proposition (substitutability) assumes that the new item takes share disproportionately from more similar items – i.e., the closer the added item is to existing items in the set, the more it "hurts" them (a negative similarity effect)."

Huber, Payne and Puto (1982)[18] note that:

> "... the similarity hypothesis asserts that a new alternative takes disproportionate share from those with which it is most similar. Researchers have shown that the similarity effect is operant for individual or aggregate choice probabilities."

Substitutability requires that rank reversals be permitted. Decision-makers must decide, and should not be told, which of these two approaches, proportionality (an open system – ideal synthesis) or substitutability (a closed system – distributive synthesis), is relevant to their evaluation. We believe that the substitution effect, is in general, more appropriate for multi-objective evaluations. Huber and Puto argue that:

> "A substitution effect will be more salient where multi-attribute decision-making occurs. It should, therefore, be most apparent in major purchases

---

[17] Huber, J. and Puto, C., 1983. Market Boundaries and Product Choice: Illustrating Attraction and Substitution Effects, *Journal of Consumer Research* Vol. 10, June, 31 - 44.

[18] Huber, J., Payne, J. W., and Puto, C., 1982. Adding Asymmetrically Dominated Alternatives: Violations of Regularity and the Similarity Hypothesis. *Journal of Consumer Research.* Vol. 9, June, 90-98.

(where attribute-based processing is more cost effective) and in product classes for which a limited number of attributes emerge that permit easy comparisons across alternatives."

Since Multi Criteria Decision-making (MCDM) and Multi Objective Decision-making (MODM) techniques like AHP are now facilitating comparisons across alternatives for more than just a limited number of attributes, the substitution effect should become even more common and the ability of a methodology to allow rank reversal should be welcomed.

Conversely, there are situations where a rank reversal would *not* coincide with the underlying preferences of the decision-makers. Suppose, for example, that a decision-maker, considering whether to buy an IBM PC compatible or an Apple MacIntosh, has decided on the IBM PC compatible. The introduction of another IBM PC compatible that is not as good on any dimension as the original PC compatible would not, for most decision makers, change the original ranking. For situations such as this, the AHP open system (ideal synthesis) should be used and will not allow a rank reversal. The following example illustrates the differences between the closed system (distributive synthesis) and open system (ideal synthesis).

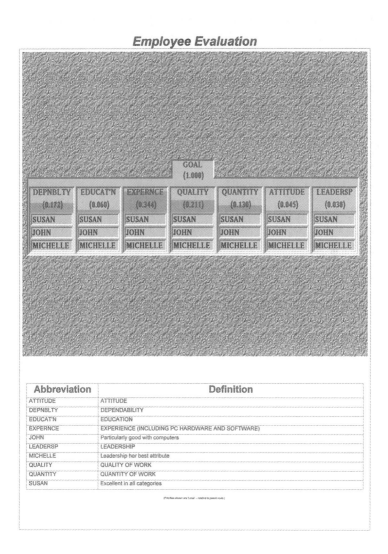

Figure 12 – Employee Evaluation with Three Alternatives

Employee Evaluation using the AHP Closed System (Distributive Synthesis)

Figure 12 contains a model used in an AHP evaluation of three employees. With the closed system (distributive synthesis) the "global" priority of each alternative "node" is the product of the node's local priority with it's parent's global priority. The overall priority for each employee is the sum of the employee's global priorities throughout the model, as shown in Figure 13. In practice there may be several additional levels in an employee evaluation model. Overall, John is the most valuable employee, primarily because of his experience with personal computer hardware and software.

Employee Evaluation

Synthesis of Leaf Nodes with respect to GOAL
Distributive Mode
OVERALL INCONSISTENCY INDEX = 0.1

LEVEL 1	LEVEL 2	LEVEL 3	LEVEL 4	LEVEL 5
EXPERNCE=.344				
	JOHN =.163			
	SUSAN =.091			
	MICHELLE=.091			
QUALITY =.211				
	SUSAN =.089			
	JOHN =.067			
	MICHELLE=.055			
DEPNBLTY=.172				
	SUSAN =.074			
	JOHN =.057			
	MICHELLE=.041			
QUANTITY=.130				
	SUSAN =.051			
	JOHN =.040			
	MICHELLE=.040			
EDUCAT'N=.060				
	SUSAN =.025			
	JOHN =.018			
	MICHELLE=.018			
ATTITUDE=.045				
	SUSAN =.018			
	JOHN =.014			
	MICHELLE=.012			
LEADERSP=.038				
	SUSAN =.015			
	MICHELLE=.013			
	JOHN =.011			

JOHN   .369
SUSAN   .362
MICHELLE .269

Figure 13 – Closed System (Distributive Synthesis) and Overall Priorities

Employee Evaluation using the AHP OPEN System (Ideal Synthesis)

In an open system (ideal synthesis), the most preferred alternative under each objective receives the full priority of the objective. Each of the other alternatives receives a priority proportional to its preference relative to the most preferred alternative. After the alternatives receive priority from each of the objectives, a subsequent normalization is performed so that sum of all of the alternatives' priorities is equal to 1.0 as can be seen in Figure 16.

The priorities in this example are such that the rank order of the four alternatives with the open system (ideal synthesis) are the same as with the closed system (distributive synthesis) shown in Figure 15. However, if we now remove Bernard, the "irrelevant alternative", and perform an open system (ideal synthesis), Susan remains the most valuable of the three employees (see Figure 17). The result is different from the closed system (distributive synthesis) where John, because of his unique abilities with computers, is the most valuable among the three employees.

Added Bernard (an irrelevant alternative)

Synthesis of Leaf Nodes with respect to GOAL
Ideal Mode
OVERALL INCONSISTENCY INDEX = 0.04

LEVEL 1	LEVEL 2	LEVEL 3	LEVEL 4	LEVEL 5
EXPERNCE=.344				
	JOHN =.344			
	BERNARD =.268			
	SUSAN =.191			
	MICHELLE=.191			
QUALITY =.211				
	SUSAN =.211			
	JOHN =.158			
	MICHELLE=.132			
	BERNARD =.053			
DEPNBLTY=.172				
	SUSAN =.172			
	JOHN =.134			
	MICHELLE=.096			
	BERNARD =.096			
QUANTITY=.130				
	SUSAN =.130			
	JOHN =.101			
	MICHELLE=.101			
	BERNARD =.029			
EDUCATN=.060				
	SUSAN =.060			
	JOHN =.043			
	MICHELLE=.043			
	BERNARD =.017			
ATTITUDE=.045				
	SUSAN =.045			
	JOHN =.035			
	MICHELLE=.030			
	BERNARD =.010			
LEADERSP=.038				
	SUSAN =.038			
	MICHELLE=.032			
	JOHN =.027			
	BERNARD =.011			

SUSAN	.303
JOHN	.301
MICHELLE	.223
BERNARD	.173

Figure 16 – Open System (Ideal Synthesis) with Four Alternatives

Employee Evaluation

Synthesis of Leaf Nodes with respect to GOAL
Ideal Mode
OVERALL INCONSISTENCY INDEX = 0.1

LEVEL 1	LEVEL 2	LEVEL 3	LEVEL 4	LEVEL 5
EXPERNCE=.344				
	JOHN =.344			
	SUSAN =.191			
	MICHELLE=.191			
QUALITY =.211				
	SUSAN =.211			
	JOHN =.158			
	MICHELLE=.132			
DEPNBLTY=.172				
	SUSAN =.172			
	JOHN =.134			
	MICHELLE=.096			
QUANTITY=.130				
	SUSAN =.130			
	JOHN =.101			
	MICHELLE=.101			
EDUCAT'N=.060				
	SUSAN =.060			
	JOHN =.043			
	MICHELLE=.043			
ATTITUDE=.045				
	SUSAN =.045			
	JOHN =.035			
	MICHELLE=.030			
LEADERSP=.038				
	SUSAN =.038			
	MICHELLE=.032			
	JOHN =.027			

SUSAN   .366 ██████████████████████████████████████
JOHN   .364 ██████████████████████████████████████
MICHELLE .270 █████████████████████████████

Figure 17 – Open System Synthesis After Removing the Irrelevant
Alternative

Summarizing, in this example (contrived for illustrative purposes), if there were only three alternatives, John would rank first using the closed system (distributive synthesis) while Susan would rank first using the open system (ideal synthesis). Since, in this illustration, the value of the employees is affected by relative abundance or scarcity of their talents (or in other words, one employee's talents can be *substituted* for another), the closed system (distributive synthesis) is more appropriate and *John should be the most valuable*! Thus, the *lack* of rank reversal with the open system (ideal synthesis) produces "flawed results".

While the rank order of the alternatives with the open system synthesis is the same for three or four alternatives, the rank order of Susan and John is different with the closed system (distributive synthesis) depending on whether Bernard is or is not included. This is due to a dilution effect caused by the Bernard, an "irrelevant alternative". The removal of Bernard causes the priority of each objective to be concentrated (the converse of a dilution of priorities when alternatives are added) under the closed system (ideal synthesis) because the total priority under each objective does not change. Furthermore, the concentration is not the same for all objectives. For, according to the similarity effect discussed previously, a new alternative would take a disproportionate share from those with which it is most similar, so conversely, the removal of an alternative would give a disproportionate share to those with which it is most similar. Since Bernard was most similar to John on the experience objective, John gains proportionately more priority if Bernard is removed and consequently John is the most preferred among the three alternatives. This makes intuitive sense since the value of John's experience with PC hardware and software has increased because it is "more" scarce if Bernard is not included.

When is scarcity germane?

When scarcity is germane a closed system (distributive synthesis) is appropriate and when it is not an open system (ideal synthesis) is appropriate. Yet, it may not always be obvious when scarcity is germane. The following questions can help determine whether to use the distributive synthesis or ideal synthesis:

Q: Is the purpose of the model to forecast, prioritize alternatives, or choose one alternative?

If the model purpose is to forecast or prioritize alternatives, then the closed system (distributive synthesis) is appropriate. If, however, the model purpose is to choose one alternative, then a subsequent question can be posed:

Q: Will alternatives not chosen still be relevant, i.e., will they still matter to you?

If the answer is yes, then the closed system (distributive synthesis) is appropriate. If not, then the open system (ideal synthesis) is appropriate.

How Significant is the Choice of Synthesis Mode in Practice? We investigated forty-four applications of the Analytic Hierarchy Process, applying the above questions about scarcity to each. In our judgment, scarcity was relevant in sixteen of the forty-four applications. Next, we compared the results of a distributive synthesis *and* an ideal synthesis for each application. Of the forty-four applications, thirty six had identical rankings of alternatives regardless of the synthesis mode. Of the remaining eight applications, six had the same first choice. The two applications for which the different synthesis modes produced different 'best' alternatives were each identified as 'closed' systems (for which the original AHP distributive synthesis was appropriate).

Summary

A multi-objective modeling approach must be able to accommodate both "closed" systems – with a fixed amount of resources and where scarcity is germane, and "open" systems – where resources can be added or removed and where scarcity is not germane. The choice of an open or closed system (distributive synthesis or ideal synthesis) for a particular prioritization, choice, or resource allocation problem is one that must be made by the decision makers – not prescribed by a methodology or its axioms. Recognizing that there are situations in which rank reversals are desirable and other situations in which they are not, a logical conclusion is that any decision methodology that always allows or always precludes rank reversals is inadequate. AHP is capable of deriving ratio scale priorities for both types of situations.

Structural adjustment / Product adjustment

Structural adjustment

Structural Adjustment. In some applications you may want to adjust the priorities of a set of nodes based on the structure of the EC tree. When the grandchildren of the current node are the alternatives, a structural adjustment *can* be made to the priorities of the children of the current node based on the total number of grandchildren. The effect of this command is to prevent diluting the importance of a grandchild simply because it has many siblings.

Consider the problem of an elderly widow who is about to write her last will and testament to provide (indirectly) for her grandchildren via her children. Disregarding preferences for children and grandchildren for the moment, the following question might arise. Should she give equal shares of her estate to each of her children, who will then distribute their shares to the grandchildren, or should her children's shares be determined by the number of grandchildren each produced?

Suppose the grandparent (the current node) wishes to leave each grandchild the same amount of money and favors each of her own children equally. If the grandparent were to leave each of her own children equal amounts of money to be passed on to the grandchildren, then the grandchildren would not receive equal amounts (see Figure 18). Those from the larger families would be penalized. An equitable distribution to the grandchildren could be achieved by adjusting the amount each child gets by the number of grandchildren they produced. Children who have produced more grandchildren get a larger priority (or amount of money) (see Figure 19).

the second set of judgments, you would turn on the Expert Choice product switch. After all judgments were entered, the priorities would be calculated as usual. However, if the product adjust switch is on these priorities will be multiplied by the previously calculated priorities (the likelihoods) and normalized appropriately. Thus the priorities of the scenarios would be based on both likelihood and importance.

Complete Hierarchy

An example of a complete hierarchy, as usually depicted in the AHP literature, is shown in Figure 20. A complete hierarchy is complete in the sense that the same objectives appear under each of the scenarios[19]. In this example priorities would be established for the scenarios by making judgments about the relative likelihood of the scenarios. Priorities would be established for the objectives by making pairwise comparisons about the

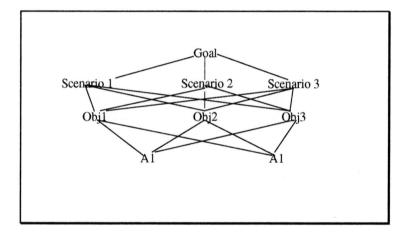

Figure 20 – Complete Hierarchy

importance of the objectives, given each of the scenarios. And priorities would be established for the alternatives by making judgments about the relative preference of the alternatives with respect to each of the objectives.

---

[19] Or if objectives appear below the goal, and the same sub-objectives appear under each of the objectives, the hierarchy would be said to be complete.

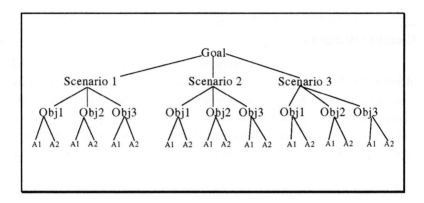

Figure 21 – Incomplete Hierarchy

An incomplete hierarchic representation of this model is presented in Figure 21. Although the hierarchy is still complete, it need not be – different objectives (or some the same and some different) could appear under each of the scenarios. The incomplete representation of this hierarchy entails another difference – that is dependence. Whereas the pairwise comparisons of the alternatives with respect to each of the objectives in Figure 20 are independent of the scenario, they are dependent in Figure 21. This dependency has two ramifications. First, it allows for more specific judgments to be made. For example, when comparing the relative preference of investment alternatives with respect to appreciation, the relative preference of a real estate investment compared to stocks could be much different for a scenario of low interest rates than for a scenario of high interest rates. The second ramification is that many more judgments must be made using the incomplete hierarchic approach.

Expert Choice represents hierarchies in the more general, incomplete form as shown in Figure 21. If however, one would like to make judgments about the alternatives irrespective of the scenarios, judgments need be made in only the leftmost plex (the nodes below SCENARIO1) and the Expert Choice complete hierarchy command[20] will replicate the plexes below the

---

[20] Invoked from the OBJ1 node below SCENARIO1.

objectives under SCENARIO1 to appear below the objectives under each of the other two scenarios.[21]

Benefit/Cost

An alternate approach to an 'achievement of objectives' framework for making decisions is to consider benefits and costs separately. Organizations have been doing 'benefit/cost' studies for quite some time. Such studies have often faltered because of the difficulty in quantifying benefits. (Costs were much easier to quantify). Our ability to use AHP to quantify *all* benefits, including those that are qualitative, and *all* costs, including qualitative costs, brings new life to benefit cost analysis.

The typical AHP model includes both benefits and costs. The *objectives* in the typical AHP model, can, if desired, be viewed in terms of *benefits* and *costs*. For example, in choosing a car, we might consider both performance and maintenance requirements as objectives. The former is clearly a benefit, while the latter is a cost. When we pairwise compare alternative cars with respect to these objectives, we ask which car is more *preferable*. A high performing car is more preferable than a low performing car. A car requiring low maintenance is more preferable than one requiring high maintenance. By asking which is more preferable, we implicitly view objectives as benefits – high performance is a benefit and low maintenance is a benefit.

Instead of including benefits and costs in a single hierarchy, a benefit/cost approach can be taken in which one hierarchy is used to measure the benefits of the alternatives, and a second hierarchy, used to measure the costs of the alternatives. The two hierarchies are similar only in that they have the same alternatives. The benefit priorities from the benefits hierarchy are subsequently divided by the cost priorities from the cost hierarchy to give a measure of benefit/cost ratio.[22]

---

[21] More generally, additional levels can appear between the objectives and the alternatives. If judgments are made for the entire plex below SCENARIO1, as well as for the objectives below SCENARIO2 and SCENARIO3, the complete hierarchy command can then be invoked from the first objective below SCENARIO1.

[22] This is mathematically meaningful because each hierarchy produces ratio scale priorities and the ratio of ratio scale numbers is a ratio scale.

Alternatives in the benefits hierarchy are evaluated such that those giving the highest benefit receive the highest priority, as is customary. In the cost hierarchy, alternatives with the higher costs should receive the highest priority, because we are trying to measure costs. To do this, we either implicitly or explicitly ask which of two alternatives is more 'costly' rather than more 'preferable' as is customary when benefits and costs are treated in one model.

The following example is a model to choose whether to build a bridge, or a tunnel across a river to continue using an existing ferry[23]. The factors involved in the benefits and costs of crossing a river are given in the two hierarchies below. They fall into three categories: economics, social and environmental. The decision is made in terms of the ratio of benefits priority to costs priority for each alternative.

The benefits hierarchy:

Determine way to cross the river yielding greatest benefits

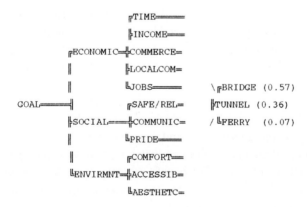

The alternative with the greatest benefit is the bridge, and the alternative with the least benefit is the ferry.

---

[23] Saaty, Thomas L. and Forman, Ernest H., *The Hierarchon - A Dictionary of Hierarchies*, The Analytic Hierarchy Process Series - Volume V, RWS Publications, Pittsburgh PA, 1993, p. A21.

The costs hierarchy:

Determine the most costly alternative for crossing the river

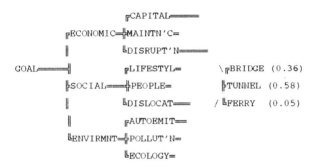

The alternative with the highest cost is the tunnel, and that with the least cost is the ferry, since it is already built.

For this example we have the following ratios of benefits/costs priorities:

Bridge 0.57/0.36 = 1.58
Tunnel 0.36/0.58 = 0.62
Ferry   0.07/0.05 = 1.28

This evaluation shows the best choice is to construct a bridge across the river as Bridge has the largest benefit to cost ratio. Note that this has taken into consideration the capital requirements in terms of dollars as well as other benefits and costs not measurable in dollars. The ferry, an existing alternative, serves as a reference point. Since the bridge benefit/cost ratio is higher than that of the ferry it gives additional support to the choice of the bridge.

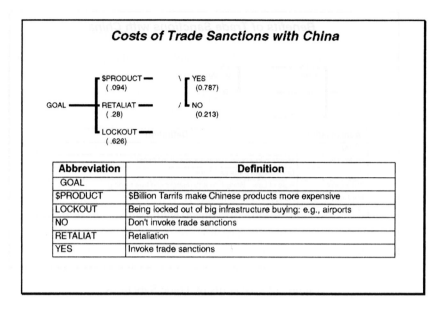

Figure 23 – Risks of Trade Sanctions

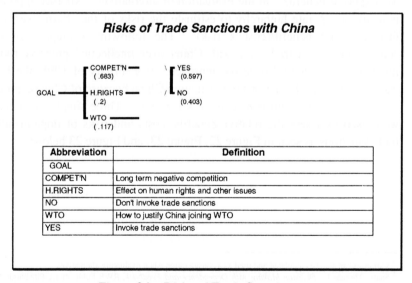

Figure 24 – Risks of Trade Sanctions

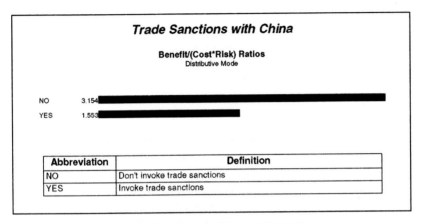

Figure 25 – Benefit/(Cost * Risk) Ratios

The benefits of imposing trade sanctions are greater than not imposing trade sanctions. However, the costs and risks of imposing trade sanctions are also greater than not imposing trade sanctions. Because benefits, costs and risks are all ratio scale measures, we can calculate the benefit/(cost*risk) ratio as seen in Figure 25. Clearly, it is better not to impose trade sanctions. This result of this evaluation by Thomas Saaty and Jen Shang was sent to several congressmen as well as the chief U.S. negotiator, Mickey Kantor. Mr. Kantor's office subsequently called Dr. Saaty congratulating him on the outcome, which coincided with the agreement reached between the United States and China.

Pairwise Comparisons versus MAUT Swing Weights

The ability for people to understand and make pairwise comparisons is one of AHP's major strengths. To appreciate this, we invite the reader to compare AHP's judgment process described on pages 72 and 77 with that used by advocates of another theory, Multi Attribute Utility Theory

(MAUT) advocates, such as Kirkwood[26], to derive weights for the objectives directly above the alternatives in a decision hierarchy.

> ...First, the single dimensional value functions have been specified so that each of them is equal to zero for the least preferred level that is being considered for the corresponding evaluation measure. Similarly, each of the single dimensional value functions has been specified so that it is equal to one for the most preferred level that is being considered for the corresponding evaluation measure.

> From these properties of the single dimensional value functions, it follows that the weight for an evaluation measure is equal to the increment in value that is received from moving the score on that evaluation measure from its least preferred level to its most preferred level. This property provides a basis for a procedure to determine the weights. ... Specifically these steps are as follows:

> Consider the increments in value that would occur by increasing (or 'swinging") each of the evaluation measures from the least preferred end of its range to the most preferred end, and place these increments in order of successively increasing value increments.

> Quantitatively scale each of these values as a multiple of the smallest value increment.

> Set the smallest value increment so that the total of all the increments is 1.

> Use the results of Step 3 to determine the weights for all the evaluation measures.

A paraphrased description of Kirkwood's application of these rules to his prototype example is:

> Suppose that the swing over the total range for Productivity Enhancement (Objective 1) has the smallest increment of value.... Suppose further that the swing over the total range for Cost Increase (Objective two) from 150 to 0 has 1.5 times as great a value increment as the swing over Productivity Enhancement from -1 to 2, and the swing over Security (Objective 3) from -2 to 1 has 1.25 times the value increment of swing over Cost increase.

---

[26] Kirkwood, C. 1997. "Strategic Decision Making – Multiobjective Decision Analysis with Spreadsheets", Duxbury Press, Belmont CA,

An alternate approach to determining weights used by MAUT is even more obscure. It involves the consideration of hypothetical alternatives and asks the decision maker to determine intermediate levels for the alternative for which they would be indifferent between that alternative and one at its maximum level. Thus instead of the swing weight questions described above, the dialog might be something like:

"Consider a hypothetical alternative that has the least preferred level for all the evaluation measures. Now suppose that you could move one and only one from its least preferred level to its most preferred level. Which would you move? Now suppose you could not move that one, which is the next one you would move? Now suppose that you could either move the second from its least preferred level to its most preferred level, or the first from its least preferred level to some intermediate level. Select the intermediate level for which you would be indifferent between the two possibilities." (This question is usually easiest to answer by considering a specific intermediate level for Security, and then adjusting this level until indifference is established).

Swing weights and other techniques such as balance beams are, in our opinion much more difficult to understand and apply then the pairwise comparisons used in AHP.

Integrating with Quantitative Methodologies

Although quantitative models, such as those characterized as Operations Research / Management Science models, have provided substantial benefits to corporations and governments over the past half century and more, many roadblocks have prevented the realization of their ultimate potential in the decision-making process.   One roadblock, the easy access to required computational resources has been eliminated – it is now possible to solve very large quantitative problems on desktop personal computers.   Another roadblock remains.   Decision-makers often lack the understanding and ability to integrate quantitative models' results with other concerns – both qualitative and quantitative. Most quantitative models provide a 'solution' to a problem formulated to represent the 'real world'.   The solution is usually framed from only one of many perspectives.   Without a synthesizing mechanism like AHP, decision-makers are left to either 'go with the model results' or with their intuition.   Most often, they go with their intuition.   By helping decision-makers synthesize the results from one or even several quantitative models with their intuition, AHP enhances the value of quantitative models. In this section we will illustrate the integration of AHP with a variety of quantitative models including linear programming, queueing, critical path method, forecasting, and integer programming.

Linear Programming

The idea for a new product must be developed into specifics.   There are usually numerous alternatives for designing each "piece" of a product, and the problem of choosing the "best" design from a very large combination of alternatives can be overwhelming.   Traditional textbook examples illustrate how linear programming can be helpful in selecting the best combination of components for a product.   Consider a problem of selecting plastic body materials for a new Sporty Convertible being designed by an auto manufacturer.   A traditional linear programming formulation might consist of an objective function to minimize costs, subject to constraints on:

- body weight – that the body weight be no more than 120 pounds,

- coverage – that there be at least 5 cubic feet of body material in order to cover the body, and

- strength – that the mixture of materials possess a strength of at least 100 pounds per square foot.

The linear programming solution to this problem would be to use 4.5 cubic feet of the standard material, .174 cubic feet of the super material, and .326 cubic feet of the lightweight material, for a total cost of $545, with a weight of 120 pounds and a strength of 100 pounds per square foot.

Table 2 – Material Characteristics

Material Description	1 Standard	2 Super	3 Econo	4 Strong	5 Lightwt
Cost/cu. Ft.	105	220	85	103	107
Weight/cu . ft.	25	15	40	55	15
Strength lbs/Sq. ft.	20	35	11	42	12

Let's reflect on where some of the relationships and parameters for this model would come from in a real world application. Minimizing cost is obviously an objective, and the coefficients of the objective function, representing the cost per cubic foot of material can be obtained from a data base of suppliers. The fact that we "must" have at least 5 cubic feet of body material to cover the body can come from preliminary design drawings of the sport convertible.

But the constraint requiring that the body weigh no more than 120 pounds is somewhat contrived since one might argue that a light body weight is an "objective" (rather than a constraint) and that we really do not know what we "must" have as a maximum body weight. We would like the body to weigh as little as possible so that the car will accelerate better and use less fuel. Then why was body weight represented as a constraint in the traditional formulation? Simply as a convenience, because linear programming allows only one objective, and we had already chosen cost minimization as that objective.

the five alternatives is shown in Figure 26.

The relative preferences of the alternatives can be determined by the decision-maker using not only the hard data about the materials, but quite probably with subjective judgments about the utility of the characteristics represented by the hard data as well. For example, when making judgments with respect to the strength objective, the decision maker might refer to Table 2 and, using his previous experience, judge that the "Econo" and "Lightwt" materials are about EQUALLY preferable in spite of the fact that the "Lightwt" is just a little bit stronger; he might then judge that the "Standard" material is STRONGLY more preferable to either, and the "Strong" material is only MODERATELY more preferable to the "Standard" material.

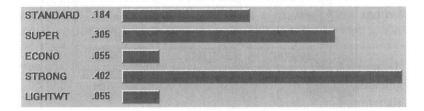

Figure 27 – Priorities with respect to Strength

These judgments and the judgments for other pairs of alternatives with respect to Strength resulted in the priorities shown in Figure 27.

Preferences with respect to Cost and Weight were developed using the Expert Choice Data mode and specifying numerical values equal to the

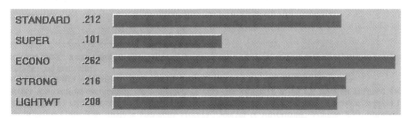

Figure 28 – Priorities with respect to Cost

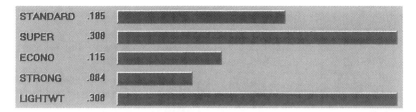

Figure 29 – Priorities with respect to Weight

reciprocals of the costs and weights of the materials.[30]   The resulting priorities are shown in Figure 28 and Figure 29.

Next, pairwise comparisons for the relative importance of the three objectives were made with the resulting priorities shown in Figure 30.

Figure 30 – Priorities of Objectives

Finally, a synthesis of the priorities of the five materials over the three objectives resulted in the priorities shown in Figure 31.

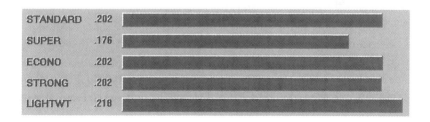

Figure 31 – Overall Material Priorities

---

[30] Reciprocals are used since low cost and low weight are preferred.

Table 3 – First LP Solution

	Standard	Super	Econo	Strong	Lightweight
Effectiveness	0.202	0.176	0.203	0.202	0.218
Decision Variables	0	0	0	0	5
Effectiveness			1.09		
Cost			535.00		
Weight			75.00		
Strength			60.00		

These priorities represent the overall relative "effectiveness" of the alternatives with respect to the three objectives. It is interesting to observe how close these measures of "effectiveness" are, especially for the top four alternatives, particularly since there were such significant differences with respect to the individual objectives.

Based on these measures of "effectiveness", we can formulate an LP model to determine the composition, at first using only the constraint that we must have five cubic feet of body material to cover the frame. Since the number of basic variables in an LP is equal to the number of constraints, it is not surprising that the "optimal" solution, shown in Table 3, is to use five cubic feet of the plastic with the highest measure of effectiveness, the lightweight plastic.

Now we must examine the solution. Is there anything that appears missing or wrong? If so, we must include additional objectives or constraints. For example, in the above, we have treated low weight and high strength more naturally as objectives, rather than as constraints as in the traditional LP formulation. But if we implement this solution, what would the cost, weight and strength characteristics of the body material be? Examination of Table 3 shows that the cost would be $535, the body weight would be 75 pounds, and the strength would be 60 pounds/per square foot. The latter is well below the 100 pounds originally thought to be the minimum required. So let's now add a constraint specifying that the

Table 4 – Modified LP Solution

	Standard	Super	Econo	Strong	Lightweight
Effectiveness	0.202	0.176	0.203	0.202	0.218
Decision Variables	0	0	0	1.33	3.67

Effectiveness	1.07
Cost	529.67
Weight	128.33
Strength	100.00

minimum strength should be 100 pounds. The modified LP, shown in Table 4, results in an optimum solution of 1.33 cubic feet of the strong and 3.67 cubic feet of the lightweight.

Not only has the strength increased to the required 100 pounds, but the cost has actually decreased from \$535 to \$529.57. This has been achieved by increasing the body weight from 75 pounds to 128.33 pounds. Since 128.33 body weight is acceptable, this solution is accepted as "optimal".

In comparing this multi-objective solution to that obtained with the traditional single objective LP approach – of minimizing cost subject to (somewhat arbitrary) constraints, it is seen that the multi-objective approach allows us to trade off cost versus weight, since this solution is lower in cost (\$529.57 vs. \$545.65) but heavier (128.33 lbs. vs. 120 lbs.) In addition, this solution uses a mixture of only two plastics as opposed to three for the traditional solution, a simplification that might result in additional savings as well.

In summary, the multi-objective approach consists of using AHP to derive measures of effectiveness for the alternatives considering more than just the single objective, cost. It then uses LP with only the obvious constraint(s) (in this case body coverage). The tentative solution is then examined to see if it is reasonable. If not, because one or more "must" objectives are obviously not met (in this example an insufficient body strength), new constraint(s) are introduced for the emerging "must(s)" and the LP solved again. In addition, judgments in the AHP model that are used to derive the measures of effectiveness of the alternatives can be re-evaluated in light of the knowledge gained by looking at the tentative

Table 5 – Measures of Performance

Number of Servers	Probability a request will have to wait	Average # of requests in queue	Average time to complete service
1	.95	18.05	20 hours
2	.31	0.28	1.29 hours
3	.01	0.04	1.03 hours

solution. Iteration continues until an "optimal" solution satisfying the multiple objectives is achieved.

Queueing Models

Consider the problem of deciding how many draftsmen with CAD/CAM equipment are needed to design new products. A queueing model provides the following measures of performance based on the number of servers (draftsmen with CAD/CAM equipment):

Having determined this, the question remains, how many servers should be used? The queueing model only helped to derive some measures of effectiveness. It did not really answer the question. A textbook exercise might state that it costs X$ per hour that the request is in queue or in service and then ask which of these three alternatives is best – a simple calculation. Simple, but unrealistic. What does it really 'cost'? One way to begin to answer this question and arrive at a decision is to list the pros and cons of each of the three alternatives as shown in Figure 6.

AHP can help management make the decision on how many draftsmen with CAD/CAM systems to use. The objectives for the decision can be extracted directly from the pros and cons:

Financial considerations
        Salaries of draftsmen
        Expense of CAD/CAM equipment
    Morale (and not stifling creativity)
        Engineers
        Draftsmen
  Risk of bottlenecks and degradation of service due to
        Absence of draftsmen
        Failure of CAD/CAM equipment
        Increased workload
Exposure to obsolescence of CAD/CAM equipment
        Within one year
        More than one year
    Personnel management
        Hiring draftsmen
        Managing draftsmen

A rational decision about how many servers (draftsmen with CAD/CAM equipment) to use must be based on objectives such as these.

arise. First, how do we estimate the "overall" worth to the firm of a product or a specific combination of products? And second, if there is a relatively large number of products, the number of combinations is extremely large. For example, if we had 20 products and 10 constraints, we would have to consider more than 30 million combinations!31

The problem can be formulated as an integer linear programming problem by defining decision variables X_i, i=1 to n, corresponding to the n products under consideration, where X_i will be equal to one if the ith product is to be produced, and zero if it is not. If we had a measure of the overall "worth" of each product to the firm, say W_i for the ith product, then we would like to maximize the sum of the worth over all products that will be included in the company's portfolio. This can be expressed as:

Maximize W1X1+W2X2+....WnXn (the worth of the products to be produced)

Subject to:
Budgetary constraint:
C1X1+C2X2+....CnXn <= Available budget

Diversification constraints:
 (i.e. at least one product in each market segment, and
 no more than two products in each market segment

Dependency constraints:
 (e.g. either both products 1 and 2 or neither)

and Xi= 0 or 1.

The remaining difficulty, that of evaluating the worth (W_i) of each of the products can be solved using AHP. This approach allows one to consider all relevant considerations in the process of determining the "best" combination of products to produce.

---

[31]Examining only the extreme points of the convex hull would require (m+n)!/(m! x n!) or 30!/(20! x 10!)points to be examined.)

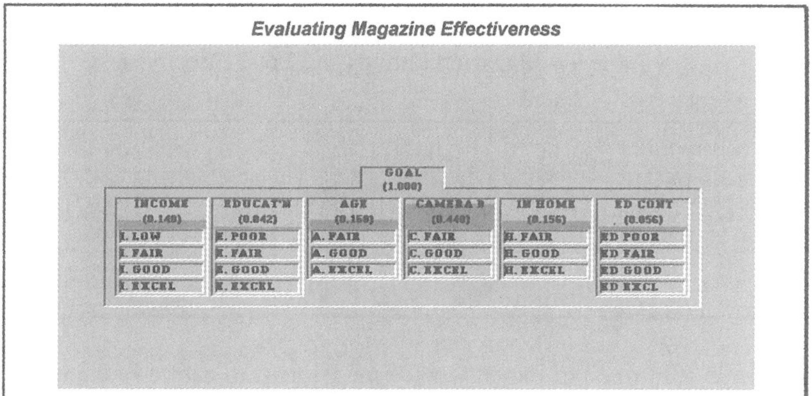

Abbreviation	Definition
A. EXCEL	MAGAZINE WITH > 60% READERS IN 18-44 AGE BRACKET IS EXCELLENT
A. FAIR	MAGAZINE WITH 40-50% READERS IN 18-44 AGE BRACKET IS FAIR
A. GOOD	MAGAZINE WITH 50-60% READERS IN 18-44 AGE BRACKET IS GOOD
AGE	% READERSHIP BETWEEN THE AGES OF 18 AND 44 YEARS OLD
C. EXCEL	MAGAZINE WITH >20% READERS PURCHASING CAMERA <1 YR IS EXCELLENT
C. FAIR	MAGAZINE WITH 10%-15% READERS PURCHASING CAMERA <1 YR AGO IS FAIR
C. GOOD	MAGAZINE WITH 15-20% READERS PURCHASING CAMERA <1 YR IS GOOD
CAMERA B	% READERSHIP THAT WERE CAMERA BUYERS WITHIN LAST 12 MONTHS
E. EXCEL	MAGAZINE WITH >60% READERS HAVING ANY COLLEGE IS EXCELLENT
E. FAIR	MAGAZINE WITH 40-50% OF READERS HAVING ANY COLLEGE IS FAIR
E. GOOD	MAGAZINE WITH 50-60% OF READERS HAVING ANY COLLEGE IS GOOD
E. POOR	MAGAZINE WITH UNDER 40% READERS HAVING ANY COLLEGE IS POOR
ED CONT	EDITORIAL CONTENT
ED EXCL	EXCELLENT EDITORIAL CONTENT MATCH
ED FAIR	FAIR EDITORIAL CONTENT MATCH
ED GOOD	GOOD EDITORIAL CONTENT MATCH
ED POOR	POOR EDITORIAL CONTENT MATCH
EDUCAT'N	% READERSHIP WITH SOME COLLEGE EDUCATION
H. EXCEL	MAGAZINE WITH >60% OF HOME READERS IS EXCELLENT
H. FAIR	MAGAZINE WITH 40-50% OF HOME READERS IS FAIR
H. GOOD	MAGAZINE WITH 50-60% OF HOME READERS IS GOOD
I. EXCEL	MAGAZINE WITH >20% OF READERS HAVING INCOME >$35,000 IS EXCELLENT

Figure 35 – Evaluating Magazine Effectiveness

Similar decisions to choosing a portfolio of products are the decision of which R&D projects to fund, and the decision of which magazines should be used for a marketing campaign.

Let us consider the choice of magazines for an advertising campaign for a 35 mm camera. Using an AHP model with the ratings approach, we can develop measures of effectiveness for each magazine with respect to objective criteria, such as income and age demographics of the readers of the magazines, as well as subjective criteria, such as editorial content.

Table 9 – Magazine Ratings and Total Effectiveness

ALTERNATIVES	INCOME .1482	EDUCAT'N .0425	AGE .1577	CAMERA B .4404	IN HOME .1557	ED CONT .0557		TOTAL
1 NATL GEOGRAPHIC	I. GOOD	E. GOOD	A. GOOD	C. GOOD	H. EXCEL	ED GOOD	||	0.311
2 NEWSWEEK	I. GOOD	E. GOOD	A. EXCEL	C. GOOD	H. FAIR	ED EXCL	||	0.331
3 SOUTHERN LIVING	I. LOW	E. FAIR	A. FAIR	C. GOOD	H. EXCEL	ED POOR	||	0.243
4 PEOPLE	I. LOW	E. FAIR	A. EXCEL	C. GOOD	H. FAIR	ED POOR	||	0.260
5 SPORTS ILLUS.	I. GOOD	E. FAIR	A. EXCEL	C. GOOD	H. GOOD	ED EXCL	||	0.346
6 TRAVEL & LEISURE	I. EXCEL	E. EXCEL	A. FAIR	C. EXCEL	H. FAIR	ED POOR	||	0.388
7 TIME	I. FAIR	E. GOOD	A. EXCEL	C. GOOD	H. GOOD	ED EXCL	||	0.327
8 U.S. NEWS	I. GOOD	E. GOOD	A. GOOD	C. EXCEL	H. FAIR	ED EXCL	||	0.402

Figure 35 illustrates an Expert Choice model used to derive such measures of effectiveness.

The pairwise comparison process yields priorities for the ratings as shown above. The global priorities are used when rating the magazines. Each magazine is given a rating with respect to each criterion. For example, with respect to the Income criterion, a magazine rated as Excellent would have .073 added to its effectiveness index, while a magazine rated Low would receive a value of .008. The ratings and total effectiveness for each magazine is shown in Table 9.

Next we must consider which combination of alternatives is "best", subject to constraints. Suppose our only constraint is budget. If we know the budgetary requirements of each of the alternatives, we can formulate an integer linear programming model as shown in Table 11.

Table 10 – Integer Programming Solution

```
X1 (NATL GEOGRAPHIC) = 1
X2 (NEWSWEEK)        = 0
X3 (SOUTHERN LIVING) = 1
X4 (PEOPLE)          = 1
X5 (SPORTS ILLUS.)   = 0
X6 (TRAVEL & LEISURE)= 1
X7 (TIME)            = 0
X8 (U.S. NEWS)       = 1
```

The final integer programming (IP) solution, shown in Table 10, concludes that advertisements should be placed in National Geographic, Southern Living, People, Travel & Leisure, and U.S. News magazines.

The "optimal" solution from the ILP formulation should not be taken as the final decision. Rather, it must be examined to see if it suggests other criteria that should be added to the AHP formulation, and/or a re-evaluation of judgments in the AHP model, and/or additional constraints for the ILP model. Iteration is performed until an acceptable, "optimal" solution is achieved.

Table 11 – Integer Linear Programming Formulation

```
Maximize  E1 R1 X1  + E2 R2 X2  +   .... + E8 R8 X8,
    where
    Magazine 1 is National Geographic,
    R1 = 21,051 (the number of readers)
    E1 = .311 (the effectiveness coefficient from the Ratings model),
    X1 will be determined and will be 1 if it is optimal to
       advertise in National Geographic, 0 otherwise,

    Magazine 2 is Newsweek
    R2 = 15,594 (the number of readers)
    E2 = .331 (the effectiveness coefficient from the Ratings model),
    X2 will be determined and will be 1 if it is optimal to
       advertise in Newsweek, 0 otherwise,
    .
    .
    .

    Magazine 8 is U.S. News
    R8 =  8,929 (the number of readers)
    E8 = .402 (the effectiveness coefficient from the Ratings model),
    X8 will be determined and will be 1 if it is optimal to
       advertise in U. S. News, 0 otherwise.

Subject to the constraint on the total advertising budget:

    346,080 X1 + 780,180 X2 + 11,370 X3 + 605,880 X4 + 965,940 X5 +
              183,216 X6 + 1,324,282 X7 + 100,740 X8 <= $1,500,000
```

The same approach can be used to determine the best combination of R&D projects for a company. Objectives or criteria such as market position, fit with strategic direction, and projected sales can be used in the AHP model. Constraints that preclude too much redundancy or require a minimum amount of research in a given area can easily be included in the ILP model.

Care must be taken to assure that the decision truly reflects management's objectives and constraints. Not only can a piecemeal analysis be difficult to synthesize into the decision process, but the results prove to be troublesome. As an example, a Fortune 500 company used AHP to rate R&D projects. They were satisfied with both the process of arriving at the priorities and the priorities themselves. However, they did not think through the resource allocation problem thoroughly and simply allocated funds from their budget to the projects in rank order until no more funding remained. This resulted in some obvious weaknesses. Some departments got very large increases in funding while others got very large decreases. The departments with large increases were happy and quiet. The departments with large decreases were unhappy and very vocal. Something was wrong with the process! Furthermore, it appeared that some research areas had an overabundance of funding while others had too little funding. With a little bit more thought about objectives and constraints, the resource allocation could have been greatly improved. One objective of the organization was to keep their employee morale high. Employee morale in those departments with large reductions in funding suffered.

Management could have included constraints in the ILP formulation that guaranteed a somewhat smoother transition from the present R&D funding to a more desirable one. For example, constraints that guaranteed that each department get at least a given percentage of the previous years allocation would have prevented any drastic changes that adversely effected employee morale. Other constraints to guarantee a minimum amount of diversification and a minimum amount of coverage to specific research areas could have easily been accommodated. Thus, with a little thought about the objectives and constraints, and with some iteration, the AHP/ILP combination is a powerful mechanism for allocating resources so as to "best" meet an organization's objectives. A more detailed discussion of resource allocation begins on page 235.

Chapter 7

Forecasting - The Forward Process [1]

Applications of the Analytic Hierarchy Process can be classified into two major categories: (1) Choice -- the evaluation or prioritization of alternative courses of action, and (2) forecasting -- the evaluation of alternative future outcomes. Up to this point we have looked at choice problems -- where the desirability of alternative courses of action were evaluated. Forecasting, the topic of this section, focuses on the evaluation of the relative likelihood of future outcomes.

It has been said that humans will forever seek three elusive goals: eternal youth (the fountain of youth), the ability to turn base metals into gold (the goose that lays the golden egg), and the ability to forecast the future with certainty. Even though we will never be able to achieve these ultimate goals, we have come a long way. We have developed technologies that have dramatically increased our expected life spans, discovered substitute metals and synthetics that are often more valuable than gold, and have developed technologies and forecasting techniques that enable us to predict such things as the next day's weather with remarkable accuracy. However, the more progress we make the more we expect. In our competitive world it is not enough to be able to forecast demand for a product better than we did ten or twenty years ago, we must be able to forecast better than our competitors today!

Historically, two separate approaches have been used for forecasting – quantitative forecasts, which employ a variety of mathematical models based on historical data, and qualitative forecasting methods that rely on intuition, personal experiences. Quantitative methods include such techniques as simple trend projection, regression models, and time series models ranging from moving averages, to Box Jenkins auto-regressive models. Qualitative methods include such techniques as a juries of executive opinion, sales force composites, delphi method, and consumer

---

[1] Choice models are sometimes referred to as "backward" processes and forecasting models referred to as "forward" models, for reasons to be explained later.

market surveys[2]. By in large, each technique produces its own forecasts (and there may be many alternative forecasts available from a single technique) and decision-makers are usually left to decide which to believe. While quantitative forecasts are more 'objective', a major limitation is that they are based solely on historical data – and there is not data for the future. Indeed, an assumption of regression analysis, one of the most often used quantitative forecasting techniques is that the results are only valid within the range of data used to estimate the parameters of the model and that range does not include the future. However, the use of historical data is, in many circumstances, far superior to using no data at all. If one is willing to assume that the future will be somewhat similar to the past, then quantitative methods may be appropriate. However, technological innovation coupled with domestic and international social changes, political changes (e.g., the break up of the Soviet Union), and economic changes (e.g., the global economy) make quantitative forecasting techniques even less reliable than they were in the past.

Occasionally we may be interested in forecasting simply because of a curiosity of what the future may bring. More often, however, we are interested in forecasting the future in order to make better decisions (by evaluating alternative courses of action). We will look at how AHP can be useful in synthesizing information in order to make better decisions under conditions of uncertainty. We will show how AHP can be used to combine forecasts (in the form of probability distributions) from a variety of factors and/or techniques. Although uncertainty cannot be eliminated, we will show how AHP can be used to derive probability distributions that, in essence, remove the uncertainty about uncertainty. The first three illustrations involve the use of AHP in conjunction with traditional quantitative forecasting techniques. The remaining illustrations involve the use of AHP as a forecasting methodology in its own right.

---

[2] Jay Heizer and Barry Render, *Production and Operations Management – Strategies and Tactics*, 3rd Edition, Allyn and Bacon, Boston, p. 124.

Illustration 1 – Synthesizing Forecasting Methods for a Composite forecast

AHP is an excellent way to combine the results of several forecasting tools to produce a single, composite forecast. Many firms benefit in using a variety of forecasting tools in tandem because the strengths of some tools offset the weaknesses in others. However, the problem in using multiple methods is how to arrive at a single numeric forecast. Recent research has indicated that a combination of forecasting approaches often produces better results than using only one approach.

Alternative approaches in forecasting future demand for a product might consist of:

- Consensus asking a group of experts, to come to a consensus on judgments about relative likelihoods (perhaps by using a Delphi approach)
- Surveys - such as sales force surveys, or buyer intention surveys
- Multiple regression
- Exponential smoothing
- Box Jenkins

Criteria such as accuracy, stability of estimates, and turning-point estimation can be used to assess the credibility of various forecasting tools. The synthesis of the model shown in Figure 1 provides weights for each of four traditional methods. These weights can then be applied to each forecast estimate in order to arrive at a weighted, composite forecast as shown in Table 1.

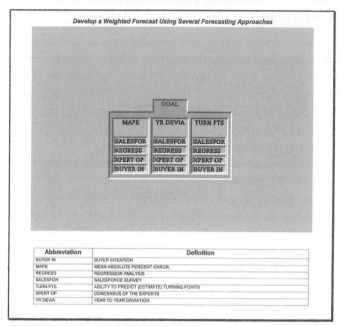

Figure 1 – Model for a Composite Forecast

Table 1 – Deriving a Weighted, Composite Forecast

Forecasting Tool	Overall Priority	Forecasted Sales	Weighted Forecast
Sales force survey	.32	3,800	1,216.0
Regression	.18	3,725	670.5
Expert Consensus	.06	4,150	249.0
Buyer intention	.44	2,725	1,199.0
Expected Sales			3,334.5

Illustration 2 – Selecting a Forecasting Method

Instead of combining the results of quantitative forecasting techniques, it may be desirable to use a forecast from only one of the many quantitative techniques available. But which one? A model to select the best forecasting technique for a particular application is shown in Figure 2. The decision maker(s) make judgments about the relative preference of the techniques with respect to objectives such as accuracy, cost, management information provided, the ability of a technique to predict turning points, and the time required to implement the technique. Judgments about the relative importance of these objectives are also made. The resulting synthesis will indicate the overall relative preference of the various techniques.

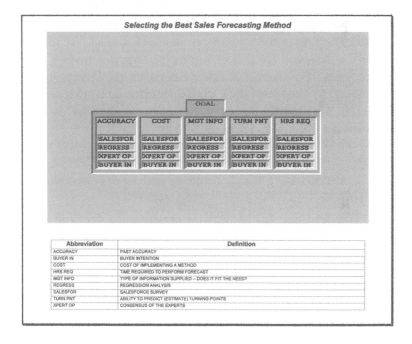

Figure 2 – Selecting A Forecasting Method

Illustration 3 – Deriving Probability Distributions

Consider an investor who is evaluating alternative stocks or options. The investor, after doing research, will form an opinion that a particular stock is likely to go up, or down. Suppose an investor is considering two alternative stocks and thinks they will both go up. Is one more likely to go up than the other? It may be that the investor feels that stock A is more likely to go up than stock B but that stock B has a greater probability of going up by more than 20 percent than does stock A. How can the investor incorporate these feelings into his or her decision process? If the investor could translate his or her knowledge about the stocks into probability distributions, he or she could then use the probability distributions in choosing among the stocks, or in even more complex decisions, choosing among alternative strategies for stock option puts and calls.

It would be unreasonable to expect the investor to specify directly the probability distribution for a stock's price performance (over a specified period of time). However, it is rather natural for the investor to express feelings about the anticipated stock's price performance via pairwise relative comparisons. For example, the investor should be able to translate his or her research about a stock into a judgment such as:

the likelihood of a stock's going up 5 percent in a given period of time is moderately more likely than that it will remain at the current price,

and, the likelihood of a stock's remaining unchanged is moderately to strongly more likely than that it will go up 20 percent.

Just as redundancy (in the pairwise comparisons) has been shown to produce accurate estimates of quantifiable physical phenomena (such as area or intensity of light), the redundancy in the investor's set of pairwise comparisons will result in probabilities that reflect the investor's judgments, which in turn are based on his or her research as well as experience. In making the pairwise comparisons, the investor will find himself or herself pressed to "think hard" and forced to question both assumptions and the

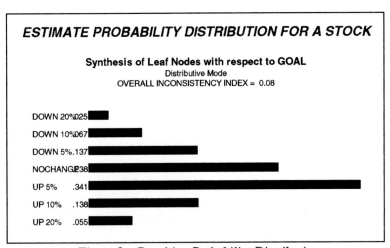

ESTIMATE PROBABILITY DISTRIBUTION FOR A STOCK

Synthesis of Leaf Nodes with respect to GOAL
Distributive Mode
OVERALL INCONSISTENCY INDEX = 0.08

DOWN 20% .025
DOWN 10% .067
DOWN 5% .137
NOCHANGE .238
UP 5% .341
UP 10% .138
UP 20% .055

Figure 3 – Resulting Probability Distribution

ESTIMATE PROBABILITY DISTRIBUTION FOR A STOCK

Node: 0

Compare the relative IMPORTANCE with respect to: GOAL <

1=EQUAL 3=MODERATE 5=STRONG 7=VERY STRONG 9=EXTREME

#	Left	9	8	7	6	5	4	3	2	1	2	3	4	5	6	7	8	9	Right
1	DOWN 20%	9	8	7	6	5	4	3	2	1	2	3	4	5	6	(7)	8	9	DOWN 10%
2	DOWN 20%	9	8	7	6	5	4	3	2	1	2	3	4	5	6	7	(8)	9	DOWN 5%
3	DOWN 20%	9	8	7	6	5	4	3	2	1	2	3	4	5	6	7	8	(9)	NOCHANGE
4	DOWN 20%	9	8	7	6	5	4	3	2	1	2	3	4	(5)	6	7	8	9	UP 5%
5	DOWN 20%	9	8	7	6	5	4	3	2	1	2	3	4	(5)	6	7	8	9	UP 10%
6	DOWN 20%	9	8	7	6	5	4	3	2	1	2	(3)	4	5	6	7	8	9	UP 20%
7	DOWN 10%	9	8	7	6	5	4	3	2	1	2	3	(4)	5	6	7	8	9	DOWN 5%
8	DOWN 10%	9	8	7	6	5	4	3	2	1	2	3	4	(5)	6	7	8	9	NOCHANGE
9	DOWN 10%	9	8	7	6	5	4	3	2	1	2	3	(4)	5	6	7	8	9	UP 5%
10	DOWN 10%	9	8	7	6	5	4	3	2	1	2	(3)	4	5	6	7	8	9	UP 10%
11	DOWN 10%	9	8	7	6	5	4	3	2	(1)	2	3	4	5	6	7	8	9	UP 20%
12	DOWN 5%	9	8	7	6	5	4	3	2	1	2	(3)	4	5	6	7	8	9	NOCHANGE
13	DOWN 5%	9	8	7	6	5	4	3	2	1	2	(3)	4	5	6	7	8	9	UP 5%
14	DOWN 5%	9	8	7	6	5	4	3	2	(1)	2	3	4	5	6	7	8	9	UP 10%
15	DOWN 5%	9	8	7	6	5	4	3	(2)	1	2	3	4	5	6	7	8	9	UP 20%
16	NOCHANGE	9	8	7	6	5	4	(3)	2	1	2	3	4	5	6	7	8	9	UP 5%
17	NOCHANGE	9	8	7	6	5	4	3	(2)	1	2	3	4	5	6	7	8	9	UP 10%
18	NOCHANGE	9	8	7	6	5	(4)	3	2	1	2	3	4	5	6	7	8	9	UP 20%
19	UP 5%	9	8	7	6	5	4	(3)	2	1	2	3	4	5	6	7	8	9	UP 10%
20	UP 5%	9	8	7	(6)	5	4	3	2	1	2	3	4	5	6	7	8	9	UP 20%
21	UP 10%	9	8	7	6	5	(4)	3	2	1	2	3	4	5	6	7	8	9	UP 20%

Figure 4 – Judgments

validity of available data. An Expert Choice model[3], as well as a typical set of comparisons and resulting probability distribution are shown in Figure 5, Figure 4 and Figure 3 respectively.

The translation of the investor's research into a subjective probability distribution is a significant accomplishment since this probability distribution can subsequently be used to evaluate investment alternatives (using criteria relevant to the investor, such as expected value, standard deviation, and the probability of gaining or losing more than a specified percent, along with other factors about the company such as its quality of management). In a sense, it can be said that this process of deriving a probability distribution removes the uncertainty about uncertainty by translating fuzzy feelings (such as research or analyst opinion that it will

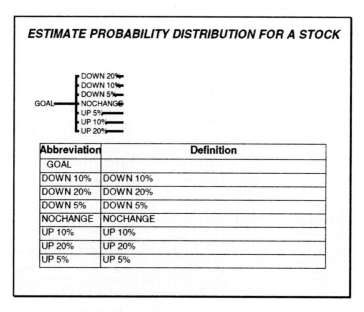

Figure 5 – Simple Model to Estimate Probability Distribution for a Stock

---

[3] More discrete intervals and subintervals can be included if desired.

probably go up a little, or a lot) into a distribution of probabilities. A distribution of probabilities is far richer and in some cases necessary when making rational choices such as deciding on stock option trades.

This approach can easily be expanded to accommodate judgments based on specific factors and to synthesize forecasts derived from different forecasting perspectives. Four common perspectives on forecasting stocks/options/futures are:

- Fundamental analysis (companies fundamentals, price earnings ratios, supply, demand, and so on.)
- Technical analysis (charts, moving averages, support and resistance levels, Elliot waves, and so on.)
- Cyclical analysis
- Historical analysis (what the price is relative to its historical highs, lows, and so on.)

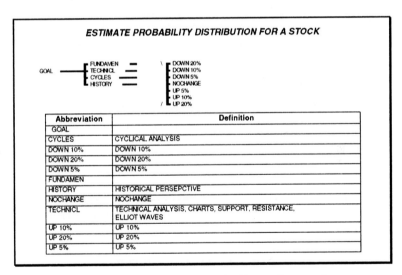

Figure 6 – Model Synthesizing Different Approaches

Some professional analysts use only one perspective, while others use a combination, trying to synthesize in their heads the likelihoods indicated by each perspective and the relative importance they attach to each perspective at a particular time. This kind of synthesis can be accomplished with AHP as shown in Figure 6.

In order to assess the relative influence in synthesizing these approaches to forecasting stocks, their relative success in both the short term and long term as well as their success in similar environments can be included in the evaluation as shown in Figure 7.

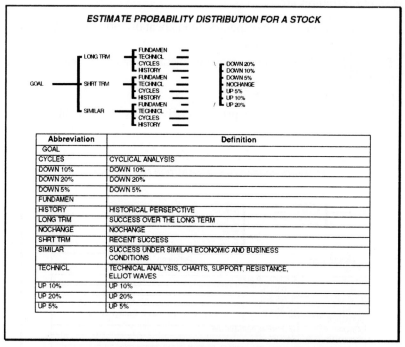

Figure 7 – Model Including Relative Influence of Approaches

Illustration 4 – Forecasting Alternative Outcomes

Many AHP forecasting models are simple, straightforward models designed to measure the relative importance of influencing factors on alternative outcomes. As an example, we will look at the following model, constructed by a retired intelligence officer one week after Iraq invaded

Kuwait. Forecasting Saddam Hussein's next move was of obvious interest. The model was used to asses the relative likelihood that Saddam Hussein would (1) stay put where he was in Kuwait, (2) invade Saudi Arabia, (3) pull his forces back to pre-invasion locations, but leave a puppet government, or (4) pull back to pre-invasion locations, without leaving a puppet government.

The factors thought to influence Saddam Hussein's behavior (his objectives) included: (1) his ego, (2) gain of land that was in dispute, (3) the power to do what he wanted to (in addition to increasing his ego), (4) revenge for the wrongs he perceived from his Arab neighbors, (5) distraction from internal problems, and (6) minimizing the risk of loss in confrontation with other powers.

Judgments were made about the relative likelihood of the outcomes with respect to each of Saddam Hussein's objectives. Following this,

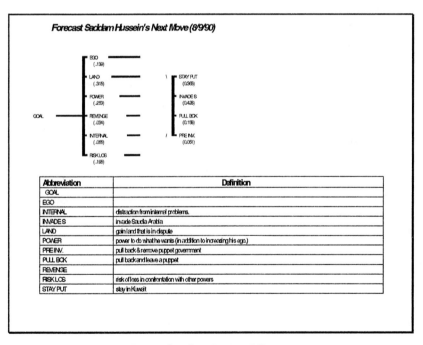

Figure 8 – Synthesis of Outcomes

judgments were made about the relative importance of Saddam Hussein's objectives. The synthesis of these judgments was that an invasion of Saudi Arabia was the most likely outcome (see Figure 8).

A look at a gradient sensitivity plot (Figure 9) for the risk of loss objective was very revealing.

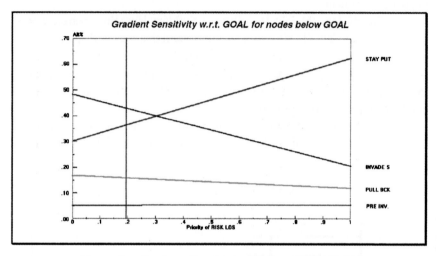

Figure 9 – Gradient Sensitivity Plot on Risk of Loss

If the risk of loss were to become more important, the most likely outcome would be for Saddam Hussein to stay put, rather than invade Saudi Arabia -- a result that is not surprising. During this time, the United States and other coalition nations were beginning to send forces into the region. About a week later, the model was revised and re-evaluated, taking into account the buildup of coalition forces (Figure 10).

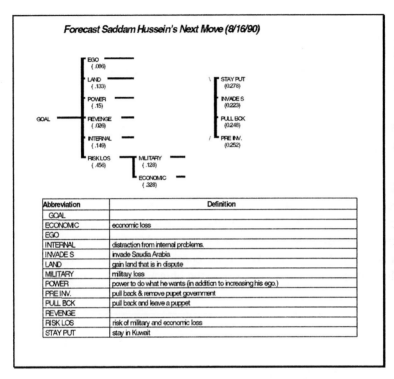

Figure 10 – Synthesis of Outcomes One Week Later

The only structural change in this model is the addition of sub-objectives under the risk of loss objective. A significant change in the evaluation of the model was due to judgments that took into account the buildup of coalition forces. The risk of loss objective was now evaluated as being much more important to Saddam Hussein than in the first model.[4] The results of this model show that the most likely outcome has changed from that of invading Saudi Arabia to staying put -- which is precisely what Saddam Hussein decided to do.

---

[4]An interesting observation, made after the Gulf War ended by General Norman Schwarzkopf, was that the press had helped the coalition efforts by giving the impression that the coalition forces were much stronger at this time than they actually were.

Two forecasting models were shown in this illustration. If the United States and the coalition forces had not already decided to build up forces in the region, the likely outcome of an invasion of Saudi Arabia would have certainly called for a choice model to evaluate alternative actions, including a force buildup.

Illustration 5 – Forecasting models interacting with choice model(s).

As an illustration of how forecasting model(s) can interact with choice models, consider the following hypothetical situation, aired by a major television network. The President of the United States must respond to terrorist demands made while the terrorists hold an oil tanker (along with some passengers) hostage off the tip of lower Manhattan. The choice model is shown in Figure 11). When one considers the relative preference of the alternatives with respect to each of the objectives, for example, the relative

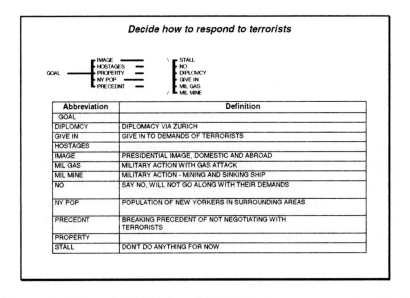

Figure 11 – Choice Model

preference of mining and sinking the ship as opposed to a gas attack with
respect to the effect on the New York population, questions arise as to what
is *likely* to happen to the New York population under
each of these alternative actions.

If there are several possibilities, each of which is affected by several

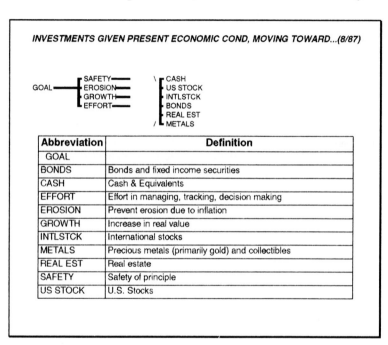

Figure 12 – Evaluation of Alternative Investments

factors, a forecasting model could be employed. Therefore, in order to
evaluate the alternatives in this model, it can be helpful to first construct
separate forecasting models for one or more of the alternatives in order to
estimate what is likely to happen if that alternative is pursued.

Illustration 6 -- Deriving Scenario Likelihoods

Another common way of incorporating uncertainty and forecasting with AHP is through scenarios. Planners use scenarios as a way of describing future conditions. Scenarios serve as a background for planning and evaluating alternative courses of action.[5] The need to include scenarios in an AHP model often becomes self-evident. The AHP model shown in Figure 12 was used to evaluate the relative attractiveness of alternative investments (cash or cash equivalents, U.S. stocks, international stocks, bonds, real estate, and precious metals), with respect to investor objectives that included safety of principle, growth, protecting against erosion from inflation, and effort required for investment management.

When considering a judgment such as "What is more important, safety of principle or growth?", the need for scenarios became apparent as the answer obviously depends on the economic environment that would ensue. Thus, economic environment scenarios were included below the goal, as shown in Figure 13.

---

[5]J. Brooke Aker, *Consumer Issues*, Presentation at The Planning Forum, April 4, 1991, New York, N.Y.

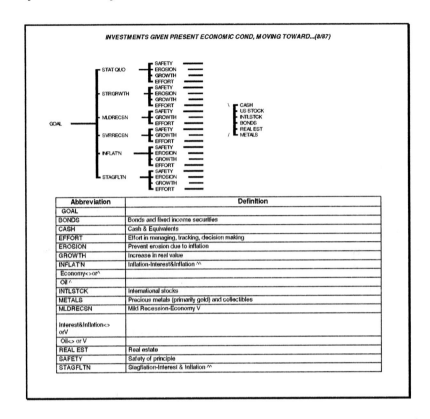

Figure 13 – Model with Economic Scenarios

Priorities for the scenarios can be derived from pairwise comparisons of the relative likelihood of the scenarios. These can be based on historical data as well as expert judgment given current conditions. Sometimes there may be ambiguity in making such judgments. For example, when judging whether a strong growth scenario is more or less likely than a mild recession scenario, the answer may depend on factors such as the Federal budget deficit, balance of trade payments, Federal monitory policy, consumer confidence, and so on. A subsidiary model including these factors can be used to resolve ambiguities (see Figure 14). The resulting priorities from the model

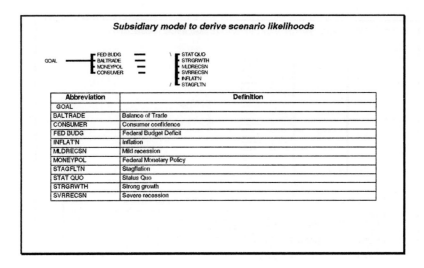

Figure 14 – Subsidiary model to derive scenario likelihoods

in Figure 14 are entered as priorities for the scenarios in the model of Figure 13.

Illustration 7 – Analytical Planning (The Forward/Backward Process)[6]

Analytical planning is a process that involves the iterative application of both forecasting and choice. On the one hand, we can look *forward* (from the present to the future) and forecast what is likely to happen. This is called the *forward process*, a primarily *descriptive* step concerned with the following kind of question: given the present actors and their policies, what *will* be (believed to be or likely to be) the future resulting from their actions? On the other hand, we can step into the future, determine what we desire, look *backward* to the present, and choose the actions or policies that will help us achieve the desired future. This is the *desired planning process*, or the *backward process* - a *normative* approach

---

[6] Saaty, Thomas L. and Forman, Ernest H., *The Hierarchon - A Dictionary of Hierarchies*, The Analytic Hierarchy Process Series - Volume V, RWS Publications, Pittsburgh PA, 1993

concerned with the question: given a desired future, what *should* our policies be to attain the future?

Complex environments with competing actors and forces may preclude us from easily achieving our desired future as set forth in the backward process. To see whether or not this is the case, the preferred actions or policies from the backward process can be incorporated into the forward process, which produces a forecast of likely futures. This forecast of likely futures can then be compared with the desired futures of the backward process. Any significant discrepancies would indicate that the desired future is not likely to be attained with the planned actions or policies. Discrepancies can be resolved by either finding other actions or policies that will bring the likely future closer to the desired future, or, if that is not possible, identifying alternative objectives for the desired future. In other words, if it is not possible to achieve particular objectives, more realistic objectives should be identified.

Thus, all hierarchic decision-making is one of three types: a forward process, a backward process, or a combination of both processes. The forward process hierarchy is used to project the *likely* or logical future. All problems of prediction fall into this class - what people prefer and what is likely to come about as a result of exercising their preferences. The backward process hierarchy is used to find promising control policies to attain a *desired* future. Problems of choice and decision, as opposed to problems of prediction, are expressions of desire. They are backward processes in which we set priorities on what is important, or on what should be important, and use it to identify the best choice to attain it.

What should we do today to prepare for tomorrow?

For the long-range planner the important question is not what should we do tomorrow, but what should we do today to prepare for an uncertain future. On the one hand, it is desirable to stay open to change and invention to attain better and more fulfilling futures. On the other hand, to cope with the future we need to design plans that will survive and be effective.

"Thankfully, Collar found a model for helping us make our priority-setting decisions - a methodology to render the ranking process more objective and systematic. It also allowed us to take any number of criteria into consideration. In short, it enabled us to deal with our situation in all of its complexity. It was called the Analytic Hierarchy Process (AHP),

"...as part of AHP, you, the decision maker, get to build the hierarchy. You establish the goal, the criteria, and the options. In so doing, you can actually bring ideas, anecdotal experience, even emotion into the process."

"Automated in the form of a relatively inexpensive software program called "Expert Choice", AHP is an extraordinarily powerful decision-making tool. It brings structure to a decision-making, yet it's flexible because you get to design a hierarchy of goals, criteria, and options customized to the particular problem at hand. It can be used with groups, and, as a collaborative effort, it can bring consensus to decision-making. It allows you to quantify judgments, even subjective ones. *It also forces you to consider the interdependencies of your criteria to meet your goals.* AHP pinpoints for you where the impacts are the highest or inconsistent. You can play "what-if" games with it..."

"AHP allows you to set priorities by taking several factors into consideration— factors that interplay and affect each other. In building the hierarchy, you can have goals and sub-goals. You can have several layers of criteria. You can also deal with several layers of options. In other words, you can address extraordinarily complex situations, ones with multi-dimensions that have interconnections every which way."

"AHP became the template we imposed on our efforts to rank the line items of the System Plan so that we could earmark funds in a much more methodical, rationally defensible way."

"All this had very real consequences. In the past, we would sometimes chase markets simply because some highly placed executive decreed we should. Usually these decrees were based on an anecdotal experience with a particular customer or industry. But with our priority ranking in hand, it became easier to fend off such unjustified dictates. ... For the first time, we could confidently articulate what businesses we were in and, more importantly, which ones we were not."

"We had come up with a process for setting priorities and, thus, for making decisions on earmarking resources. It's a rare organization that doesn't find itself in need of some similarly systematic process. In today's competitive global marketplace, where almost everyone is finding themselves having to do more with less, figuring how much money should be spent where may be one of a manager's most difficult tasks. But the problems and pain can be obviated by setting priorities. Its simple: Before you decide how to budget, you've simply got to know what's most important, especially in reaching your organization's overarching goals in a holistic, balanced way. As straightforward as that sounds, however, it's hardly a simple task. Making decisions today depends on taking into consideration any number of interdependent goals, criteria, and options. As we proved though, relying on a model can make the job of setting priorities to allocate resources much more methodical and objective and, therefore, much more credible and defensible."

The details of how they did it are not presented in *The Silverlake Project*, although the authors do discuss some specifics of what they did. We will next present the details of several approaches to allocating resources that can be used to fit in with any organization's objectives and constraints. Before looking at the details, it is important to once more focus on the big picture—what needs to be done when allocating resources and what the consequences of a rational, systematic resource allocation methodology can be. Bauer, Collar, Emilio, and Tang, authors of *The Silverlake Project, write:*

"Making tradeoffs is a fact of organizational life, especially in an era of doing more with less. So priorities have to be set. But those priorities must be determined on the basis of the enterprise's overall objectives. Resource decisions need to be made holistically, that is, with their consequences to the entire enterprise and all its parts in mind."

"Setting priorities - priorities that will serve as a guide to resource decisions— shouldn't be a matter of guesswork. It must be done through a process that's as systematic as possible. And one which produces repeatable results. This is precisely what we did—not only in allocating resources, but ultimately, in determining the shape of the entire Silverlake Project."

Methodology Overview

There are a variety of ways to achieve a systematic, rational, and defensible allocation of resources that will provide a competitive advantage to an organization. The methodology discussed below is quite flexible and can be adapted to a wide variety of situations and constraints. As outlined above, the methodology consists of the following steps[4]:

1. Identify/design alternatives

2. Identify and structure the organization's goals and objectives

---

[4] Keep in mind that these 'steps', are part of a 'process', in which iteration is extremely important.

3. Prioritize the objectives and sub-objectives

4. Measure each alternative's contribution to each of the lowest level sub-objectives

5. Find the best combination of alternatives, subject to environmental and organizational constraints

Identify/design alternatives

Expertise in the art and science of identifying and/or designing alternatives lies in the domain of the decision makers, who have many years of study and experience to bear on this task. Our goal here is not to tell them how to do this, but, instead, to help them better measure and synthesize in order to better capitalize on their knowledge and experience.

Even if alternatives have already have been identified, e.g. R&D project proposals as responses to a request for proposal (RFP), it might be possible to augment or redesign these as part of the 'process'. For example, if, after one 'iteration' of the resource allocation methodology for allocating funds to internal R&D project proposals, it may be to the organization's benefit to make known the 'preliminary' allocation as well as the details of the evaluation so that proposors can revise their proposals, and, in the process, improve their contribution to the organization's objectives. Of course, there are rules that must be employed in this context to insure fairness. For example, government agencies may, by law or regulation, have to limit the process to one iteration with no opportunities for the proposors to 'improve' their proposals. Such laws and regulations sacrifice 'quality' for 'fairness'. While rules, laws or regulations that limit feedback and iteration are intended to make the process 'fair', the tradeoff between 'fairness' and 'quality' of results should be carefully considered when deciding on the 'rules' for the resource allocation process.[5]

Instead of deciding which alternatives to fund and not to fund, as in the case of R&D project selection, a more common resource allocation activity is the periodic allocation of an organization's basic budget. Here, the alternatives are not which departments to fund, but instead, at what level

---

[5] The choice of procurement rules is itself a multi-objective decision that should be addressed before the actual procurement process begins.

should each department be funded.   Each department, or organizational unit, can design their operation at alternative levels of funding, e.g., equal to last years funding, 10% above last years funding level, 10% below last years funding level, 20% above, etc. If an organization faces a budget cut, say 10%, for example, cutting each organizational unit by 10% (sometimes called across the board cuts) may seem fair, but it is not competitive. It stands to reason that in today's fast changing world, in order to be competitive, some units should be cut perhaps 50%, 80% or entirely, in order to increase the budgets of other units by significant amounts. The resource allocation methodology presented below makes this a practical approach.

Identify and structure the organization's goals and objectives

The main message of this book is that decisions must be made on the basis of achievement of objectives. And so it is with resource allocation decisions. As Bauer, Collar, Emilio, and Tang advise in The Silverlake Project, "priorities must be determined on the basis of the enterprise's overall objectives. Resource decisions need to be made holistically, that is, with their consequences to the entire enterprise and all its parts in mind." And so the entire enterprise's goals and objectives must be addressed. This may not seem easy to do in a large enterprise or organization; however, it can be done the same way that large organizations are typically organized, that is, hierarchically.

Most organizations already have a statement of goals and objectives (sometimes organized as values, goals, and objectives). A good bet is that they are already structured hierarchically. Where are they kept? In some organizations they might be framed and hung on the walls to help remind employees and inform customers of the organization's values, goals and objectives. In other organizations they might be in 'the blue book' or 'the black book' that is referred to from time to time. It is important to study these goals and objectives to see if they are 'living' or long forgotten soon after they were drafted. If they are still living, and up to date—taking into account the fast changes in business and society, (locally, nationally, and globally), they will serve as the driving force behind the allocation of resources.   Otherwise, they must be revised, brought back to life, and continually examined to keep them current.   Once people realize that the enterprise's overall objectives will serve as the basis for the allocation of resources, there will be a keen interest in keeping them current and relevant!

The hierarchy of objectives, sub-objectives, sub-sub-objectives, and so on, must be broad enough to encompass every existing or desired activity that is part of the resource allocation process.   If not, proponents of an activity will not be able to show where and how much the activity can contribute to the organization's objectives.   Once more, we need to be open to iteration since it might not become obvious that specific objectives were overlooked until the activities are rated in a subsequent step of the process.

Top level executives understand and can best make judgments about the relative importance of the main organizational objectives, and possibly the sub-objectives.   They know very little about the detailed alternatives vying for funding.   Lower level management and operational personnel can best make judgments about the relative importance of the lowest level sub-objectives and about how much contribution each alternative contributes to the lowest level sub-objectives.   They often don't appreciate or understand top management's strategic direction or change in direction. The systematic approach presented below makes it possible to synthesize knowledge, experience, and insights across many levels within a large organization, something that has not been possible to do in the past.   Without such a synthesis, it is virtually impossible to achieve a rational, competitive allocation of resources.

Prioritize the objectives and sub-objectives

The relative importance of the objectives and sub-objectives must be established in order to make a rational allocation of resources.   Neglecting to do so is a mistake.   Assuming that all the main objectives are equally important is a mistake. The pairwise comparison process and team methods discussed in this text provide a straightforward, informative, and reliable way to prioritize the organization's objectives.   Remember, this is a 'process'. After establishing priorities for the organization's objectives, and subsequently deriving a 'preliminary' allocation based on these priorities, the priorities and judgments that served to derive the priorities should be re-examined and revised as necessary. The prioritization of the organization's objectives during the resource allocation process leads to another important benefit. In top management's quest for excellence and response to shifts in direction brought about by changes in the environment and competitive forces, what better way is there to convey their priorities to the organization at large? If these priorities are not conveyed, it is almost inevitable that individuals or departments which formerly provided valuable services to an organization, will, because of ignorance of changes in the organization's primary objectives or their relative importance, someday be surprised to find their contributions are no longer of value.

Measure Alternatives' Contributions

Having prioritized the organization's objectives and sub-objectives, the next step is to evaluate how much each proposed activity (or each possible level of funding for each activity) would contribute to each of the lowest level sub-objectives. This could be done by a pairwise comparison process, but because there will normally be many, possibly hundreds or thousands of activities or levels of funding, the ratings approach is customarily used.

Find the Best Combination of Alternatives

After prioritizing the organization's objectives and sub-objectives, and rating the contribution of the competing activities to the lowest level objectives, we have ratio scale measures of the relative contribution of each alternative to the overall objectives of the organization. We claim that there is no way to rationally allocate resources without such measures and suggest that the derivation of such measures for a large, diverse organization without the approach detailed here is almost impossible to accomplish! We will next consider two different basic situations in which we seek to find the best combination of alternatives for the allocation of resources. In the first situation, which we will refer to as Discrete Alternative Resource Allocation, each project/activity is a separate or discrete unit. (There may be a variety of dependencies between these units.) For example, we might be allocating resources to discrete proposals in response to an RFP. In the second situation, which we will refer to as Activity Level Resource Allocation, each project or activity is represented at one or more levels of funding but an additional constraint is that each project can be funded at only one level. (Here too there may be a variety of dependencies between projects,).[6] For example, each department of an organization may design several alternative levels of funding; the resource allocation methodology is to find the levels for each department that produces the best overall results for the organization. For each of these two situations we will look at two different approaches, one that focuses on the maximization of benefit/cost and the other that focuses on the maximization of benefit.

Discrete Alternative Resource Allocation

George Washington University Academic Computing Advisory Committee

We will illustrate the allocation of resources to alternative projects/activities with a rather small, but typical example. The Academic Computing Advisory Committee of the George Washington University had $15,000 available to fund proposals relating to the use of computers. After publishing a short RFP, eleven proposals were received. The total amount requested for all the proposals was $34,430. The committee, consisting of nine faculty members had to decide which of the proposed projects to fund. Can you imagine getting nine faculty members to agree?

After discussing 'criteria' or, what we prefer to call 'objectives', the following Expert Choice model was developed:

---

[6] After looking at these two situations, it will be easier to understand the general situation which is simply a hybrid of the two.

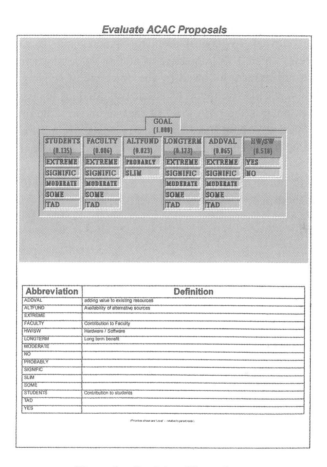

Figure 1 – Decision Hierarchy

Through a process of discussion and pairwise comparisons (the committee used keypads to enter individual judgments, which were then aggregated) the priorities of the objectives (shown in Figure 1) were derived. (A complete discussion of group or team decision-making begins on page 115). Since the committee's focus was on computer hardware and software, and since some of the proposals were only peripherally related to hardware and software the HW/SW objective was judged to be the most important. Expected long-term benefits to the University were second most important, followed by contribution to student and faculty activities (learning, research etc.) The objective of adding value to existing resources was next in importance, followed by the objective of funding projects for which there was little likelihood of alternative funding sources. Note that the priorities possess the ratio level of measurement. The priority of the HW/SW objective is 2.99 times the priority of the second most important objective, long-term benefits to the University. Had an ordinal scale of six items been used, the most important objective would have a value of 6, the next most important objective a value of 5, and the ratio would have been only 6/5 or about 1.2.

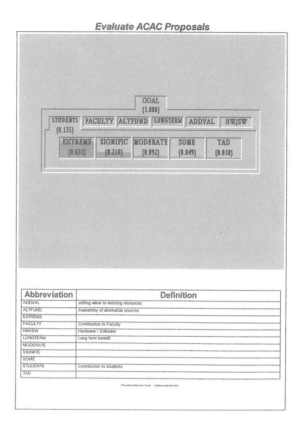

Figure 2 – Intensities

The intensities below each of the objectives were also prioritized with pairwise comparisons. For example, a project that is judged to make an extreme contribution to students will receive a priority for that contribution of about 63 times that of a project that makes only a 'tad' of a contribution to students, as can be seen in Figure 2. This is quite different than an ordinal scale where the ratio would be 5 to 1 instead. The intensities and their scale can be different under each of the objectives. The intensities for the alternative funding sources is shown in Figure 4.

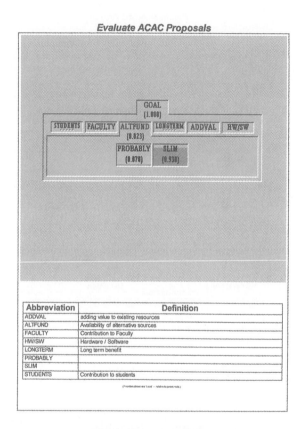

Figure 3 – Alternative Funding

After the objectives and intensities are prioritized, each of the alternative projects is rated with respect to each of the lowest level objectives, as shown in Figure 4.

Alternatives	TOTAL	COSTS	STUDENTS .1350	FACULTY .0859	ALTFUND .0225	LONGTERM .1730	ADDVAL .0654	HW/SW .5182
Proposal One	0.684	2,000	0.417	0.241	0.384	SIGNIFIC	0.320	YES
Proposal Two	0.598	1,622	0.202	0.146	0.422	0.116	0.160	YES
Proposal Three	0.742	1,515	0.782	SIGNIFIC	PROBABLY	0.395	0.285	YES
Proposal Four	0.762	1,280	0.709	SIGNIFIC	PROBABLY	0.490	0.490	YES
Proposal Five	0.090	7,500	0.055	0.121	PROBABLY	0.295	0.212	NO
Proposal Six	0.079	4,375	0.134	0.136	PROBABLY	0.202	0.117	NO
Proposal Seven	0.722	3,187	0.672	SIGNIFIC	PROBABLY	SIGNIFIC	SIGNIFIC	YES
Proposal Eight	0.575	565	0.490	0.256	PROBABLY	0.329	0.373	0.780
Proposal Nine	0.647	4,000	0.220	0.220	0.868	0.220	0.345	YES
Proposal Ten	0.709	3,300	0.380	0.256	PROBABLY	0.468	0.541	YES
Proposal Eleven	0.647	5,086	0.395	0.167	0.589	0.212	0.175	YES

Figure 4 – Combined Ratings

The entries in the columns representing the objectives (STUDENTS, FACULTY, etc.,) are either one of the intensities for that column (for which we derived is a ratio scale value) if all nine faculty members agreed on the rating, or a decimal value which represents the average of the intensities of the nine faculty members. The values in the Total column are ratio scale measures of the contribution each project is expected to make to the organization's objectives, or, as Bauer et. al assert:

> "Before you decide how to budget, you've simply got to know what's most important, especially in reaching your organization's overarching goals in a holistic, balanced way."

In this simple example, there are only six 'overarching goals' or objectives, each represented by a column in the matrix. In a typical large organization there may be hundreds of columns, structured hierarchically.

What does the total value .684 for Proposal One in Figure 4 mean? By itself nothing, but it means a great deal when compared to the total values for the other alternatives—Proposal One contributes about 8.7 times as much as Proposal Six, for example. Because the totals are ratio scale numbers, we can normalize without changing the ratios. The totals in Figure 4 are normalized such that an 'ideal' alternative, one that rated best in every column would have a value of 1.0. Figure 5 shows the two other normalizations: one normalized so that the best alternative is 100%, and another normalized so that the priorities add to 1.0. Any of these three

Alternatives	% OF MAX	PRIORITY
Proposal One	89.813	0.109
Proposal Two	78.493	0.096
Proposal Three	97.377	0.119
Proposal Four	100.000	0.122
Proposal Five	11.747	0.014
Proposal Six	10.397	0.013
Proposal Seven	94.798	0.115
Proposal Eight	75.505	0.092
Proposal Nine	84.901	0.103
Proposal Ten	93.106	0.113
Proposal Eleven	84.942	0.103

Figure 5 – Percent of Maximum

normalizations of the projects' expected[7] total benefit could be used in determining the best allocation of resources. How the numbers are used depends on the circumstances and constraints of the situation. If, for example, each project could be partially funded and would produce benefits in proportion to the amount funded, we might decide to allocate the $15,000 to the projects on the basis of the normalized priority column, so that Project One would get 10.9%, Project Six 1.3% and so on. However, the assumptions here are that each project requires a given amount of funding (expressed as Costs in Figure 4) in order to deliver the benefits in the total column—that is, we can not fund a project at some fraction of its stated cost[8]. How then should we decide which projects to fund? We will look at two approaches, depending on whether we are interested in achieving the highest benefit/cost ratio or the highest benefit.

---

[7] We refer to the benefits as 'expected' because the ratings were made on the basis of what the projects would be expected to contribute. A more formal 'expected' contribution could be derived by including scenarios between the goal and top level objectives in the AHP model and making judgments about the relative likelihood of each of the scenarios.

[8] Mechanically, it is just as easy, perhaps even easier, to perform the resource allocation allowing for partial funding of projects.

Alternatives		Benefit	Cost	B/C	Cum C.	Cum B.
Alt 008	Proposal Eight	0.092	565	162.832	565	0.092
Alt 004	Proposal Four	0.122	1280	95.313	1845	0.214
Alt 003	Proposal Three	0.119	1515	78.548	3360	0.333
Alt 002	Proposal Two	0.096	1622	59.186	4982	0.429
Alt 001	Proposal One	0.109	2000	54.500	6982	0.538
Alt 007	Proposal Seven	0.115	3187	36.084	10169	0.653
Alt 010	Proposal Ten	0.113	3300	34.242	13469	0.766
Alt 009	Proposal Nine	0.103	4000	25.750	17469	0.869
Alt 011	Proposal Eleven	0.103	5086	20.252	22555	0.972
Alt 006	Proposal Six	0.013	4375	2.971	26930	0.985
Alt 005	Proposal Five	0.014	7500	1.867	34430	0.999

Figure 6 – Benefit Cost Ratios

Benefit/Cost Ratios—Sort and Allocate

Given the benefits and the costs, we can easily calculate the benefit/cost ratios, and sort from high to low as shown in Figure 6.[9] We can then allocate funds to the projects starting with the project with the highest benefit/cost ratio and continuing until the $15,000 budget is used up. This will produce the largest benefit/cost ratio while funding as many projects as possible within the budget constraint. Looking at the cumulative cost column, we see that if we were to do this, we would fund Projects 8, 4, 3, 2, 1, 7 and 10. Projects 9, 11, 6 and 5 would not be funded.

Figure 7 contains a benefit/cost efficient frontier graph produced with Team Expert Choice. Notice that the curve is concave, signifying diminishing marginal benefit as additional projects are selected with lower benefit/cost ratios.

---

[9] The b/c ratios have been multiplied by 10^6.

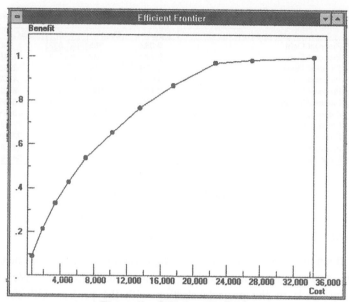

Figure 7 – Efficient Frontier

Before adopting this methodology, we should see when it makes sense to seek the highest cumulative benefit/cost ratio as our objective and when it doesn't. If we assume that an organization will consistently follow the philosophy of maximizing its cumulative benefit/cost ratio, then over time, they will also maximize their benefits[10]. This statement also assumes that there will be other comparable opportunities for additional resource allocations in the future, so whatever portion of the budget that is not expended will provide benefits commensurate with those activities currently being funded. However, these assumptions are not always valid and it is dangerous to take the maximization of benefit/cost ratios for granted. An example illustrating the danger of using a benefit/cost maximization will be presented after looking at the benefit optimization methodology.

---

[10] As compared to any other allocation that produces a lower benefit/cost ratio and, in the long run, allocates approximately the same total amount.

Maximizing Benefits -- Optimization

Another method for allocating resources seeks to find that combination of projects or activities that maximizes the total benefits without exceeding the given budget.[11] This problem can be formulated as a zero-one integer mathematical programming problem, sometimes referred to as a knapsack problem. Most spreadsheet programs today contain algorithms for solving such problems.[12] We will illustrate the solution to the preceding resource allocation exercise using the Solver tool in Microsoft's Excel. Mathematically, the optimization problem formulation is as follows:

Maximize $.109X_1 + .096X_2 + .119X_3 + \ldots\ldots + .103X_{11}$ (Benefits)

subject to: $2000X_1 + 1622X_2 + 1515X_3 + \ldots\ldots + 5000X_{11} <= 15000$ (Cost)

where: $X_1, X_2, X_3, \ldots\ldots X_{11} >= 0$

    and $X_1, X_2, X_3, \ldots\ldots X_{11} <= 1$
    and $X_1, X_2, X_3, \ldots\ldots X_{11}$ are integer.

The following steps will setup and solve the problem with Expert Choice and Microsoft's Excel:

I-a) From Expert Choice's ratings module, select the first three columns: (Alternatives, Priorities, Costs).
Then do an Edit Copy.
I-b) Start Excel and do an Edit Paste to the Excel spreadsheet.
I-c) Add a column with the heading DV's for the decision variables. The decision variables will be adjusted by the algorithm to be either 0, if a project is not to be funded, or a 1 if the project is to be funded. Put the value of 1 in each element of this column (for illustrative purposes only).
I-d) Add another column with the heading F.Benefits (for funded benefits). Enter a formula in the row corresponding to the first alternative in this column that multiplies the decision variable cell by the priority cell

---

[11] Compared to the ambiguity of what maximizing the cumulative benefit/cost ratio really accomplishes , the objective of maximizing benefits is straightforward, understandable, and doesn't depend on questionable underlying assumptions.
[12] Problems involving hundreds of alternatives might require special purpose optimization programs.

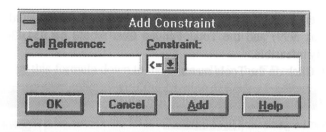

Figure 10 – Constraint Dialog Box

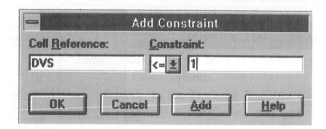

Figure 11 – Decision Variables <=1

Click the Add button and the Add Constraint dialog box (Figure 10) will appear:

1) Type DVS in the left box (Cell Reference); select <= in the middle box; and type 1 in the right box.
Then click Add to add another constraint.

2) Type DVS in the left box; select >= in the middle box; and type 0 in the right box (see Figure 11). Then click Add to add a third constraint.

3) Type DVS in the left box; select INT in the middle box; and then click Add to add a fourth constraint. (Note: Later versions of Solver have a 'Binary' option which can be used instead of steps 1-3 to specify that the decision variables must be integer values of 0 or 1).

4) With the left box active, click on the Total F.Costs in the Spreadsheet; select <= in the middle box; and type 15000 in the right box.[13]

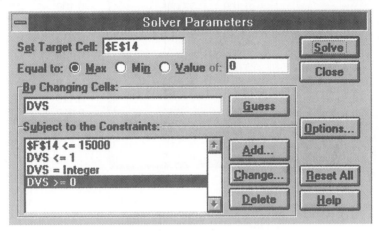

Figure 12 – Specified Parameters

Then press OK. The Parameters should look like Figure 12.

IV-a) Click on Options, select Assume Linear, then OK.

IV-b) Click on Solve. (If a message box appears stating the maximum iteration limit was reached, select Continue). When the Solve Results box appears, click the OK button.

The Spreadsheet should look like the Figure 13.

---

[13] Instead of entering $15000 as a constant, it can be entered into a cell which is referenced in right hand side of the constraint dialog box.

	A	B	C	D	E	F
1	Alternatives	PRIORITY	COSTS	DV's	F.Benefit	F.Cost
2						
3	Proposal One	0.109	2,000	1	0.109	2000
4	Proposal Two	0.096	1,622	1	0.096	1622
5	Proposal Three	0.119	1,515	1	0.119	1515
6	Proposal Four	0.122	1,280	1	0.122	1280
7	Proposal Five	0.014	7,500	0	0	0
8	Proposal Six	0.013	4,375	0	0	0
9	Proposal Seven	0.115	3,187	1	0.115	3187
10	Proposal Eight	0.092	565	1	0.092	565
11	Proposal Nine	0.103	4,000	0	0	0
12	Proposal Ten	0.113	3,300	1	0.113	3300
13	Proposal Eleven	0.103	5,086	0	0	0
14				Totals:	0.766	13469

Figure 13 – Solver Results

The results are exactly the same as those when we sorted by benefit/cost ratio (which you can easily do in this spreadsheet as well). Is this true in general? Usually, but not always. It will be true if, the available funding (in this case $15,000) is exactly equal to one of the values in the cumulative cost column of the sorted benefit/cost display. If this is not the case, the organization might be better off (realize a greater total benefit) by replacing one or more higher benefit/cost ratio projects with two or more lower benefit/cost ratio projects.

We can perform the above optimization for different values of available funding and plot the results. To do this, we first add a cell to the Excel spreadsheet representing the limit on available funding and modify the constraint to reference this cell instead of the $15000 as we did earlier. See Figure 14 and Figure 15.

If we first enter a very large limit for the funds available, we get the

Alternatives	PRIORITY	COSTS	DV's	F.Benefit	F.Cost	
Proposal One	0.109	2,000	1	0.109	2000	
Proposal Two	0.096	1,622	1	0.096	1622	
Proposal Three	0.119	1,515	1	0.119	1515	
Proposal Four	0.122	1,280	1	0.122	1280	
Proposal Five	0.014	7,500	0	0	0	
Proposal Six	0.013	4,375	0	0	0	
Proposal Seven	0.115	3,187	1	0.115	3187	
Proposal Eight	0.092	565	1	0.092	565	
Proposal Nine	0.103	4,000	0	0	0	
Proposal Ten	0.113	3,300	1	0.113	3300	
Proposal Eleven	0.103	5,086	0	0	0	
			Totals:	0.766	13469	15,000
						Available

Figure 14 – Cell With Funding Limit

solution shown in Figure 16 in which all proposals are funded for a total cost of $34,430. Next, changing the amount available to be 1 dollar less than 34,430, we get the solution shown in Figure 17 in which all but Proposal five is funded for a total cost of $26,930.

Figure 15 – Constraint for Funding Limit

Alternatives	PRIORITY	COSTS	DV's	F.Benefit	F.Cost	
Proposal One	0.109	2,000	1	0.109	2000	
Proposal Two	0.096	1,622	1	0.096	1622	
Proposal Three	0.119	1,515	1	0.119	1515	
Proposal Four	0.122	1,280	1	0.122	1280	
Proposal Five	0.014	7,500	1	0.014	7500	
Proposal Six	0.013	4,375	1	0.013	4375	
Proposal Seven	0.115	3,187	1	0.115	3187	
Proposal Eight	0.092	565	1	0.092	565	
Proposal Nine	0.103	4,000	1	0.103	4000	
Proposal Ten	0.113	3,300	1	0.113	3300	
Proposal Eleven	0.103	5,086	1	0.103	5086	
			Totals:	0.999	34430	99,999
						Available

Figure 16 – Solution for Very Large Limit

Alternatives	PRIORITY	COSTS	DV's	F.Benefit	F.Cost	
Proposal One	0.109	2,000	1	0.109	2000	
Proposal Two	0.096	1,622	1	0.096	1622	
Proposal Three	0.119	1,515	1	0.119	1515	
Proposal Four	0.122	1,280	1	0.122	1280	
Proposal Five	0.014	7,500	0	0	0	
Proposal Six	0.013	4,375	1	0.013	4375	
Proposal Seven	0.115	3,187	1	0.115	3187	
Proposal Eight	0.092	565	1	0.092	565	
Proposal Nine	0.103	4,000	1	0.103	4000	
Proposal Ten	0.113	3,300	1	0.113	3300	
Proposal Eleven	0.103	5,086	1	0.103	5086	
			Totals:	0.985	26930	34,429
						Available

Figure 17 – Solution for Limit of 34,429

If we continue to change the amount available to be one dollar less than the total cost of the previous solution, we will generate the series of points shown in Figure 18. Given a level of available funding, the best solution is that point at, or to the left of the available funding level.

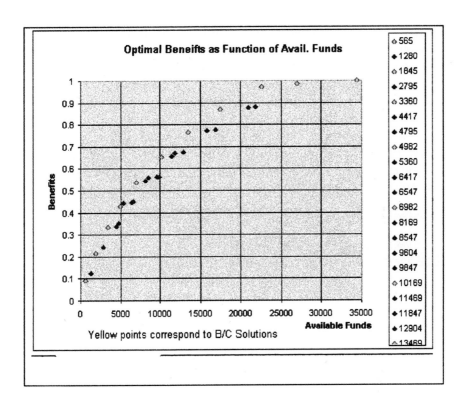

Figure 18 – Optimal Benefits vs. Available Funding

The yellow points in Figure 18 correspond to the points on the Benefit/Cost efficient frontier in Figure 7. The points in benefit optimization plot that do *not* correspond to any points in benefit/cost efficient frontier will be 'hidden' when making a resource allocation using benefit/cost. This may or may not be significant. Suppose, for example, $1300 of funding was available. The benefit maximization method yields a benefit of .122 at a cost of $1280, while the benefit/cost method yields a benefit of .092 at a cost of $565. Which solution is better, the solution produced by the method that maximizes the cumulative benefit/cost ratio or the solution produced by the method that maximizes total benefit? Is the 56% increase in costs justified by the 25% increase in benefits? If the amount expended doesn't matter[14], then any increase in total benefit is an improvement and the solution that maximizes total benefit is better. However, the benefit/cost ratio of the maximum benefit solution is smaller, and this may seem 'suboptimal' to those who have been taught to maximize the benefit/cost ratio. The danger of maximizing the benefit/cost ratio when benefit is more appropriate is well illustrated with the following example.

Consider a situation where you can invest in either of two business opportunities: (A) you can invest one dollar and get ten dollars back, and (B) you can invest 50 dollars and get 100 dollars back. However, you have only 50 dollars to invest. Both the benefit/cost solutions and the maximum

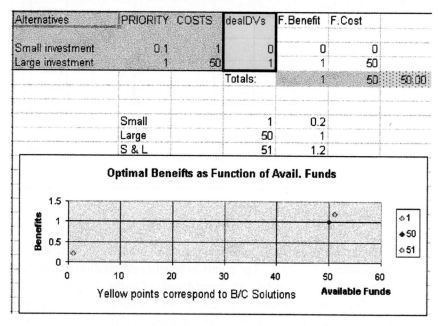

Alternatives	PRIORITY	COSTS	dealDVs	F.Benefit	F.Cost
Small investment	0.1	1	0	0	0
Large investment	1	50	1	1	50
			Totals:	1	50	50.00
	Small		1	0.2	
	Large		50	1	
	S & L		51	1.2	

Figure 19 – Optimization vs. Benefit/Cost

---

[14] As an aside, there are organizations that prefer to spend as much of their budget as possible to prevent having the budget decreased the following year.

benefit solutions as a function of the amount to invest are plotted in Figure 19. While all three solutions points are achieved following a maximum of benefits, only the two points shown in yellow are achieved following a maximization of benefit/cost. In particular, if 50 dollars is available for investing, the maximization of benefit solution is to invest $50 (recommending that $50 be invested for the $100 return), while the nearest point in yellow to the $50 for the maximization of benefit/cost is at $1 (suggesting that $1 be invested for a $10 return).

A variation of this situation is that there is no limit on available funding, but you must choose either (A) or (B), but not both. If you had to make (and possibly justify) the decision based on benefit/cost ratios, you would choose the first proposition, because a benefit/cost ratio of 10 is better than a benefit/cost ratio of two. However, the maximization of benefit solution (shown in Figure 20) is to choose the second proposition wherein you

	Alternatives	PRIORITY	COSTS	ChoiceDV	F.Benefit	F.Cost
1						
2						
3	Small investment	0.2	1	0	0	0
4	Large investment	1	50	1	1	50
5				Totals:	1	50
6						
7		Either small or large		1		

Figure 20 – Optimum is Large Investment

would walk away with a 50-dollar profit rather than a 9-dollar profit. Clearly, he benefit/cost ratio approach produces the wrong answer. In general, whenever unexpended funds from the resource allocation are not relevant, the benefit/cost ratio approach is not applicable.

Another example of the inappropriateness of maximizing the benefit/cost ratio is related to the knapsack problem designation given to this type of optimization. Suppose a camper is planning to take a knapsack of books on a trip. The knapsack can only hold a certain volume of books and each book has a different expected benefit15 to the camper. Which books should the camper take so as to maximize the total benefit? There will likely be some slack or unused volume in the knapsack., but slack is not one of the campers objectives. The camper 's objective is clearly to maximize the value of the books. The ratio of the total benefits of the selected books to the amount of volume used is really not of any significance. If, after tentatively selecting the books, the knapsack were replaced with one a bit larger, the camper might be able to remove a previously selected book and replace it with a larger book that has more value but a lower benefit/volume ratio. This would increase the campers overall objective, maximizing benefit. The increase in occupied volume from replacing the smaller book by the larger is of no consequence so long as the new volume constraint is not violated.

The problem can be made more complex by introducing other factors such as weight and /or cost. These factors can be considered as objectives and/or constraints. For example, suppose the camper had a budget of $X for books. This constraint can easily be added to the mathematical programming problem along with the volume constraint and an optimal solution (combination of books) can be found. This optimal will maximize the total value of the books without exceeding either the volume or cost constraints.

Would cost also be an objective in addition to a constraint? It depends on the situation. If the camper were deciding which books to take from his existing library, cost would *not* be an objective. If the camper were told he could spend up to but no more than $X to purchase books, then cost would *not* be an objective. If the camper were given $X from which he could purchase books, with any remaining funds retained by the camper, then cost *would be* an objective.

The assumptions necessary to formulate the resource allocation to fit a real world situation can best be identified by focusing on objectives. In particular, answering the question of whether cost is an objective as well as a constraint can best be answered by asking if cost, or the unexpended funds of the resource allocation, have significance to the decision makers. The

---

[15] The expected benefits can be derived with an AHP model.

following are three examples where cost (or unexpended funds) would not be considered as an objective:

Military campaign: In a military campaign, the objective is to get maximum military effectiveness; dollars not spent are virtually meaningless. Would military decision-makers be concerned with unexpended money if that would in any way decrease their effectiveness (even though the overall benefit/cost ratio is decreased)?

Small business competition: Suppose a small business in a competitive environment has extended its credit to limit. The managers feel they need to be as competitive as possible. Any increase in competitiveness is worth the extra cost, provided money is available. Having funds unexpended is really not part of the objective.

Government department's budget: money not spent can't be spent the next year[16].

Cost as a constraint and/or an objective:

When allocating resources, it is usually obvious when cost is a constraint – e.g., an organization is constrained to work within a given budget (although they can often try to justify increases to the budget). It is not so obvious, when allocating resources, if cost is also an objective.

What is cost anyway? A primitive society without money will engage in trade with barter. An advanced society has markets that, in equilibrium, equate cost with value. Two people trading hand made goods in a primitive society might take the following factors (or objectives) into account when contemplating a trade:
1. production time
2. value of component parts
3. tangible benefits
4. intangible benefits (e.g., artistic value)
5. value for future trades (e.g., have monetary value, such as art).

---

[16] An interesting twist to this situation: not only is any money not spent *not* carried over to next year, but the under-spending is likely to result in a *decrease* in next year's budget. Now cost again becomes an objective, but the objective is to spend as much as possible!

In a sense, the value (or cost) of something being traded is a synthesis of objectives. More advanced societies attempt to translate this value into dollars with monetary and market systems. But there may not be a market to place a value on a proposed new weapon system. Or, even if a market does exist, the market value may not represent the value to an individual or organization. Hence the need for organizations to be able to synthesize multiple objectives when allocating resources. It does not necessarily follow that the 'market value' or cost of an alternative is commensurate with the value of that alternative to an organization.

How to proceed if costs (or unexpended funds) are an objective as well as a constraint:

Cost can be included in the hierarchy so that the total benefit of each alternative includes the objective of low cost. (Judgments would be made comparing the relative importance of cost and the other factors, e.g., author's reputation, interest in the subject of the book, etc.; intensities defined and prioritized for the price objective, and ratings made for the cost of each book.) This is analogous to including cost along with other objectives such as style, comfort, and performance when choosing a car.

Don't include cost in the hierarchy (because sometimes people find it easier to make comparisons about benefits without having to consider cost17. Instead, optimize over a range of total budget constraint values, plotting the maximum benefit vs. cost for each of the solutions. Such a plot is called an "efficient frontier". The decision-maker examines this efficient frontier and decides which point is most desirable. This approach is preferred by those who feel that decision-makers sometimes find it easier to make judgments about objectives without considering costs.

Still another way to address cost as an objective is to add the percentage of unused budget as a variable in the objective function. The coefficient of this variable must either be estimated (which may be difficult to do) or treated as a parameter.

---

[17] Although when selecting a car, people don't seem to have any difficulty with low price as one of the objectives.

Flexibility of Benefits Optimization Approach:

The benefits optimization approach to resource allocation is extremely flexible. Constraints can be added to fit almost any managerial need. For example, The Air Force Cost Center added constraints to guarantee that each division received some minimum amount of funding. The Northeast Fisheries Center added constraints to regulate the rate of change in budget cutbacks so that members of the organization would not feel that the rug was about to be pulled out. They added a constraint for each division that guaranteed that the division total funding would be at least X% of the prior years funding, and solved the optimization of benefits for different values of X. The larger the value of X, the smaller the maximum will be. The smaller the value of X, the more flexibility there is to increase funding in areas that contribute more to the organization's objectives. Management then examined the plot of total benefit versus guarantee percent to determine what the percent should be and implemented the corresponding resource allocation. Resource allocation must be a dynamic, iterative process. By examining intermediate results, and modifying either or both of the AHP hierarchy or optimization formulation, an organization can express its unique musts and wants to find an allocation of resources that is rational and makes sense.

Constraints for dependencies

Two **mutually exclusive activities** i and j can be represented by a constraint such as:

$X_i + X_j <= 1$

This can easily be extended to three or more mutually exclusive activities:

$X_i + X_j + X_k + ... <= 1$

A constraint to specify that **one from a set** of activities must be selected can be modeled by including a mutually exclusive constraint as above, plus a constraint of the form:

$X_i + X_j + X_k + ... = 1$

Constraints representing Synergy

Saaty and Peniwati[18] have illustrated how constraints can be used to represent both positive and negative synergy. Consider the formulation presented above:

Maximize $.109X_1 + .096X_2 + .119X_3 + ... + .103X_{11}$ (Benefits)

subject to: $2000X_1 + 1622X_2 + 1515X_3 + ... + 5000X_{11} <= 15000$ (Cost)

where: $X_1, X_2, X_3, ... X_{11} >= 0$

  and $X_1, X_2, X_3, ... X_{11} <= 1$
  and $X_1, X_2, X_3, ... X_{11}$ are integer.

Suppose a group of activities (for example A_1 and A_2) taken together contribute more than the sum of the activities taken separately. Define the combined activity A_{12} to be A_1 and A_2 together. Suppose this activity were added to the Expert Choice model and the derived priority is **.250**. This would represent a positive synergy since individually activities A_1 and A_2 contribute $.109 + .096 = .205$. A negative synergy, perhaps due to overlap of contribution, would be indicated by a priority for A_{12} of less than .205. The optimization can be formulated by adding a decision variable, call it $Z_{1,2}$, where a resulting value of $Z_{1,2} = 1$ means that the combination of A_1 and A_2 is to be included. However we must add additional constraints to assure what Saaty refers to exclusion and duplication.

Exclusion means that if an activity is performed exclusively (alone), no other combination containing the activity can be performed. Thus, for each activity that is a member of a combination, the decision variable corresponding to the activity performed alone plus all other decision variables representing the combinations does not exceed 1.

Duplication assures that for each combination, there is no other combination of variables that duplicates the combination.

---

[18] Saaty, T.L. and Peniwati, K. "The Analytic Hierarchy Process and Linear Programming in Human Resource Allocation", *Proceedings of the Fourth International AHP Symposium*, Vancouver, 1996.

Thus, for the previous example, we would have:

Maximize $.109X_1 + .096X_2 + .119X_3 + \ldots\ldots + .103X_{11} + \mathbf{.250\ Z_{1,2}}$ (Benefits)

subject to:

$2000X_1 + 1622X_2 + 1515X_3 + \ldots\ldots + 5000X_{11} + \mathbf{3622\ Z_{1,2}} <= 15000$ (Cost)

and constraints for exclusivity:

    $\mathbf{X_1 + Z_{1,2} <=1}$ **for activity 1 with combination $Z_{1,2}$**
    $\mathbf{X_2 + Z_{1,2} <= 1}$ **for activity 2 with combination $Z_{1,2}$**

and a constraint to prevent duplication:

    $\mathbf{X_1 + X_2 <= 1}$

to prevent duplication of combination $Z_{1,2}$.

where: the decision variables are non negative integers:

    $X_1, X_2, X_3, \ldots\ldots Z_{1,2} >=0$

    $X_1, X_2, X_3, \ldots\ldots Z_{1,2} <=1$
    $X_1, X_2, X_3, \ldots\ldots Z_{1,2}$ are integer.

Another, perhaps simpler representation of constraints representing Synergy

Identify each set of activities with synergistic effect (either positive or negative). For each set, define up to $2^n -1$ decision variables representing all meaningful combinations of the activities. The cost and benefit of each possible combination represent the synergistic cost and benefit respectively. Only one constraint must be added for each set of synergistic activities – the sum of the 2^n variables must $= 1$. This approach results in more decision variables but fewer constraints. To apply this technique to the example above, lets represent the combinations of activity 1 and activity 2 by the four decision variables $Z_{0,0}$, $Z_{0,1}$, $Z_{1,0}$, and $Z_{1,1}$, where the first subscript refers to activity 1, the second subscript refers to activity 2, and a 0 for the subscript means that the activity is not included while a 1 means that it is included. So, for example, if $Z_{1,1}$ is 1, then both activity 1 and activity 2 are to be undertaken. The formulation using these variables would be:

Maximize $.109Z_{1,0} + .096Z_{0,1} + \mathbf{.250\ Z_{1,1}} + .119X_3 + \ldots + .103X_{11}$
(Benefits)
subject to:
$2000\ Z_{1,0} + 1622\ Z_{0,1} + \mathbf{3622\ Z_{1,1}} + 1515X_3 + \ldots + 5000X_{11} <= 15000$
(Cost)
and the additional constraint:

$\mathbf{Z_{0,1} + Z_{1,0} + Z_{1,1} <=1}$
where the decision variables are non-negative integers:
$Z_{0,1}, Z_{1,0}, Z_{1,1}, X_3, \ldots X_{11} >=0$
$Z_{0,1}, Z_{1,0}, Z_{1,1}, X_3, \ldots X_{11} <=1$
$Z_{0,1}, Z_{1,0}, Z_{1,1}, X_3, \ldots X_{11}$ are integer.

A more elaborate example

Suppose, as a more elaborate example, an additional synergistic combination of $\mathbf{A_2}$ and $\mathbf{A_3}$ produces a combination represented by decision variable $Z_{2,3}$, with a benefit of **.275**. Furthermore, an additional synergistic combination of $\mathbf{A_1}$, $\mathbf{A_2}$ and $\mathbf{A_3}$ produces a combination represented by decision variable $Z_{1,2,3}$ with a benefit of **.400**.

Maximize $.109X_1 + .096X_2 + .119X_3 + \ldots\ldots + .103X_{11} + \mathbf{.250\ X_{12} + .275\ Z_{1,3} + .400}$
$\mathbf{Z_{1,2,3}}$ (Benefits)

subject to:

$2000X_1 + 1622X_2 + 1515X_3 + \ldots\ldots + 5000X_{11} + \mathbf{3622\ X_{12} + 3137\ Z_{1,3} + 5137}$
$\mathbf{Z_{1,2,3}} <= 15000$ (Cost)

and constraints for exclusivity:

$\quad\quad\quad X_1 + Z_{1,3} <= 1$ **for activity 1 with combination X_{12}**
$\quad\quad\quad X_1 + Z_{1,2,3} <= 1$ **for activity 1 with combination X_{14}**
$\quad\quad\quad X_2 + Z_{1,3} <= 1$ **for activity 2 with combination X_{13}**
$\quad\quad\quad X_2 + Z_{1,2,3} <= 1$ **for activity 2 with combination X_{14}**
   and a constraints to prevent duplication:
$\quad\quad\quad X_1 + X_2 <= 1$ **to prevent duplication of combination X_{12}.**
$\quad\quad\quad X_2 + X_3 <= 1$ **to prevent duplication of combination X_{13}.**
$\quad\quad\quad X_1 + X_2 + X_3 <= 1$ **to prevent duplication of combination X_{14}.**
$\quad\quad\quad X_{12} + X_3 <= 1$ **to prevent duplication of combination X_{14}.**
$\quad\quad\quad Z_{1,3} + X_1 <= 1$ **to prevent duplication of combination X_{14}.**

where the decision variables are non-negative integers:
$X_1, X_2, X_3, \ldots\ldots, Z_{1,3}, Z_{1,2,3} >= 0$
$X_1, X_2, X_3, \ldots\ldots, Z_{1,3}, Z_{1,2,3} <= 1$
$X_1, X_2, X_3, \ldots\ldots Z_{1,3}, Z_{1,2,3}$ are integer.

The alternative formulation for this more elaborate example would be:
Define $2^3 - 1$ or seven decision variables representing the combinations of activities 1, 2 and 3, where $Z_{1,0,0}$ represents doing activity 1 but not two or three, $Z_{0,1,0}$ represents doing activity 2 but not 1 or 3, $Z_{1,1,0}$ represents doing activities 1 and 2, but not 3, and so on. The formulation would be:

Maximize $.109Z_{1,0,0} + .096Z_{0,1,0} + .119Z_{0,0,1} + \mathbf{.250\ Z_{1,1,0} + .275\ Z_{1,0,1} + .400\ Z_{1,1,1}}\ldots\ldots + .103X_{11}$
subject to:

$$2000\ Z_{1,0,0} + 1622\ Z_{0,1,0} + 1515\ Z_{0,0,1} + \mathbf{3622\ Z_{1,1,0}} + \mathbf{3137\ Z_{1,0,1}} + \mathbf{5137\ Z_{1,1,1}} \ \dots\ + 5000X_{11} <= 15000 \quad \text{(Cost)}$$

$$Z_{1,0,0} + Z_{0,1,0} + Z_{0,0,1} + Z_{1,1,0} + Z_{1,0,1} + Z_{0,1,1} + Z_{1,1,1} <= 1.$$

where the decision variables are non-negative integers:

$Z_{1,0,0}, Z_{0,1,0}, \dots Z_{1,1,1}, X_4, \dots X_{11} >= 0$

$Z_{1,0,0}, Z_{0,1,0}, \dots Z_{1,1,1}, X_4, \dots X_{11} <= 1$

$Z_{1,0,0}, Z_{0,1,0}, \dots Z_{1,1,1}, X_4, \dots X_{11}$ are integer.

An example with two sets of synergistic activities.

Suppose activities $A_1, \dots A_{100}$ were being considered. Further suppose there are two sets of synergistic activities, the first set including activities A_1, A_2, A_3, and A_4 and a second set including activities A_8, A_9, and A_{10}.

For the first set, suppose the following combinations of A_1 through A_4 are possible: each activity by itself, or the following synergistic combinations (either positive or negative synergy):

A_1 with A_2

A_2 with A_3 with A_4

For this first set, define a subset of 2^4 - 1 or 15 variables:

$Z_{1,0,0,0}$,	which,	if	set	to	1,	signifies	A_1,	but	not	A_2,	A_3,	or	A_4
$Z_{0,1,0,0}$,	which,	if	set	to	1,	signifies	A_2,	but	not	A_1,	A_3,	or	A_4
$Z_{0,0,1,0}$,	which,	if	set	to	1,	signifies	A_3,	but	not	A_1,	A_2,	or	A_4
$Z_{0,0,0,1}$,	which,	if	set	to	1,	signifies	A_4,	but	not	A_1,	A_2,	or	A_3

$Z_{1,1,0,0}$, which, if set to 1, signifies A_1 and A_2 but not A_3, or A_4

$Z_{0,1,1,1}$, which, if set to 1, signifies A_2, A_3, A_4, but not A_1

- These variables are included in the objective function and functional constraints with the appropriate benefit and cost coefficients. Additionally, a constraint:

$Z_{1,0,0,0} + Z_{0,1,0,0} + Z_{0,0,1,0} + Z_{0,0,0,1} + Z_{1,1,0,0} + Z_{0,1,1,1} <= 1$ insures that only one of the combinations will be selected.

For the second set, suppose the following combinations of A_8 through A_{10} are possible: each activity by itself, or the following synergistic combinations (either positive or negative synergy):

A_8 with A_9 with A_{10}

A_9 with A_{10}.

For this first set, define a subset of 2^3 - 1 or 7 variables:

$W_{1,0,0}$,	which,	if	set	to	1,	signifies	A_8,	but	not	A_9,	or	A_{10}
$W_{0,1,0}$,	which,	if	set	to	1,	signifies	A_9,	but	not	A_8,	or	A_{10}
$W_{0,0,1}$,	which,	if	set	to	1,	signifies	A_{10},	but	not	A_8,	or	A_9
$W_{1,1,1}$,	which,	if	set	to	1,	signifies	A_8,	with	A_9	and	A_{10}

$W_{0,1,1}$, which, if set to 1, signifies A_9 with A_{10} but not A_8.

These variables are also included in the objective function and functional constraints with the appropriate benefit and cost coefficients. Additionally, a constraint:

$W_{1,0,0} + W_{0,1,0} + W_{0,0,1} + W_{1,1,1} + W_{0,1,1}$ <=1 insures that only one of the combinations will be selected.

Constraints for different types of 'costs'

Additional constraints can easily be added for other 'costs'. For example there may be one constraint for dollar costs, another for personnel, and still another for space. Each such constraint can also be specified for multiple time periods.

Orders of Magnitude Considerations

Care must be taken when allocating resources to alternatives that differ in cost by several orders of magnitude. If for example, the cost for some alternatives are in the 1-10 thousand dollar range while the cost for others are in the hundreds of millions of dollars, then the benefit measure must be capable of spanning a commensurate range ratio. This would not be the case with a narrow hierarchy (one that doesn't encompass a wide range of objectives) or intensities that do not span ranges that can adequately reflect the difference in contribution of very inexpensive alternatives and very expensive alternatives. One approach, then, is to construct an evaluation hierarchy that is both broad -- so that expensive alternatives can be recognized for their contributions over a broad range of sub-objectives while inexpensive alternatives will be recognized only for the more narrow areas to which they contribute. The evaluation hierarchy should also contain numerous rating intensities so as to span as wide a range of measure as possible, perhaps even two orders of magnitude.

It may be difficult or impractical to do this in some circumstances, so another approach, and one that is similar to the traditional way organizations allocate funds hierarchically, is to divide the alternatives into categories from low cost to high cost and allocate separately within each category. For example, if projects are being considered that range in cost from 5 thousand to 8 million dollars, the projects can be organized into categories 1-10K, 10K-100K, 100K-1M and 1M-8M. The question then arises as to how much of the total budget is to be allocated to each category. This can be addressed various ways. One would be with a hierarchy to derive priorities for each category's contribution to the organizations objectives. The total funding can then be multiplied by the resultant priorities to determine how much will be allocated within each category. Another way would be to allocate funding to each category based on the ratio of the total cost of the projects in each category to the total costs of all projects, and multiply the funding amount in each category by the ratio of the total funding available to the total cost of all projects.

Summary of B/C Ratios vs. Optimization of Benefits:

B/C Ratios:
Cost is an objective because it goes into B/C ratio.
If cost (or unexpended funds) is not an objective, then B/C ratio should not be used.
     examples: Military, Competitive business; government agency
Pros: Easy to Solve.
Cons: Can lead to wrong answers if applied blindly (assumptions difficult to verify).

Can only deal with one constraint.

Optimization of Benefits:

Cost may not be an objective, or
Cost is an objective. If so, can do one of the following:
1. include cost as an objective in the hierarchy, or
2. consider cost as a constraint and optimize benefits over a range of total cost constraint values, plotting the maximum benefit vs. cost for each of the solutions. Such a plot is called an "efficient frontier". The decision maker examines this efficient frontier and decides which point is most desirable; or
1. add percentage of unused budget as variable in optimization the objective function.

Pros: Easy to verify assumptions
        Can include many types of constraints
        Very flexible
Cons: Computationally difficult
        May have to explain why replacing a higher b/c alternative with a more costly but lower b/c alternative as budget is increased, is in the best interests of the organization.

Comparison of results from maximizing b/c ratio and maximizing benefits:

* Results are often quite close
* Identical results if budget limit corresponds to a cumulative cost break value
* Drastically different results are possible, especially in situations where cost, or unexpected funds are not important.

Activity Level Resource Allocation

Whereas in discrete alternative resource allocation, each alternative (e.g., research proposal) is discrete from (although possibly related to) the other alternatives, activity level resource allocation considers one or more *levels* of funding for each alternative (e.g., department). For example, each department in an organization can be considered for funding at current funding levels, +/- 5%, +/- 10%, etc. A plan is developed specifying the type and extent of activities each department would perform at each level of funding. An AHP model is used to evaluate the expected contribution to the organization's objectives for each alternative level of funding. A prototype of an activity level resource allocation problem will be used to illustrate a heuristic incremental benefit/cost approach as well as a maximization of total benefit approach.

Consider an organization with four departments, Marketing, Production, Operations, and Maintenance. Each department submits plans for how they would operate with a bare minimum number of people, with the current number of people, and with a moderate increase from current funding level. The organization has six major missions, which we will refer to as Mission A through Mission F. To keep the example simple, we will assume that the objectives within each mission include responding to day to day needs and activities, total quality efforts, and long term development. An Expert Choice model with mission priorities derived from pairwise comparisons is shown in Figure 21.

Intensities were defined for rating how much each alternative level of funding for each department would contribute to each of the objectives within each mission. A portion of the RATINGS model is shown in Figure 22. Notice that each 'line item' is a level of funding within a department. Departments are identified by a common alphanumeric prefix before the delimiter, in this case a colon. The costs are shown in thousands of dollars. The Total column represents the un-normalized total expected contribution of that line item (department at a specified level of funding) toward the organization's overall objectives. Objectives for which no contribution is expected at a specified level of funding are left blank.

Personnel Allocation

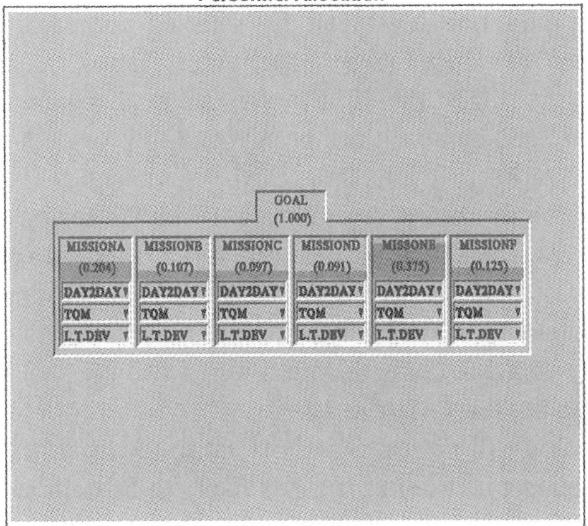

GOAL
(1.000)

MISSIONA	MISSIONB	MISSIONC	MISSIOND	MISSONE	MISSIONF
(0.204)	(0.107)	(0.097)	(0.091)	(0.375)	(0.125)
DAY2DAY	DAY2DAY	DAY2DAY	DAY2DAY	DAY2DAY	DAY2DAY
TQM	TQM	TQM	TQM	TQM	TQM
L.T.DEV	L.T.DEV	L.T.DEV	L.T.DEV	L.T.DEV	L.T.DEV

Abbreviation	Definition
DAY2DAY	Responding to day to day needs and activities
L.T.DEV	Long term development
MISSIONA	
MISSIONB	
MISSIONC	
MISSIOND	
MISSIONF	
MISSONE	
TQM	Total quality efforts

(Priorities shown are 'Local' — relative to parent node.)

Figure 21 – Organizational Objectives

MISSIONA | DAY2DAY

EXTREME	SIGNIFIC	LARGE	MODERATE	TAD
1 (1.000)	2 (.483)	3 (.276)	4 (.162)	5 (.028)

	Alternatives	TOTAL	COSTS	MISSIONA-DAY2DAY	TQM	L.T.DEV	MISSIONB-DAY2DAY	TQM	L.T.DEV	MISSIONC-DAY2DAY	TQM
				.0680	.0680	.0680	.0350	.0350	.0350	.0324	.0324
1	Marketing: 1 Person	0.055	80	MODERATE			MODERATE			LARGE	
2	Marketing: 2 People	0.342	160	LARGE	LARGE	MODERATE	LARGE	LARGE	LARGE	LARGE	SIGNIFIC
3	Production: 2 People	0.062	140	MODERATE			MODERATE			TAD	
4	Production: 3 People	0.260	210	LARGE	LARGE	MODERATE	MODERATE	LARGE	SIGNIFIC	MODERATE	LARGE
5	Production: 4 People	0.406	280	LARGE	LARGE	LARGE	LARGE	SIGNIFIC	MODERATE	LARGE	LARGE
6	Operations: 3 People	0.050	225	SIGNIFIC			LARGE			MODERATE	
7	Operations: 4 People	0.290	300	EXTREME	MODERATE	LARGE	SIGNIFIC	SIGNIFIC	MODERATE	LARGE	LARGE
8	Operations: 5 People	0.400	350	EXTREME	LARGE	SIGNIFIC	EXTREME	SIGNIFIC	LARGE	LARGE	LARGE
9	Operations: 6 People	0.547	400	EXTREME	LARGE	SIGNIFIC	EXTREME	SIGNIFIC	SIGNIFIC	SIGNIFIC	SIGNIFIC
10	Maintenance: 3 People	0.063	90	LARGE			LARGE			MODERATE	
11	Maintenance: 4 People	0.305	120	SIGNIFIC	MODERATE	SIGNIFIC	LARGE	LARGE	MODERATE	LARGE	LARGE
12	Maintenance: 5 People	0.416	150	EXTREME	LARGE	LARGE	LARGE	SIGNIFIC	SIGNIFIC	LARGE	LARGE
13	Maintenance: 6 People	0.766	180	EXTREME	EXTREME	EXTREME	SIGNIFIC	SIGNIFIC	SIGNIFIC	SIGNIFIC	SIGNIFIC
14											

Figure 22 – Activity Level Ratings

Benefit/Cost Ratios

Because only one level can be selected for each department, the maximization of cumulative benefit/cost ratios is not nearly as straightforward as for the discrete resource allocation situation. The following heuristic approach has been found to provide a reasonably good allocation. We begin by funding each department at its lowest level of funding, thereby producing a combination with the lowest total benefit and lowest total cost. We look for the best choice of department to increase to its next level of funding. We make the choice by choosing the department with the highest incremental benefit/cost ratio from its present level of funding. We continue doing this until we exceed the total budget, and then go back to the last level of increase.

This method will not necessarily result in the maximum benefit subject to the total budget constraint, but it is likely to be quite close. One of the practical difficulties in implementing the method occurs when a department's contribution fails to follow a diminishing marginal rate of return curve. Theoretically, the law of diminishing returns states that the incremental benefit from an increase in one unit of cost should be a non-increasing function. If this assumption is violated, then a relatively low incremental benefit/cost ratio at some level of funding can 'hide' a higher incremental benefit/cost ratio from being seen by the algorithm. To avoid this difficulty, a recursive procedure is used to remove the lower incremental benefit/cost level(s) from consideration.

The initial lowest cost allocation consists of the lowest levels for each department as shown in Figure 23, Figure 24, and Figure 25.

The values in the Benefit column in Figure 23 are normalized equivalents of the total values in Figure 22 – normalized so that, if each department were funded at the maximum level, the total would be 100. The >>> symbol in Figure 25 suggests that if additional funds beyond the $535K are to be allocated, then the Maintenance department should be increased to a higher level of funding.

	Activity	B	C
1	Marketing: 1 Person	2.648	80.000
2	Marketing: 2 People	16.595	160.000
3	Production: 2 People	3.014	140.000
4	Production: 3 People	12.602	210.000
5	Production: 4 People	19.712	280.000
6	Operations: 3 People	2.832	225.000
7	Operations: 4 People	14.050	300.000
8	Operations: 5 People	19.781	350.000
9	Operations: 6 People	26.551	400.000
10	Maintenance: 3 People	3.079	90.000
11	Maintenance:4 People	14.773	120.000
12	Maintenance: 5 People	20.172	150.000
13	Maintenance: 6 People	37.142	180.000

Figure 23 – Each Activity At Lowest Level

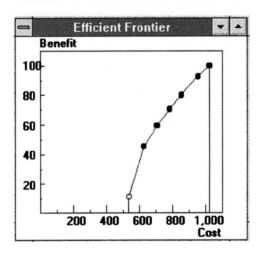

Figure 24 – Efficient Frontier

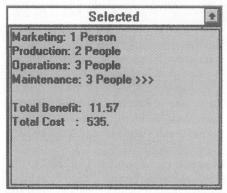

Figure 25–More Maintenance If More Funding

Suppose we didn't know this, but asked the Department managers to meet and decide. Suppose they decided to increase the Operations Department to four people. The results would be as shown in Figure 26 and Figure 27. The total benefit has increased from 11.57 to 22.79[19] and the total cost has increased from $535K to $610K.

	Activity	B	C
1	Marketing: 1 Person	2.648	80.000
2	Marketing: 2 People	16.595	160.000
3	Production: 2 People	3.014	140.000
4	Production: 3 People	12.602	210.000
5	Production: 4 People	19.712	280.000
6	Operations: 3 People	2.832	225.000
7	Operations: 4 People	14.050	300.000
8	Operations: 5 People	19.781	350.000
9	Operations: 6 People	26.551	400.000
10	Maintenance: 3 People	3.079	90.000
11	Maintenance:4 People	14.773	120.000

Figure 26 – Seat of the Pants Decision

---

[19] Since the benefit scale is a ratio level of measure, we can say that this is about a 100% increase in total benefit.

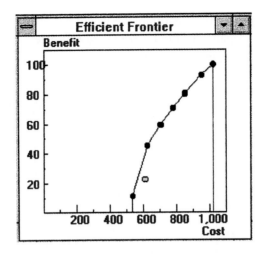

Figure 27 – Below the Efficient Frontier

	Activity	B	C	
1	Marketing: 1 Person	2.648	80.000	
2	Marketing: 2 People	16.595	160.000	
3	Production: 2 People	3.014	140.000	
4	Production: 3 People	12.602	210.000	
5	Production: 4 People	19.712	280.000	
6	Operations: 3 People	2.832	225.000	
7	Operations: 4 People	14.050	300.000	
8	Operations: 5 People	19.781	350.000	
9	Operations: 6 People	26.551	400.000	
10	Maintenance: 3 People	3.079	90.000	
11	Maintenance: 4 People	14.773	120.000	
12	Maintenance: 5 People	20.172	150.000	
13	Maintenance: 6 People	37.142	180.000	

Figure 28 – Incremental Benefit Cost Allocation

But if we followed the algorithm, we would have increased funding in the Maintenance Department from 3 people to 6 people[20]. The results are shown in Figure 28, Figure 29, and Figure 30.

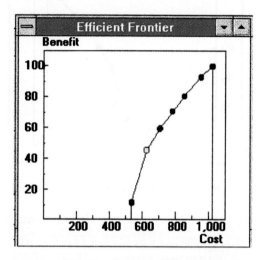

Figure 29 – Back on the Efficient Frontier

Thus, increasing funding in the Maintenance Department from 3 people to 6 people, rather than increasing the funding in the Marketing Department from 1 person to 2 people, would result in almost double the benefit (45.64 vs. 22.79) for only a slightly extra cost ($625K vs. $610K). The >>> symbols in Figure 30 indicate that the next increase should be in the Marketing Department. Following the algorithm would result in the points shown on the efficient frontier plot in Figure 29.

---

[20] Staffing levels of 4 and 5 were skipped because the incremental benefit/cost for this department did not follow the law of diminishing returns.

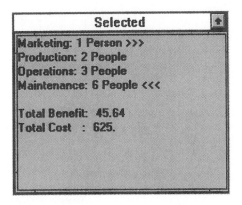

Figure 30 – Change Indicators

Maximizing Benefits -- Optimization

The problem formulation for the maximization of benefit approach that we used for the discrete alternative resource allocation extends easily to the activity level resource allocation case. We want to find that combination of activity levels that maximizes the total benefits without exceeding the given budget.[21] This problem, is formulated as a zero-one integer mathematical programming problem, sometimes referred to as a multiple choice knapsack problem. The formulation for the prototype activity level resource allocation presented above (refer to Figure 22 and Figure 23) is as follows:

Maximize $2.648X_{1,1} + 16.595X_{1,2} + 3.014X_{2,1} + 12.602X_{2,2} + 19.712X_{2,3} +$

$$+..... + 3.079X_{4,1} + 14.773X_{4,2} + 20.172X_{4,3} + 37.142X_{4,4}$$
(Benefits)[22]

subject to: $80X_{1,1} + 160X_{1,2} + 140X_{2,1} + 210X_{2,2} + 280X_{2,3} +$

---

[21] Here, as in the discrete alternative resource allocation case, maximizing the cumulative benefit/cost ratio really is more straightforward and understandable than the incremental benefit/cost approach. Furthermore, it doesn't depend on questionable underlying assumptions. However, the computation complexity, even with high speed computers, is sometimes a concern.

[22] The coefficients of the objective function correspond to the normalized benefit column of Figure 23 (normalized so that the total benefit is 100 if each department were funded at the maximum level). Alternatively, the un-normalized values in the total column of Figure 22 could have been used.

Decision By Objectives

	A	B	C	D	E	F	G
1	Alt/Levels	PRIORITY	COSTS	LDV's	F. Benefit	F.Cost	
2							
3	Marketing: 1 Person	2.648	80	0	0.00	0.00	
4	Marketing: 2 People	16.595	160	1	16.60	160.00	
5	Production: 2 People	3.014	140	1	3.01	140.00	
6	Production: 3 People	12.602	210	0	0.00	0.00	
7	Production: 4 People	19.712	280	0	0.00	0.00	
8	Operations: 3 People	2.832	225	0	0.00	0.00	
9	Operations: 4 People	14.05	300	1	14.05	300.00	
10	Operations: 5 People	19.781	350	0	0.00	0.00	
11	Operations: 6 People	26.551	400	0	0.00	0.00	
12	Maintenance: 3 People	3.079	90	0	0.00	0.00	
13	Maintenance:4 People	14.773	120	0	0.00	0.00	
14	Maintenance: 5 People	20.172	150	0	0.00	0.00	
15	Maintenance: 6 People	37.142	180	1	37.14	180.00	
16				Totals:	70.80	780.00	800.00
17							Available
18	Constraints to assure one and only one level for each Alternative:						
19	Marketing	1					
20	Production	1					
21	Operations	1					
22	Maintenance	1					

Figure 31–Activity Level Optimization

$$+..... + 90X_{4,1} + 120X_{4,2} + 150X_{4,3} + 180X_{4,4} \qquad <= \text{Budget} \qquad \text{(Costs)}$$

where: $X_{1,1}, X_{1,2}, X_{2,1}, ... X_{4,4} \quad >=0$

$$X_{1,1} + X_{1,2} \qquad = 1$$

$$X_{2,1} + X_{2,2} + X_{2,3} \qquad = 1$$

$$X_{3,1} + X_{3,2} + X_{3,3} + X_{3,4} = 1$$

$$X_{4,1} + X_{4,2} + X_{4,3} + X_{4,4} = 1$$

and $X_{1,1}, X_{1,2}, X_{2,1}, ... X_{4,4} \; <=1$
and $X_{1,1}, X_{1,2}, X_{2,1}, ... X_{4,4}$ are integer.

contains an Excel spreadsheet in which the optimization is performed. The values correspond to the optimal solution for an available budget of $800K. Columns A, B, and C were copied and pasted from the Expert Choice Ratings sheet. The level decision variables (designated as LDV's) are contained in Column D. Column E contains formulas for Funded Benefits. For example, the formula in cell E3 is =D3*B3. Column F contains formulas for Funded Costs. For example, the formula in cell F3 is =D3*C3. Cell G16 contains the available funding, presently set at $800K. Cells B19 through B22 each contain the sum of the decision variables for the respective activity. For example, cell B19 contains the formula: =SUM(D3:D4).

The solver parameters are shown in Figure 32. The target cell, E16, is the sum of the funded benefits. The By Changing Cells are the level decision variables. The five constraints are as follows:

1. B19:B22 = 1 insures that one and only one level will be funded for each alternative.

2. F16<=G16 constrains total spending.

3. The level decision variables are less than or equal to 1.

4. The level decision variables are integer.

5. The level decision variables are non-negative.

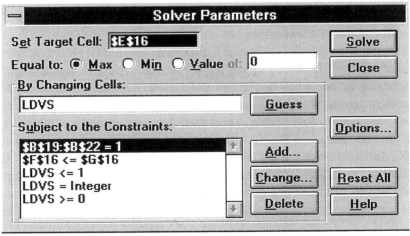

Figure 32 – Optimization Parameters

The AHP process is used to derive priorities for the organization's objectives as well as the alternatives that compete for resources. Once priorities are derived, either a benefit/cost or maximization of benefit approach can be used. The former offers some computational benefits whereas the latter is more robust and flexible. We have presented methodologies for discrete alternative resource allocation as well as for activity level resource allocation. The former is particularly useful when considering new activities, such as proposals for research and development. The latter can easily be applied in any organization that does periodic resource allocation. It is particularly useful as an alternative to 'across the board cuts' when an organization is faced with budget cutbacks[23] since 'across the board cuts' will eventually lead to the demise of an organization that faces competition in a changing environment. Instead, this rational

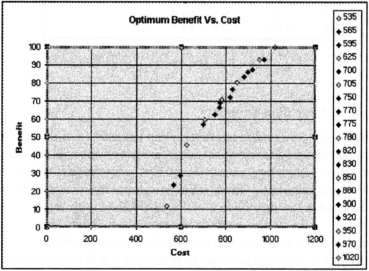

Figure 34 – Optimum Benefit Vs. Cost

---

[23] Although resource allocations during stable or increasing budgets do not concern management as much as cutbacks, the need to gain and maintain a competitive advantage should make this activity just as important as when budgets are being reduced.

resource allocation methodology will help identify those departments that should receive increased funding even when the overall budget is being decreased. The methodologies are extremely flexible and can be implemented piecemeal -- yielding incremental improvements over the organization's current resource allocation "methodology". Improvement may come just from prioritizing the organization's objectives, and / or from evaluating the expected contributions at different levels of funding for each department.

Implementation of the complete methodology, including the combinatorial optimization problem will require iteration so that the intermediate 'solutions' can be questioned, challenged, and modified by:

•changing the AHP model and / or

•changing judgments and / or

•adding or modifying constraints in the optimization.

The 'final' solution should not only be mathematically 'optimal', but intuitively appealing to those who will have to live and compete with the resulting levels of funding.

Chapter 9

Meetings, Meeting Facilitation and Group Support Systems (GSS)

Groups and meetings

Many organizations focus on individual job descriptions and individual incentives even though a majority of an individual's time is spent in group activities. Much of an organization's productivity is the result of group work. Groups, and meetings in particular, can, if conducted properly, be a positive force as opposed to being viewed as a necessary nuisance. Ask people at meeting –"how many of you enjoy going to meetings?" – and you will achieve greater consensus than perhaps for any other question or issue at the meeting.

Researchers have already studied groups extensively, as evidenced by the list of variables and characteristics of contained in Table 1.

Table 1 – Characteristics identified by researchers[1]

Member characteristics	Group characteristics	Organizational & environmental context characteristics
values	work group norms	organizational environment in which the group operates
personality	socio-political structure	setting in which the group operates
gender	degree of individual dominance	group's task circumstances

---

[1] Unisys Corporation, *Group Support Technologies*, A study prepared for Organizational Planning and Development Division, Office Of Human Resource Development, Federal Aviation Administration, Cambridge, MA, January 1990, p. 30-32.

Member characteristics	*Group characteristics*	*Organizational & environmental context characteristics*
skills	group cohesiveness (including degree of cooperation vs. Competition)	spatial arrangement of the group to other elements of the environment
knowledge	density of the group (composite of group size, room size and interpersonal distances)	degree of technological support for performing its functions
experience	size of the group (small, medium, large)	degree of information support provided
age	whether the group is formally or informally defined	reward systems for the group
race	whether the group meets face-to-face or not	reward systems for the individuals
status	previous history of the group length of time the group has existed stability of the group experience with task type outcomes of previous decisions	networks to which its members belong (social, political, information-exchange, decision-making, expertise, persuasion)
socioeconomic background	purpose for which the group was formed	whether communication is synchronous or non-synchronous
competence	stage of task/purpose development	outcomes
social needs	proximity of its members	
self - esteem	group's political orientation	
motivation	type and degree of leadership	

Member characteristics	Group characteristics	Organizational & environmental context characteristics
ability to work in groups	group's task characteristics complexity degree of structure degree of definition formal vs. Informal planned vs. Unplanned	
attitudes about working in the group	kinds of tasks the group engages in planning creativity and idea generation idea structuring preference mixed motive consensus building communication	
attitudes about other group members	structure of the group process order of sub-tasks timing	
	depth and quality of task processing number of alternatives generated and considered criteria used for evaluation of alternatives	
	scheduling of group activities	
	length of group sessions	
	goals of the group	
	degree of group synergy	

Member characteristics	Group characteristics	Organizational & environmental context characteristics
	group's productivity	
	degree of type and group member participation	
	type and degree of facilitation	
	degree of anonymity	
	spatial arrangement of the group to each other	
	degree of consensus	
	time to make decisions	
	communication characteristics degree of clarification degree of information exchange non-verbal communication degree of task-oriented communication degree of socially-oriented communication	

However, many organizations have ignored paying attention to groups. Forces and trends that should convince an organization to pay more attention to groups are contained in Table 2.

Group work and meetings often involve creativity, decision-making or problem-solving. Decision-making and problem solving often begin with a creative exploration of the problem domain. The missing element in creativity that is present in decision-making is the one of Choice. The missing elements in problem solving are implementation and review.

Table 2 – Why pay more attention to groups?[2]

> • Estimates of the cost of coordination run as high as 30 - 40% of the United States Gross National Product.
>
> • Studies of management work have demonstrated its group nature – as much as 80% of managerial time is spent in meetings
>
> • The fast pace of industry consolidations has resulted in changes in the size, scope and structure of organizations, resulting in a need to combine functions and support the communication of dispersed groups.
>
> • Globalization of the marketplace, due in part to the greater effectiveness and lowered cost of communication technologies, has increased the need for smoother functioning of dispersed groups that require both synchronous and asynchronous communication.
>
> • The intensification of strategic thinking and integration of functions as necessary conditions for survival has created the need for tighter inter and intra-organizational links.
>
> • The importance of product quality as a driver of market success and strategic advantage has resulted in a trend toward the use of concurrent engineering to address the need for capturing design logic across time periods and group boundaries.
>
> • The growth of knowledge has resulted in an inability for individuals to have sufficient knowledge and expertise upon which to make a decision in which sufficient confidence can be placed. Groups of specialists are becoming necessary to form complete knowledge maps.

Experienced managers are well aware that the outcome of decision-making (the implementation process) may not be what decision-makers intended.

---

[2] Unisys Corporation, *Group Support Technologies*, A study prepared for Organizational Planning and Development Division, Office Of Human Resource Development, Federal Aviation Administration, Cambridge, MA, January 1990, p. 11.

Table 3 – Problem Solving, Decision-making and Creativity

Problem Solving	Decision-making	Creativity
Intelligence Problem finding, identification, definition and diagnosis	Intelligence	Preparation Incubation
Design Identification / design / generation of alternative solutions	Design	Illumination Verification
Choice	Choice	
Implementation Of the chosen solution		
Monitoring, Reviewing and Maintaining Solution progress		

Table 3 shows the relationship between models of creativity, decision-making, and problem solving. [3]

A group decision-making situation has, by its very nature, unique benefits and trade-offs. On the positive side, group decision-making allows room for diverse inputs from multiple sources, bringing the ideas that may not otherwise have been considered. Group decision-making can help ensure the acceptance of a decision in an organization by including more members in the decision process, thus fostering an environment for achieving consensus. On the other hand, these varying perspectives can lead to disagreements and decision-making difficulties. Furthermore, it can be problematic to take all of the group members' input accurately into account during the decision-making process. A decision-maker sometimes has the option of choosing whether to decide alone, or in some combination with others in the organization. Some options include: (1) making the decision

---

[3] Ibid., p 19.

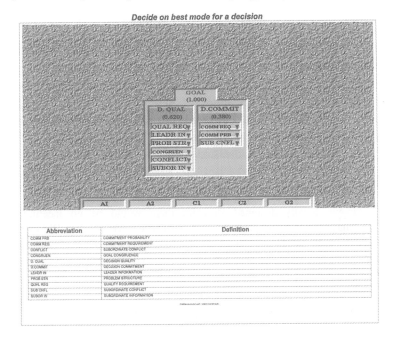

Figure 1 – Deciding on best mode for a decision

totally alone without consulting anyone, (2) collecting information from subordinates without telling about issue, then deciding alone, (3) consulting with subordinates on an individual basis about an issue, then deciding alone, (4) consult with a group about an issue, then deciding alone, and (5) meeting with a group, sharing information, and having the group decide. Some of the considerations in deciding which option is best for a particular decision are shown in Figure 1. The last option, meeting with a group and having the group decide, is sometimes considered too 'risky' by some decision makers. However, with the proper decision support technologies, a decision- maker can greatly improve the likelihood that the group will choose an alternative that best meets his/her objectives. The technologies must be able to cope with all of the complexity of an individual decision (discussed earlier) and then some.

In making group decisions, not only is it necessary to synthesize multiple, often conflicting objectives of a single decision maker, but a group decision requires a synthesis over numerous decision makers, each with differing values.   Group decisions also tend to entail greater risk or opportunity than individual decisions.

Group decisions typically require numerous meetings. Meetings can be categorized as either information meetings or decision meetings.   While both types will be discussed, decision meetings will be emphasized in this chapter.

Peter Drucker observed the following about meetings[4]:

"In an ideally designed structure there would be no meetings. Everybody would know what he needs to know to do his job. We meet because people holding different jobs have to cooperate to get a specific task done.   We meet because the knowledge and experience needed in a specific situation are not available in one head, but have to be pieced together out of the experience and knowledge of several people."

Douglas McGregor recognizes the lasting importance of meetings[5]:

"Fads will come and go. The fundamental fact of man's capacity to collaborate with his fellows in the face-to-face group will survive the fads and one day be recognized. Then, and only then, will management discover how seriously it has underestimated the true potential of its human resources."

---

[4] Peter Drucker, *The Effective Executive,* 1967
[5] Douglas McGregor, The Human Side of Enterprise

Michael Schrage observed that[7]: "Individual genius may spot fertile ground, but it takes a collaborative community to cultivate and harvest it." Information meetings can involve a large number of people, are typically arranged in classroom or auditorium style seating, involve one way communication with some Q&A, and emphasize content. Decision-making meetings have traditionally been limited to fifteen or fewer people, but with new meeting facilitation technologies, can involve many more people. Decision-making meetings are typically arranged in a conference room style, involve interactive communication, and may place as much or more emphasis on process as on content.

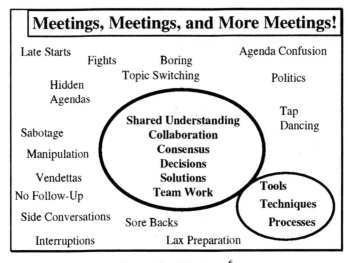

Figure 2 – Meetings[6]

---

[6] Source: Meeting Facilitation Seminar notes – Peter Beck and Ernest Forman, Expert Choice Inc., Pittsburgh, Pa.
[7] Michael Schrage, *No More Teams*, 1995

Dissatisfaction with outcomes of meetings

Numerous studies have documented widespread dissatisfaction with the process and outcomes of meetings.[8] Researchers have identified a variety of structured procedures and guidelines that can help overcome meeting problems. External process facilitation and group support systems are two means of applying effective procedures outside of relying on meeting members themselves to do so. Research results have shown that GSS can positively impact group processes resulting in improved task outcomes and improved relational outcomes[9]. There is also evidence to indicate that flexibly applied process facilitation by external facilitators can supplement and/or enhance GSS effectiveness. In an excellent discussion of group facilitation and group support systems[10], Bostrom, et al. addresses the question of how to effectively plan, coordinate, and direct the work of group members who are using a GSS, an activity they call facilitation. We summarize their discussion below.

What is a meeting?

A meeting can be viewed as a goal or outcome-directed interaction between two or more people (teams, groups) that can take place in any of four environments:

- same time/same place (face-to-face)
- same time/different place
- different time/same place
- different time/different place
- By far, most meetings today take place in the same time/same place environment. Support technologies are making the other three environments more prevalent. Phone and video conferencing for same time/different place; computerized storage and retrieval for

---

[8] "Group Facilitation and Group Support Systems" Robert Bostrom, Robert Anson, and Vikki, K. Clawson, in *Group Support Systems - New Perspectives*, Edited by Leonard M. Jessup and Joseph S. Valacich, McMillan, New York, 1993.
[9] Ibid., p156.
[10] Ibid., p146.

different time/same place and, coupled with telecommunications, for different time/different place.

There are three primary roles played at decision meetings. The "leader", or meeting owner, establishes meeting objectives, participates in meeting planning, and often has primary responsibility for the meeting outcomes. The "participants" contribute their skills, talents and experience and are responsible for generating ideas, analyzing information, helping to arrive at a decision, and often are responsible for implementing action plans. A "facilitator", who might be the meeting leader or an external person, introduces tools, processes and techniques to help people work together.

Meeting Model

Meetings (and sequences of meetings) can last anywhere from a fraction of an hour, to months or even years. A meeting is an interaction that:

- utilizes a set of *resources* (people, technology)

- to transform the group's *present problem* into its *desired future state* (accomplishing specific meeting outcomes)

- through a series of *action steps* (agenda)

The action steps (agenda) can be described in terms of a core set of generic *activities* for any meeting task. For example, to accomplish a particular topic, a group might:

generate information;

organize the information into alternatives;

evaluate and select alternatives; and

discuss (communicate) their actions

GSS tools and other meeting technology can be classified in terms of the activities they support, for example, brainstorming to generate alternatives, structuring to organize information, and evaluation to choose the most preferred alternative.

Meeting Outcomes: Relational as well as Task

The task, or content outcomes of a meeting concern the *what* of a meeting and are most visible. Four types of task processes include:

- generating alternatives

- choosing among alternatives

- negotiating

- executing chosen alternatives

Conflict is more prevalent in tasks, which must decide issues where there is more than one 'right' answer, tasks, which must reconcile divergent values, and interests, and competitive tasks.

Less obvious than the task outcome, but always important, are how participants *feel* about or *react to* aspects of the meeting, including:

- how participants feel about or react to the content (the task)

- feelings that group members have toward each other (interpersonal)

- rapport, openness, trust, and cohesiveness in the group

- feelings about the interactions (process) – e.g., agenda, activities, GSS

- feelings about themselves and their contributions (self)

The objective is to create and maintain positive emotions that promote working together effectively. In an effective meeting , negative affect (feeling or emotion as distinguished from cognition, thought, or action) is not avoided, but instead refocused in a positive direction. Many facilitators comment that no affect (i.e., no energy) is their biggest problem.

A Meeting Facilitation Framework

Bostrom's[11] meeting facilitation framework helps in understanding the objects, functions and targets of a meeting. The framework consists of *facilitation sources*, performing *functions* on *meeting targets* (see Figure 3). The **sources** can be people (a group member, a group leader or an external facilitator) or technology (a GSS). The **functions** are facilitiative acts or behaviors such as organizing and energizing. And the meeting

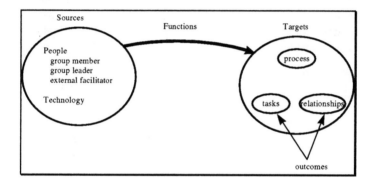

Figure 3 - Meeting Sources, Functions and Targets [1]

targets are what the facilitative acts are trying to influence, including how the group does its work (process), the content of work (task) and/or how the group works together (relationships). The latter two targets, task and relationships are referred to above as the meeting outcomes.

Many meetings emphasize task outcomes. Members are brought together primarily for their **task** content expertise and judgment. The term consultant rather than facilitator is normally be applied to a third party individual who is brought in with specific task expertise. Most people use the term meeting facilitation to denote intervention to the group **process** or **relationships**. As an example, a facilitation source (external individual,

---

[11] Ibid., p156.

group member, or technology) may facilitate a meeting process by suggesting that ideas be contributed in a round robin fashion or providing an anonymous brainstorming capability. However, technology can also play a content facilitation roles such as information retrieval, information processing, content analysis and content synthesis.

Lacking an external facilitator or GSS, a group member or leader facilitator who also has meeting content expertise has three responsibilities: task-related discussions, group processes, and group relationships. Bostrom claims that this triple responsibility and lack of facilitation skills is the major reason why traditional meetings are so often found to be inefficient and ineffective.

Facilitative functions are groupings of facilitative acts or behaviors and include such things as:

- organizing

- initiating structure

- summarizing

- clarifying

- harmonizing

- energizing

It is convenient to categorize facilitation functions into two general categories – **structure** and **support**. For example, an external facilitator (source) may need to influence how the group creatively interacts (process target) by applying a brainstorming technique (**structure**). The facilitator would manage (**support**) the brainstorming structure by acting as the recorder and by carefully summarizing each contribution.

Structure facilitation functions include:

- role specialization (participants are assigned specific roles such as devils advocate)

- rules to follow

- procedures

- techniques

Support facilitation functions or activities are designed to maintain, reinforce, promote and adapt the structures being used. They encourage effective behavior and deal with disruptive influences. The heart of good facilitation support is effective communication skills. Support activities in meetings are carried out through communication acts using verbal, nonverbal, and GSS channels.

Facilitation activities by meeting stage[12]

Although one person is the primary facilitator for a particular meeting, facilitation can be shared to some extent by all attendees. A GSS is a set of tools used by the facilitator and the group to help accomplish meeting outcomes. The primary facilitator, and not the GSS, must shape and guide the meeting process. The meeting process is often iterative – some meetings never "end" – but instead follow a continuing cycle of:

pre-meeting activities

meeting activities

post-meeting activities

Pre-meeting activities

It is important to design or plan the meeting before it convenes. The facilitator works with the group leader to develop a meeting design. An effective design focuses on formulating the problems and outcomes to be addressed and developing an appropriate meeting agenda of the topic activities to be undertaken. Meeting participants are selected and informed about meeting preparation. Participants' roles (facilitator, decision makers, etc.) and meeting ground rules are established. Although critical to the success of a meeting, the pre-meeting stage is often neglected or under-emphasized in practice – one of the biggest benefits of the introduction of a GSS is that it forces people to pay careful attention to the meeting design

---

[12] Ibid., p150.

During Meeting activities

During the meeting both task and relational activities must be accomplished. A meeting is usually divided into three phases opening, during, and closing. When opening the meeting (meeting setup), the facilitator must clarify the meeting objectives and get agreement from the attendees about the meeting purpose, agenda, process, and ground rules. During the meeting, the primary responsibility of the facilitator is to help the group adapt and execute the agenda to accomplish the task outcomes (e.g., choose the best alternatives, or develop an action plan) and to ensure that positive affect and constructive relationships are developed and maintained. This may entail providing focus, regulating traffic, stimulating discussion and insuring participation, maintaining process flexibility, and dealing with problem people. The facilitator must remain objective and protect participants and the group leader from attack. Participants' responsibilities during the meeting include getting to the meeting on time, keeping an open mind, sharing ideas and judgments, and adhering to ground rules.

Stimulating Discussion

Draw people out and encourage discussion.
How do you feel about ...
What are your thoughts on ...
What prompted your reaction ...
How did you feel when you learned that ...
What are some other approaches to ....

Help in gaining understanding - paraphrase.
Let me see if I understand you position. Are you saying that ...
I don't understand. Are you saying that ...
Let me paraphrase what I think you are saying .....
What I am hearing you say is ... Is that right?

Encourage Participation
Jim, how do you see that ...
Mary, would you state that another way ...
Before we go on, I would like to hear from Jane ..
Jerry, do you understand what Peter said?
We haven't heard from Fred. Any thoughts on this ..

Summary
Can someone summarize that?
I have lost track. Can someone summarize?
Jim does not agree? Can you summarize your ..

Clarification
Is it clear now? Can we look at it another way?
It is still not clear to me. Help me understand

Sanity Check the Task with the group:
Is this the right problem ..
Are these the most important criteria ..
Are these really our goals ...
Do we have all the stakeholders ....

Other Interventions:
Ask for Examples
Test for Consensus
Do a quick survey
Take a Break
Suggest a technique or tool
Be supporting (this is hard work)
Question Assumptions
Confront Differences

Figure 4 – Stimulating Discussion

Chapter 10

Feedback

Intuitive and Formal Feedback

In some (but not necessarily all) choice decisions, the importance of the objectives may depend on the alternatives being considered. This dependence can be accommodated either with formal feedback calculations or, in most cases, intuitively by the decision maker(s). Consider the following example. Suppose you are the mayor of a medium size city. The city council has just approved funding for a bridge that will connect the eastern and southern districts– saving the residents 30 minutes in commuting time. You announce that the winning proposal will be chosen using a formal evaluation methodology in which the proposals will be evaluated on the basis of strength and aesthetics. In order to be fair, you will, before receiving any bids, specify which of the two objectives will be more important. It seems obvious[1] that strength is much more important than aesthetics and you publicly announce that strength will be the most important objective in choosing the winning proposal.

Subsequently, two alternative designs are proposed for the new bridge. Bridge A is extremely save (as safe as any bridge yet built in the State) and beautiful. Bridge B is twice as strong as bridge A, but is UGLY!. Your hands are tied – you have announced that the most important objective is strength and, as the example below will illustrate, you must choose the ugly bridge. The bridge is built and many town residents are reminded of your decision at least twice a day. You lose the next election and will be wary of formal evaluation methodologies for the rest of your life. Yet formal evaluation methodologies are, as we have already seen, necessary to cope with the complexity of most crucial decisions. The answer is not to avoid formal evaluation methodologies, but to use them in ways that make sense!

Evaluation methodologies that neglect the dependence of objective priorities on the alternatives being considered are sometimes mandated by

---

[1] It would be difficult to defend a position that the strength of the bridge is not more important than aesthetics.

regulations.   For example, government organizations sometimes have regulations that mandate that evaluation weights be established and announced before a request for proposal is issued.   In our simple two objective example above, the Mayor would have had to declare that strength was more important than aesthetics and then have had to chose the ugly bridge, which, he intuitively knew was the wrong choice.   But intuition alone is not adequate in real world decisions because the numerous competing factors of the decision challenge man's cognitive abilities to adequately evaluate and process the information.   Hence we must rely on decision models when evaluating alternatives, but we must use them in ways that make sense – intuitively and logically.   If we need to incorporate feedback between alternatives and objectives, but fail to do so, our intuition will tell us that there is something wrong with the tentative conclusion. Recognizing this, we can incorporate the necessary feedback through iteration, or through mathematical means with a 'supermatrix.'   Lets see how this can be done using the bridge selection problem discussed above.

Top Down Evaluation of Bridge Selection AHP Model

A top down evaluation of an AHP model for the Mayor's simple two objective decision would proceed as follows. Before examining the alternatives, most rational people would judge safety to be much more important than aesthetics. Suppose the Mayor judged safety to be extremely more important than aesthetics as shown in Figure 1 and Figure 2.

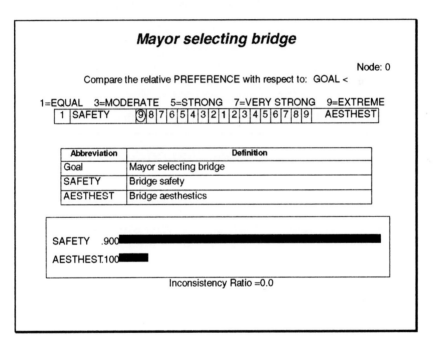

Figure 1 – Importance of Safety vs. Aesthetics

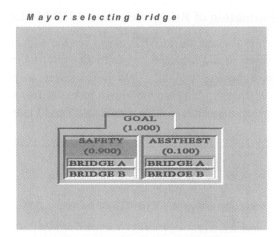

Figure 2 – Model for Bridge Selection

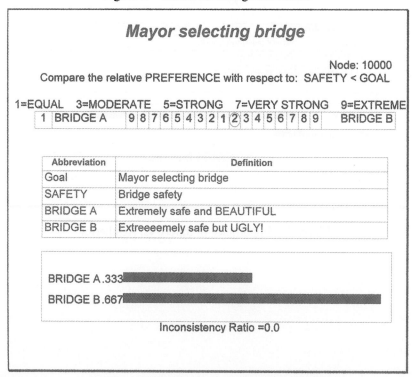

Figure 3 – Preference with respect to Safety

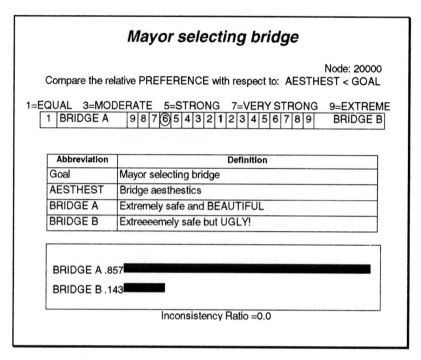

Figure 4 – Preference with respect to Aesthetics

Judgments about the preference for the bridges and resulting priorities are shown in Figure 3 and Figure 4. A synthesis using the top down approach is shown in Figure 5. This result, using a top down approach with no iteration, is counter-intuitive! Why should we choose an ugly bridge when we can choose one that is both safe and beautiful?

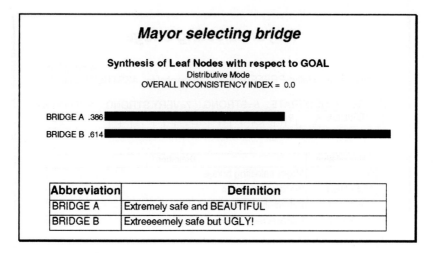

Figure 5 – Top Down Synthesis without Iteration

Top Down and Bottom Up

The 'top down' approach entails evaluating the importance of the objectives before evaluating the alternative preferences. A 'bottom up' approach, on the other hand, would consist of the evaluation of alternative preferences with respect to each objective before evaluating the relative importance of the objectives. If the decision-maker had used a bottom up approach instead, he/she would have learned that although design B is stronger than design A, both designs far exceed all safety standards. Furthermore, the decision-maker would have learned that design A is beautiful and while design B is ugly. Subsequently, while considering the relative importance of strength and aesthetics, the decision-maker might reasonably decide that aesthetics is more important than strength – see Figure 6. The resulting synthesis – see Figure 7, shows that Bridge A is now more preferable, a result that is also intuitively appealing.

This example illustrates that, if the decision-maker does not already know enough about the alternatives being evaluated, a bottom up approach will provide the necessary information so that reasonable judgments can be made about the relative importance of the objectives.

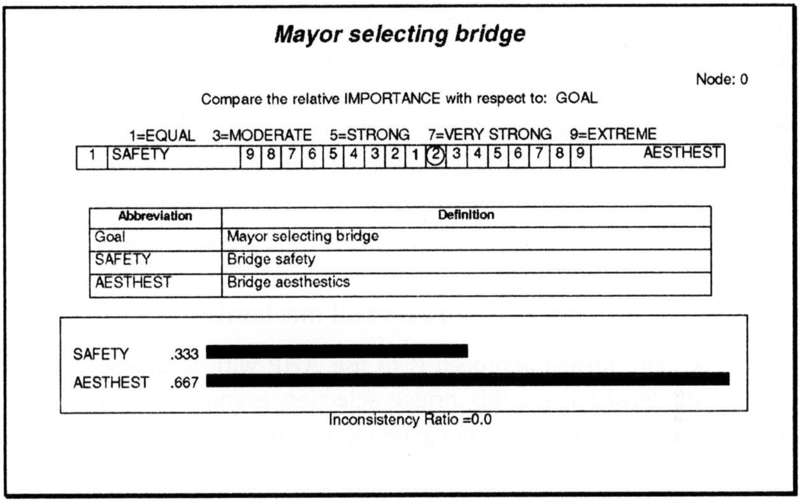

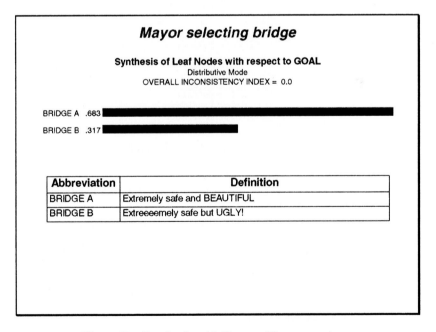

Figure 6 – Importance of Objectives with Bottom Up approach

Figure 7 – Synthesis with Bottom Up approach

Even if a top down approach is used, no harm will result provided the decision-maker examines the tentative model results and questions its reasonableness.[2] In this example, the Mayor would, after synthesizing the first time, realize that the choice of the ugly bridge is counter-intuitive. Now knowing that both bridges are more than adequately safe he or she should re-evaluate his or her judgments. Doing so will result in the obviously correct choice of Bridge A.

AHP with Feedback −A more formal mechanism

A more formal approach is to use AHP with feedback[3]. An AHP model with feedback for this bridge selection example would, instead of asking the decision maker to compare the relative importance of safety and

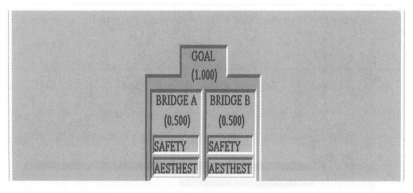

Figure 8 – Upside down Hierarchy

aesthetics with respect to the 'goal', instead ask for judgments about the relative importance of safety and aesthetics first with respect to Bridge A, and then with respect to Bridge B. We can think of this as turning the hierarchy in Figure 2 upside down, ignoring the priorities of the alternatives, and making judgments about the importance of the objectives with respect

[2]As should always be done!
[3]Saaty, T.L., *Fundamentals of Decision Making and Priority Theory with The Analytic Hierarchy Process*, 1994, RWS Publications, Pittsburgh, PA., p38.

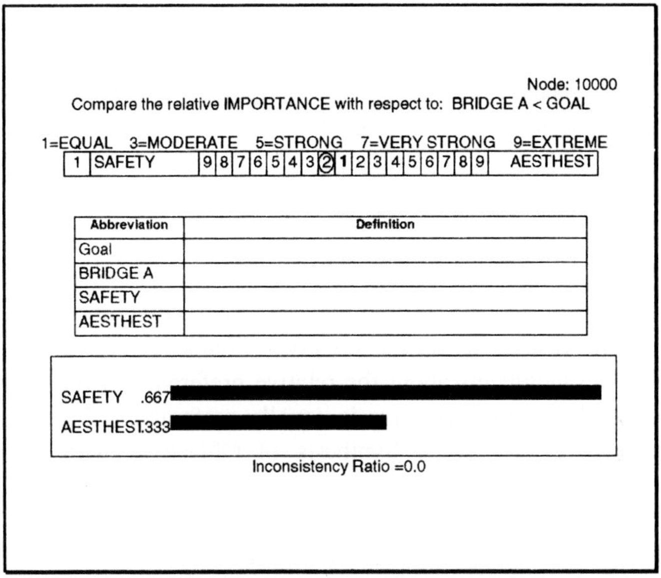

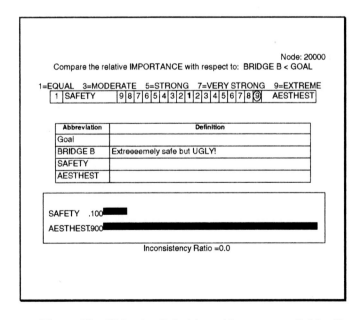

Figure 9 – Objective Priorities with respect to Bridge A

Figure 10 – Objective Priorities with respect to Bridge B

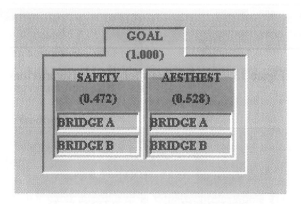

Figure 16 – Substituting 2nd Synthesis Priorities

Table 1 – Iterative Objective and Alternative Priorities

Iteration# / Alt or Obj	BridgeA or Safety	BridgeB or Aesthetics
2nd Alt:	.610	.390
3rd Obj:	.446	.554
3rd Alt:	.624	.376
4th Obj:	.454	.546
4th Alt:	.619	.381
5th Obj:	.451	.549
5th Alt:	.621	.379
6th Obj:	.452	.548
6th Alt:	.620	.380
7th Obj:	.451	.549
7th Alt:	.621	.379

By iteratively synthesizing the models in Figure 8 and Figure 12, each time replacing the priorities of the nodes below the goal with the priorities of the synthesized dual model, we converge on the priorities shown in Table 1. The alternative priorities derived above with a formal approach to feedback are similar to those derived using intuitive feedback (see Figure 7) where the judgments about the relative importance of the objectives were made with respect to the goal *after* examining the alternatives. The formal approach to feedback differs in that judgments about the relative importance of the objectives are made with respect to each alternative, rather than with respect to the goal. The iterations required for the formal feedback calculations can be carried out by a computer in the form of supermatrix calculations.

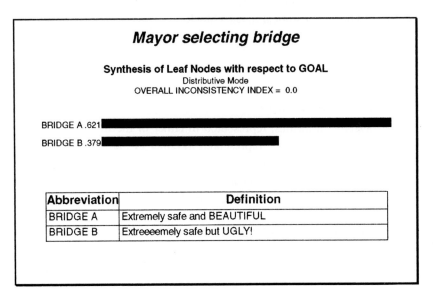

Figure 17 – Priorities after Iterating

Supermatrix for feedback

A supermatrix can be constructed and used to assess the results of feedback. Instead of iterating as we did above for illustrative purposes, the priority vectors for the alternatives with respect to each objective (from Figure 3and Figure 4) as well as the priority vectors of the importance of the objectives with respect to each alternative (from Figure 8 and Figure 9), are used to form a 'supermatrix' as follows:

```
0.     0.     0.667  0.1
0.     0.     0.333  0.9
0.333  0.857  0.     0.
0.667  0.143  0.     0.
```

The final priorities for both the objectives and alternatives are obtained by multiplying this matrix by itself numerous times[4] until the columns stabilize and become identical in each block[5]:

```
0.452  0.452  0.     0.
0.548  0.548  0.     0.
0.     0.     0.621  0.621
0.     0.     0.379  0.379
```

The objective priorities, represented in either of the first two columns, and the alternative priorities, represented in either of the last two columns, are the same as those achieved with iterative syntheses of the two models (Table 1). The supermatrix approach allows a great more deal of flexibility to incorporate feedback as we shall see shortly.

Intuitive versus formal feedback

It is possible to arrive at similar results using either a bottom up approach or top down followed by bottom up, where feedback occurs in the decision makers thought process, or a formal methodological approach

---

[4] These calculations can be performed for feedback between adjacent levels using Team, or, more generally for any type of feedback using the ECNet software described later in this chapter.
[5]Saaty, T.L., *Fundamentals of Decision Making and Priority Theory with The Analytic Hierarchy Process*, 1994, RWS Publications, Pittsburgh, PA., p40.

where feedback is modeled in a supermatrix of priority vectors. Feedback is deeply ingrained in human functioning. Our ability to move from one part a room to another without falling over pieces of furniture (or even more remarkably to run, intercept and hit a moving tennis ball before it bounces twice within the confines of the court) rests in our brain's ability to continually process information based on cognition and our senses, and to give the appropriate commands to our muscles. Information is continually fed back so that, for example, adjustments to the current path are made based on our desires about our destination, present position, obstacles in our path, forecast of what will happen, and so on. Halfway across the room we might decide to change our destination realizing that the chair we had started out for will likely be taken by another person by the time we arrive. There is no question that humans can mentally process information incorporating feedback.   Our ability to make judgments about the importance of objectives based on our knowledge of alternatives is an example of such feedback. However, there are also situations where we can benefit with a decision aid that formally incorporates feedback.   An increased understanding of what our minds can do easily and what we find difficult will be important so that we can employ the proper balance of cognition and decision aids. Our ability to catch a ball, or (for some humans) to think several moves ahead in a game of chess is truly remarkable. On the other hand, psychologists have shown that the human mind has very limited abilities. We function very well without decision models for the vast majority of our decisions. Yet our everyday decision rules or common simplistic strategies are often not adequate for making crucial decisions. In the example presented above, our intuition is more than adequate in selecting the best of two bridges given the two alternatives and two objectives of safety and aesthetics. However intuition alone would not be adequate if there were several alternatives and many tradeoffs to consider involving perhaps ten, twenty, or fifty objectives. We need to continue to investigate and learn more about human abilities and limitations in making complex decisions so that we can provide decision support where it is needed and in ways that best augment, rather than replace human thinking. The Analytic Network Process (ANP) is a step in that direction.

The Analytic Network Process

Saaty has extended the Analytic Hierarchy Process to incorporate various types and degrees of feedback – a process referred to as the Analytic Network Process or ANP[6]. The ANP is the first mathematical theory that makes it possible for us to deal systematically with all kinds of dependence and feedback. The reason for its uniqueness is the way it elicits judgments and uses measurement to derive ratio scales. Priorities measured on ratio scales are necessary for performing the basic arithmetic operations of adding within the same scale and multiplying different scales meaningfully as required by the ANP. The ANP provides a framework of clusters of elements connected in any desired way to investigate the process of deriving ratio scales priorities from the distribution of influence among elements and among clusters. The distribution of influence is represented by interactions and feedback within clusters (inner dependence) and between clusters (outer dependence). The AHP is a special case of the ANP. Although some decision problems are best studied through the ANP, it is not true that forcing an ANP model always yields better results than using the hierarchies of the AHP. There are examples to justify the use of both. We have yet to learn when the shortcut of the hierarchy is justified, not simply on grounds of expediency and efficiency, but also for reasons of validity of the outcome.

The ANP is implemented in the software ECNET[7] and is a coupling of two parts. The first consists of a control hierarchy or network of criteria and subcriteria that control the interactions in the system under study. The second is a network of influences among the elements and clusters. The network varies from criterion to criterion and a supermatrix of limiting influence is computed for each control criterion. Finally, each of these supermatrices is weighted by the priority of its control criterion and the results are synthesized through addition for all the control criteria.[8] We will

---

[6] Saaty, T.. L. *Decision Making with Dependence and Feedback, The Analytic Network Process*, 1996, RWS Publications, Pittsburgh, PA.

[7] ECNET was developed jointly by Ron Chan and Thomas Saaty.

[8] In addition, a problem is often studied through a control hierarchy or system of benefits, a second for costs, a third for opportunities, and a fourth for risks. The synthesized results of the four control systems are combined by taking the quotient of the benefits times the opportunities to the costs times the risks to determine the best outcome.

deal only with the second part right now and take as our only control
criterion the benefits to be derived from the alternatives under consideration.

A Car buying example with Feedback

Consider a car buying example where the objectives are Initial Cost,
Repair Costs, and Durability and the alternatives are American cars,
Japanese cars and European Cars. A traditional hierarchy for this problem is
shown in Figure 18.

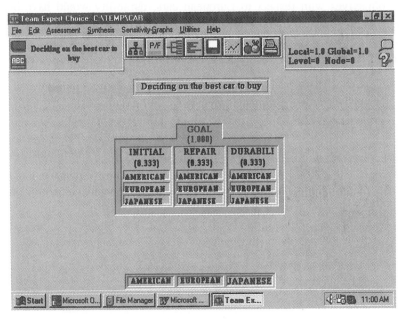

Figure 18 – The First Car Model Hierarchy

An upside down hierarchy

Instead of making judgments about the relative importance of the objectives with respect to an 'overall goal', it might be more meaningful (although more time consuming) to make such judgments with respect to each of the alternatives. In essence, you have turned the first hierarchy upside down. The model is shown in Figure 19. For example, as of the early 1990's, when you thought of American cars, the low initial cost would have been more important than durability. On the other hand, when comparing the objectives with respect to European cars, durability would have been more important than initial cost. And when you thought of Japanese cars, requiring fewer repairs would have been more important than initial cost or durability. The result of this model is the prioritization of the objectives.

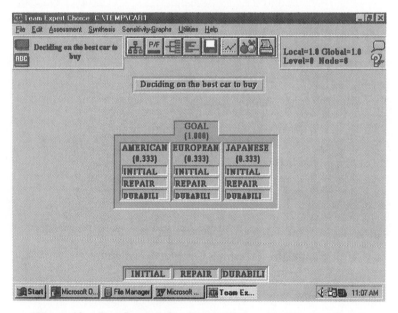

Figure 19 – The Second Car Model Hierarchy (Upside-down)

Combining the Two Hierarchies in a Feedback Network Model

The implicit interactions among factors in the two hierarchies above is what we mean by feedback and dependence. Just as we iterated between two related models in the bridge example earlier, we can do the same for this car buying example. In general, however, we can best handle these considerations by modeling the problem as a network. What if one currently owns a particular kind of car (American, European, or Japanese), would that not somehow influence our perceptions, and hence judgments about, repair costs and durability? Those judgments may in turn may cloud our judgments about the various manufacturers.

Influences in hierarchies only flow in one direction--downward. The 'Goal' of a traditional hierarchy can be thought of as a 'source' of water. The water is distributed to the objectives, then to the sub-objectives, and so on, down to the alternatives. The relative amount of water collected by each alternative determines the alternative's priority. Water never flows 'out' of the alternatives in the traditional hierarchical model.9 The feedback network model, however, differs in that water flowing into the alternatives also flows out. The water flowing out can be 'fed back' to the objectives (as well as other elements in a more elaborate network). The 'steady state' water flow in a network is continuous – water flows out of the objectives, into the alternatives, then flows out of the alternatives into the objectives. There is no need for a 'goal' node as a source of water because the alternatives no longer act as absorbing 'sinks'.

Network models do not have levels such as goal, objectives, and alternatives. Instead, the elements (or nodes) in a network model are grouped into clusters, such as an objectives cluster and an alternatives cluster. The feedback model for this car example has two clusters:

OBJECTIVES containing the objectives Initial Cost, Repair Cost and Durability.

ALTERNATIVES containing the alternatives American, Japanese and European.

---

9 The 'supermatrix' representation of a traditional hierarchy must have an identity matrix in that portion of the matrix representing the alternatives to indicate that the alternatives are 'sinks' for what flows in.

Links in a Feedback Network Model

The flow of influence in a feedback network model is specified by links. A link from one element, such as an objective, to other elements, such as alternatives, specifies that influence can flow from the former to the latter, and that pairwise comparisons will be made to indicate the relative amount of influence that flows from the former to each of the latter. Conversely, when pairs of elements can be meaningfully compared with respect to another element, then a link from the latter to the former is appropriate.

One way to identify ALL possible links is to consider each element and identify all other pairs of elements that can logically be compared with respect to the element being considered. This approach can lead to a very complex structure that might take an inordinate amount of time to evaluate. Another approach is to add links only for those situations where influence is apparent.

Each objective in the car network example has a link to the three alternatives to indicate the flow of influence from the objective to the alternatives. Pairwise comparisons will be made to determine the relative influence that the objective has on the relative preferences of the alternatives.

Similarly, each alternative in the car network example has a link to the three objectives to indicate the flow of influence from the alternative to the objectives. Pairwise comparisons will be made to determine the relative influence that the alternative has on the relative importance of the objectives.

Clusters themselves become linked when elements within them are linked. When a cluster is linked to more than one other cluster, comparisons will also have to be made for the relative influence of the latter clusters on the former.

Two Kinds of Questions to Answer in Making ANP Comparisons

When making pairwise comparisons in an ANP model the questions are formulated in terms of dominance or influence. When comparing a pair of elements in one cluster with respect to an element in another (or the same) cluster, we ask either:

Which element of the pair has greater influence?, or

Which element or the pair is influenced more?

The same type of question should be used throughout the evaluation.

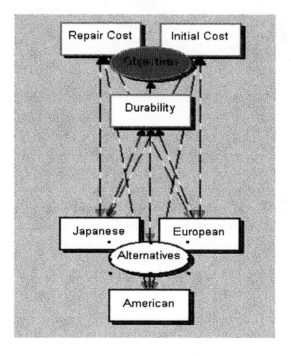

Figure 20 – Cluster Centric View of Car Network

The clusters, elements and links for the car example is shown in Figure 20 and Figure 21, the former a cluster centric view and the latter an orbital

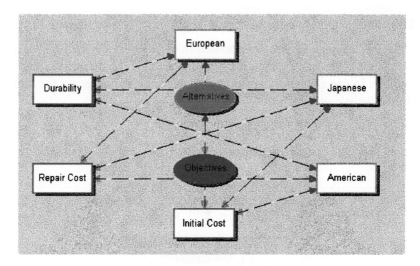

Figure 21 – Orbital View of Car Network

view. A model is said to have outer dependence when elements are linked to elements in another cluster. A model also has inner dependence when elements are linked to other elements in their own cluster. There is no inner dependence in this example.

In the ANP, just as in the AHP, we are usually looking for a prioritization of alternatives as a result. Thus, in general, every feedback model should include a cluster of elements that will be our alternatives.

Summary of Steps in Building a Feedback Network

We have to:

identify the clusters as they relate to the problem
identify the elements within each cluster
identify dependencies among the elements and link them
elicit judgments on the elements
elicit judgments on the clusters (if necessary) synthesize the result

Chapter 11

Empowered for the Future

Everything That Counts

We have examined the implicit difficulties in making important complex decisions, in forecasting the future, and in allocating resources. We have seen how the Analytic Hierarchy Process can provide significant advantage in overcoming these difficulties. We have seen how AHP can be applied so that everything that counts *can* be counted (measured on a ratio scale to be more precise) and how, through intelligent model representation of an organization's objectives, to *avoid counting* everything that can be counted.

Beyond Buzzwords

In *Reinventing the Business*[1], Roy Harmon wrote the following about a business trend called business process reengineering:

> "It is my fervent (but undoubtedly vain) wish that the latest buzzwords-of-the-month, 'reengineering' or 'business process reengineering,' will disappear from routine business conversation – just as their hundreds of faddish predecessors have – and that they will not be replaced by new and equally short-lived crazes. ... We consultants and authors are guilty of perpetuating the largely nonsensical buzzword creation... Unfortunately, there is little in the world that is really new. In fact, most 'new' publications, valuable as they may be, incorporate virtually all of the best of their predecessors. Nevertheless, quantum improvements are being achieved through the application of established methods, and implementation of these tried and proven techniques should be the ongoing goal of every organization and all of its personnel."

We believe that AHP is not just another contemporary management trend, but can be applied to *all* past and future management trends. While AHP is a relatively 'new' as a methodology, it is comprised of parts that

---

[1] Roy L. Harmon, *Reinventing the Business,* The Free Press, New York, NY, 1996 pg xxiv.

have been with us for a long time – hierarchical organization of complexity, pairwise comparisons, eigenvectors, and measurement theory. The parts, however, have been crafted so they fit together into a methodology that we confidently believe will be embraced far into the future. Why do we say this?   Because, unlike other management crazes that address specific management needs such as quality, reengineering or budgeting, AHP is a fundamental methodology that allows individuals and organizations to better structure complexity and synthesize both qualitative and quantitative factors that are part of *every* management process.   We are hopeful that the reader will be able to apply AHP to future management trends that develop.   To help in this endeavor, we have provided examples of how AHP can be applied to current and past management trends in Appendix I. Additionally, two case studies are included in Appendix II.

We have shown how AHP, as a fundamental methodology, can be applied to: decision making by focusing on objectives; to forecasting by measuring and synthesizing alternative influencing factors and their relative impacts; and to resource allocation by measuring benefits that reflect the true objectives of the organization, not just what could traditionally be counted.

Empowered

The processes and techniques contained in this book should empower you to see the world with more clarity than you were able to before. While others get bogged down in complexity, you will be able to structure complexity into coherent clusters, to assess (measure) relative importance, likelihoods and preferences.   You will be able to not only make better decisions based on the achievement of objectives, but will be able to communicate the rationale to others.   You will be able to engage others in the process, create cooperative teams, and share power in ways that will make you more powerful.

Appendix I

Contemporary Management Trends

We illustrate in this appendix how AHP can be applied to several management processes / trends of the past and encourage the reader to extend these notions to new management trends that emerge in the future.

Strategic Planning

Strategic planning has many facets, several of which are facilitated with AHP. J. Heizer, B. Render (Production and Operations Management: Strategies and Tactics, Allyn Bacon, 1993 p25,26) describe the strategy development process as follows:

> "In order to develop an effective strategy, organizations first seek to identify opportunities in the economic system. Then we define the organization's mission or purpose in society -- what it will contribute to society. This purpose is the organization's reason for being, that is, its mission. Once an organization's mission has been decided, each functional area within the firm determines its supporting mission. .. "We achieve missions via strategies. A strategy is a plan designed to achieve a mission. .. A mission should be established in light of the threats and opportunities in the environment and the strengths and weakness of the organization."

AHP can assist an organization in selecting among alternative missions, in selecting among alternative strategies, and in allocating resources to implement the chosen strategy. Strategic planning involves a "forward process" of projecting the likely or logical future and a "backward" process of prioritizing desired futures. The backward process affords people an opportunity to expand their awareness of what states of the system they would like to see take place, and with what priorities. Using the backward process, planners identify both opportunities and obstacles and eventually select effective policies to facilitate reaching the desired future.

Total Quality Management

Total Quality Management (TQM), a business process that became extremely popular in the mid to late 1980's, dates back several decades to the work of W. Edwards Demming, who, after World War II, went to Japan to teach quality. Demming insisted that employees could not produce products that on the average exceeded the quality of what the *process* was capable of producing. He emphasized the use of statistical techniques as the fundamental tool for improving the process. These techniques, known as statistical process control, differ somewhat from traditional statistics. Traditional statistics usually assume that there is a probability distribution for a population and is concerned with estimating the parameters of the distribution. Statistical process control, on the other hand, does not assume that there is a 'stable' probability distribution, but that, in fact, the mean and or variance of the distribution might be changing – that is, the process may be out of control. The first concern in statistical process control is to ascertain that the process is 'in control', and if not, determine what needs to be done to stabilize the system. Then, and only then, is attention turned to determining whether the system is 'process capable – capable of producing output that is within defined specification limits. Demming insisted that the use of intuition alone was not adequate to achieve quality. He gave examples to illustrate that without some theoretical basis, such as the use of statistics, the application of 'common sense' ways to improving quality often lead, surprisingly, to a reduction in quality. He was fond of saying that without a theory "Off you go to the Milky way".

Total quality management grew to encompass many other ideas and concepts. So many, in fact, that it is often difficult to say what TQM doesn't encompass. The historical shift in quality focus can be seen in Table 1. Another view of TQM is the categorization as three vertices of a triangle shown in Figure 1.

The meaning of the word 'total' is often misunderstood – it does not refer to total quality, but instead is a translation from the Japanese terminology for 'company -wide'. A consequence of organizational growth and compartmentalization has been the inability of any one 'department' to make an effective impact on quality improvement without cooperation and

involvement of other departments. One vertex of the TQM triangle in
Figure 1 is a concerted company-wide–effort to break down organizational
barriers such as:

- poor communication or lack of communication
- lack of overall mission and goals
- competition between departments, shifts, areas, ...
- too many levels of management that filter information
- decisions and resource allocation without regard to social memory

- Statistical Process Control
    - measurement of 'variables' and 'attributes'
- Quality Improvement
    - Pareto Analysis – is only a first step – too simplistic
    - cause and effect diagrams
        - Fishbone diagrams are AHP models in disguise
        - hierarchical structure allows many levels
        - can translate expert judgment into ratio scales
- Product and process design
- Pricing

Malcom Baldridge Award

Quality is multidimensional. The basic capabilities of AHP –structuring complexity, measurement, and synthesis over multiple dimensions – are applicable to numerous aspects of TQM. First of all, quality is multi-dimensional, as is illustrated by the Malcom Baldridge criteria shown in Figure 2[1].

---

[1] The Malcom Baldridge National Quality Award, United States Department of Commerce, Technology Administration, Gaithersberg, MD, 1996.

```
AWARD CRITERIA - ITEM LISTING
Categories/Items                                          Point Values

1.0 Leadership                                                90
        1.1 Senior Executive Leadership                      45
        1.2 Leadership System and Organization               25
        1.3 Public Responsibility and Corporate Citizenship 20
2.0 Information and Analysis                                  75
        2.1 Management of Information and Data                20
        2.2 Competitive Comparisons and Benchmarking         15
2.3 Analysis and Use of Company-Level Data                   40
3.0 Strategic Planning                                       55
        3.1 Strategy Development                              35
        3.2 Strategy Deployment                              20
4.0     Human Resource Development and Management            140
        4.1 Human Resource Planning and Evaluation           20
        4.2 High Performance Work Systems                    45
        4.3 Employee Education, Training, and Development     50
        4.4 Employee Well-Being and Satisfaction             25
5.0 Process Management                                       140
        5.1 Design and Introduction of Products and Services 40
        5.2 Process Management: Product and Service Production
                and Delivery                                 40
        5.3 Process Management: Support Services              30
        5.4 Management of Supplier Performance               30
6.0 Business Results                                         250
        6.1 Product and Service Quality Results              75
        6.2 Company Operational and Financial Results        110
        6.3 Human Resource Results                           35
        6.4 Supplier Performance Results                     30
7.0 Customer Focus and Satisfaction                         250
        7.1 Customer and Market Knowledge                    30
        7.2 Customer Relationship Management                 30
        7.3 Customer Satisfaction Determination              30
        7.4 Customer Satisfaction Results                    160
TOTAL POINTS                                                1000
```

Figure 2 – Baldridge Award Criteria

Some of these dimensions are quantitative and some are qualitative. Also notice the hierarchical structuring of the Baldridge criteria. The criteria have been clustered just as in an AHP model – with no more than seven, plus or minus two elements in any cluster. In the message to executives, the Baldridge guidelines state:

"The Criteria's seven Categories and 24 Items focus on requirements that all business – especially those facing tough competitive challenges – need to thoroughly understand. The Criteria address all aspects of competitive performance in an integrated and balanced way."

The 'integration' requires synthesis, the 'balance' is achieved through appropriate priorities for the seven categories and 24 items. The criteria and sub-criteria are, according to the Baldridge guidelines, 'not only to serve as a reliable basis for making Awards but also to permit a diagnosis of each applicant's overall performance management system." The weights 'assigned' by the Baldridge committee vary from year to year and are used to score the applicants for the award. How these weights are determined is not specified. For the purpose of a competition, establishing rules, including arbitrary weights as in this case, is adequate. However, these weights should *not* be used as a diagnosis of each applicant's overall performance – since the weights obviously should be tailored to the industry and company being assessed. A far more meaningful set of weights can be *derived* through pairwise comparisons as discussed in this book.

Assessing the Voice of the Customer

Quality, like beauty, is in the eyes of the beholder. But deciding who's eyes we look into and ascertaining what these eyes are looking at are not always easy to determine. We include here, a brief example developed by Zultner & Company, called "Before the House – The Voices of the Customers in QFD[2]" (The 'House' refers to the House of Quality in TQM parlance. Consider a small 'Mom and Pop" restaurant. To be 'successful', should they focus on the tastiness of the food, serving large portions, providing comfortable surroundings, or making their restaurant a happening place? They want to 'listen' to the voice of the customer, but which customer? They service families, students, singles, and senior citizens.

---

[2] Richard Zultner, Software QFD, Princeton N.J., 1991.

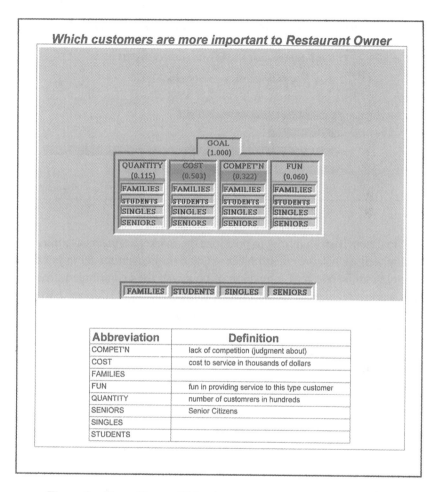

Figure 3 – From Owner Objectives to Market Segment Priorities

Furthermore, shouldn't *their* objectives influence how they operate their business? Making a profit is of course, a given, but having enjoyment from running the business, or 'fun', is one of the main reasons they decided to open a restaurant in the first place.

Zultner & Company developed two very simple, but powerful AHP models that together, are effective in assessing the voice of the customer.

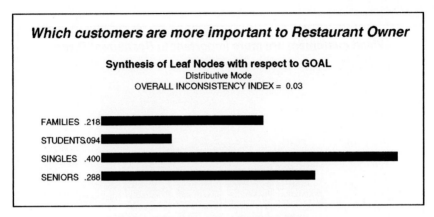

Figure 4 – Market Segment Priorities

The first model(see Figure 3) to prioritize the market segments as a function of how well each serves their objectives, and the second model to prioritize the restaurant services as a function of how well they contribute to each of their market segments. Some of the priorities in Figure 3 were based on data, while others were based on verbal judgments.

The synthesis of this simple model produces priorities for the market segments as shown in Figure 4. These priorities are transferred to second model, shown in Figure 5, that leads to the derivation of service priorities shown in Figure 6.

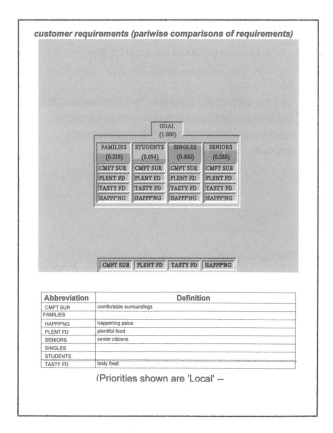

Figure 5 – Prioritizing Services

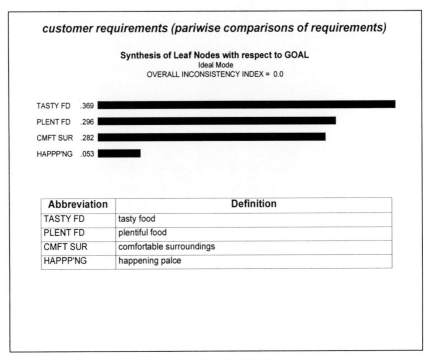

Figure 6 – Synthesis

The application of AHP to derive priorities for a firm's products or services is both simple and sound. Simple because the purpose of each of the models is straightforward and easily understandable. Sound, because the priorities that are derived are ratio scale priorities and ratio scale priorities

are required for the results to be mathematically meaningful!

Value Based Value Pricing

A second aspect of the consumer oriented focus stage of TQM developed by Knowledge Management Group[3] is called value based value pricing. Value Based Value Pricing is an analytical methodology developed

---

[3] Strategus, Inc. 23, Hunters Lane, Nashua, NH.

to support pricing of products or services. The assumption is that the customer is the only judge that really matters in establishing the value of a product or service. The factors affecting buyers' decisions are better understood through a thorough and quantified analysis of customer needs and preferences. Value Based Value Pricing enables users to achieve this objective through an integration of behavioral analysis and value engineering, much more powerful and precise than cost justification or investment evaluation techniques.

Value Based Value Pricing is implemented in three steps. The first one (Customer Driven Value Analysis) analyzes what customers want and establishes values of these wants. The second step (Competitive Value Analysis) compares how well different companies satisfy customer requirements. The third step (Competitive Value Pricing) allows for the planning of pricing methodologies that take into account both competitive forces and also how well customers value the products or services offered.

Value Based Value Pricing offers additional collateral benefits. The information collected can be used to focus resources on the functionality of products and services that offer higher value to customers. Functionality that is not, or not often enough, appreciated by customers can be discarded. Marketing and sales strategies can be built around the elements that offer the best value to customers. Value Based Value Pricing can be used by buyers as well to analyze the relative value of multiple responses to a request for products or services.

Value Pricing

The method makes use of the AHP to structure and quantify value to customers. It enables the user to structure the functionality of a product or service into mutually interacting elements and then to synthesize them by measuring the priority of the functional elements. The result is a list of functional attributes carrying weights established through a rigorous analysis with the user. For example, a company asked for a computerized order entry system. Small size, appealing design, and high reliability were among the specifications. When asked, the customer listed reliability as more important than size or appearance. A company called Systems

Integration, needed a better understanding of the customers priorities in order to develop a pricing for its product proposal.

Order Entry System	Size	Design	Reliability	Priority
Size	1	7	1/7	0.1912
Design	1/7	1	1/9	0.0480
Reliability	7	9	1	0.7608

A Value Analysis workshop with the customer revealed that reliability was very strongly more important than size, and extremely more important than design. The AHP verbal scale and eigenvector priority computation method were used to derive the priorities of the customer wants.

Competitive Value Analysis

The priorities established through *Customer Driven Value Analysis* are used as input to the next tool, *Competitive Value Analysis.* The ability of different companies to satisfy requirements according to priority values established by the customer is compared through a simple process – rating the companies on a 1-10 scale for each of the functional attributes. In the example illustrated in the table, the System Integrator appeared at a disadvantage after a first analysis by being last in two of the three required characteristics. The relative importance of reliability to the customer and the competitive strength in this field showed that, in reality, the System Integrator was 23% better than Company B, and 36% better than Company A.

Order Entry System	Priority	Company A	Company B	Syst. Integr.
Size	.19	7	5	2
Design	.05	5	9	2
Reliabili ty	.76	5	6	9
Competitive Value		5.38	5.96	7.32

An even more robust way to arrive at such results is to perform pairwise comparisons of the companies with respect to each of the functional characteristics and derive priorities using the AHP eigenvector technique. In fact, the first two steps, Customer Driven Value Analysis, and Competitive Value Analysis, can be combined into one simple AHP model to derive relative values for competing company products. This model is shown in Figure 7. The relative importance of what the customers want (size, design, reliability in this example) are derived with pairwise comparisons and the relative value of the competing companies with respect to each of the customer wants also derived with pairwise comparisons. A synthesis of the competing company values over the customer wants is shown in Figure 8.

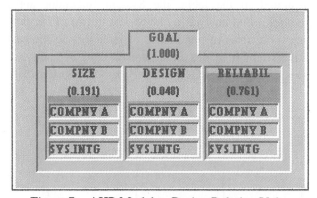

Figure 7 – AHP Model to Derive Relative Value

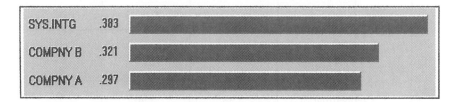

Figure 8 – Synthesized Company Values

Competitive Value Pricing

Decisions about pricing depend upon a number of considerations. Questions must be answered about how aggressive a company wants to be in gaining market share or maximizing profit. The measurement of competitive value from step 2 allows for a better understanding of the price range available for a decision.

The first step is to assign an arbitrary number to the price of the company offering the lowest value. In our example, we assume that Company A has a basic ratio of value to price of 1 and indicate it by drawing two vectors of the same length in a diagram. Company B offered a price higher than Company A, but the higher price was more than offset by the higher value offered. When pricing for value, the issue is not to compete against the lowest price, but against the best value to price ratio. The System Integrator started by puffing on the diagram a vector indicating the relative value of its products, and a vector equal to its price. The decision about pricing lies between two points. Point X indicates the same price as Company B. This price is acceptable for a very aggressive competitive posture, because System Integrator would offer a much higher value for the same price. Price X would also offer the minimum profit for System Integrator. Price Y assumes that System Integrator will offer the same value/dollar as Company B. It maximizes profit, but it does not offer any specific competitive advantage to System Integrator. The final decision was made for a price at a point between X and Y.

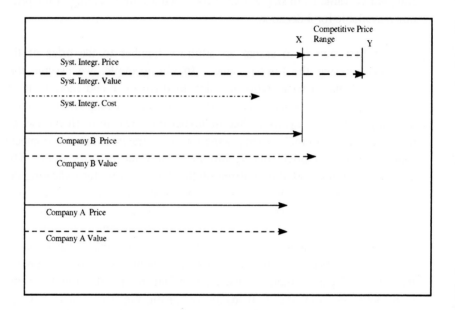

Figure 9 – Value Pricing

Another way to view the value pricing decision is to set lower and upper bounds as follows.   The lower bound, or aggressive pricing is determined either by the cost to produce the product (break-even price), or even lower if the firm is willing to lose money in order to capture market share.   The upper bound is found with the following relationship:

$$P \le \frac{V}{\max(V_i / P_i)} \text{ where:}$$

P is the maximum price such that the company's product value to price ratio is at least as large as any of the competitors,

V is the company's product value,

P_i is the price of competitor i's product,

V_i is the value of competitor i's product.

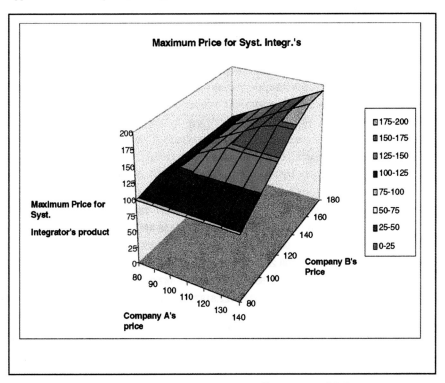

Figure 10 – Maximum Product Price vs. Competitors' Prices

A two way data table and chart are shown below in Table 2 and Figure 10 respectively.

The problem – and it is widespread – comes when managers of Zero Defects programs make a virtue of this necessity. They grow accustomed to thinking about product quality in terms of acceptable deviation from targets – instead of the consistent effort to hit them. Worse, managers may specify tolerances that are much too wide because they assume it would cost too much for the factory to narrow them. Consider the case of Ford vs. Mazda (then known as Toyo Koygo). Ford owns about 25% of Mazda and asked the Japanese company to build transmissions for a car it was selling in the United States. Both Ford and Mazda were supposed to build to identical specifications; Ford adopted Zero Defects as its standard. Yet after the cars had been on the road for a while, it became clear that Ford's transmissions

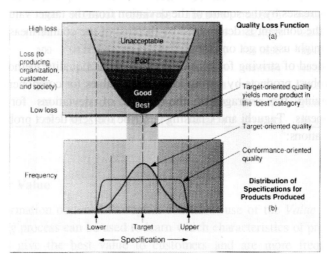

Figure 11 – Quality Loss Function

were generating far higher warranty costs and many more complaints about noise. Imagine that in some Ford transmissions, many components near the outer limits of specified tolerances – that is, fine by definitions of Zero

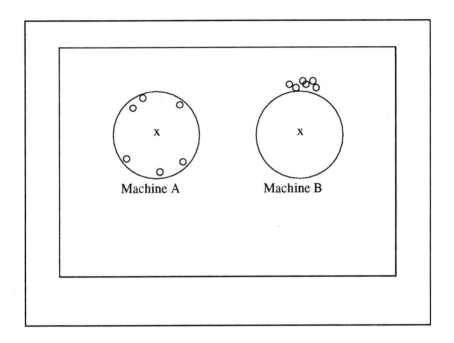

Figure 12 – Specification limits and 'defects'

Defects – were randomly assembled together. Then, many trivial deviations from the target tended to "stack up." An otherwise trivial variation in one part exacerbated a variation in another. Because of deviations, parts interacted with greater friction than they could withstand individually or with greater vibration than customers were prepared to endure. Mazda managers worked on the assumption that robustness begins from meeting exact targets *consistently* – not from always staying within tolerances.

Of course, the Mazda managers' assumptions of meeting exact targets consistently is hardly ever possible in the strict sense of its meaning.

However, it is almost always possible to come 'closer' to a target by applying additional resources. Rather than saying how close is close enough, the Taguchi approach centers around a Quality Loss Function that measures the 'loss' due to poor quality is a function of the *distance* from the target. A *distance* measure of closeness is a ratio scale measure – in contrast to the traditional good-defect measure or 0,1 which is an ordinal measure.
The Quality Loss Function, seen at the top of Figure 11 takes the general form of a quadratic formula – loss increasing as the square of the deviation from the target value – and includes customer dissatisfaction, warranty and service costs; internal inspection, repair, scrap costs, as well as costs to society[6]. Notice the difference between quality measured with the quality loss function (top of Figure 11) compared to traditional conformance-oriented quality measures (bottom of Figure 11).

Figure 12 contains another illustration of how setting specification limits[7] can lead to inferior performance. Suppose 'x' marks the target and the circle represents the 'specification limit', outside of which a part is considered to be a 'defect'. We would conclude that there are no defects for machine A, but numerous defects for machine B. Even if no corrective action were taken for parts produced with Machine B (there would be no reason to consider corrective action for Machine A because all parts are with the specification limits), products built with parts from Machine B would function no worse than those produced by Machine A since the distances from the target are about the same.

Even though Machine B is producing all defects while machine A is producing no defects, the Machine B situation is actually preferable to the Machine A situation for two reasons. The first is that by considering only whether or not parts are within specification limits, there is a clear indication for Machine B that corrective action may be warranted, an indication that cannot help but improve the product. The second reason is that there may be a simple x, y corrective action that will move most parts produced with Machine B very close to the target, while such a simple corrective action would not be available for Machine A.

---

[6] Jay Heizer and Barry Render, *Production and Opertions Management – Strategic and Tactical Decisions*, 4th Edition, Prentice Hall, p. 89.
[7] Or using aspiration levels or musts in decision problems

If the specification limit had been set a bit further out there would be no corrective action indicated for either Machine B or Machine A. A question that should come to mind is how can we avoid being subjected to the vagaries of an arbitrarily set specification limit?   Instead of using specification limits and the (ordinal) defect/no defect approach, we can look at the (ratio scale) distances from the target. The need for corrective action would be evident for both Machines. Furthermore, this need would not be subject to producing different results for slight changes in an arbitrarily set specification limit.

Taguchi's quality loss function approach relies on such 'ratio scale' measures of distance from target. However, 'distance' measures are not always easy to acquire because (1) there are typically a number of factors (or different dimensions) that need to be combined, and (2) some of the factors might be quantitative while others might be qualitative. The Analytic Hierarchy Process provides a way to derive and synthesize ratio scale measures of distance from the target on each of the applicable dimensions of product or service quality– leading to a practice of "continuous improvement." AHP hierarchies can be used to evaluate alternative approaches to producing a product or service during design or re-engineering phases, or to measure the relative outputs of the process during system operation. An outline of the use of AHP in deciding how best to move toward ones' targets is presented next.

Prioritizing Defects and Evaluating Solutions with AHP

Suppose an organization has a mission with several (numerous) specified objectives, some of which were more important than others. Also suppose the organization identifies a set of 'defects' in its processes, defects that hamper the achievement of the mission objectives. (The defects can be thought of as deviations from 'targets' discussed above). Further suppose the organization has identified a set of 'solutions' that can be applied to mitigate defects. How can the organization decide which solutions to implement subject to budgetary constraints?

A rational approach to such a problem requires ratio scale measure of the relative importance of the mission objectives; ratio scale measures of the impacts of the defects on the mission objectives, and ratio scale measures of the mitigating effects of the solutions on each of the defects. AHP can be applied to derive such ratio scale measures, which can then be used in a resource allocation optimization. The process is described next.

A hierarchy of mission objectives, sub-objectives, sub-sub-objectives, is established. Since the defects, d_i i= 1, 2, ... n will typically be too large in number to compare in a pairwise fashion, rating intensities can be defined for the lowest level of the hierarchy. The intensities will be used to rate the impact that each defect has on each of the lowest level sub-objectives.

After pairwise comparisons are made to derive ratio scale priorities for the factors in the hierarchy, ratio scale priorities are derived for the defects by rating each defect against the lowest level subobjectives in the hierarchy. We will refer to the priority of the ith defect as d_i below.

We turn now to the set of possible solutions, s_1, s_2, ... s_m each with a cost c_1, c_2, ... c_m. Considering each defect in turn, we must determine the fraction of the defect that each applicable solution can mitigate. If 'engineering' judgment is not adequate to estimate this factor, an AHP hierarchy can be constructed to derive ratio scale measures for the importance of the factors that contribute to the defect, as well as ratio scale measures for the relative effectiveness of the solutions in addressing each factor. If many solutions are applicable, the ratings approach can be used. An 'ideal' solution, one that would mitigate each factor entirely, is included in the set of solutions being evaluated so that the resulting priorities can be normalized – dividing by the priority of the ideal solution – in order to translate the priorities of the solutions to percent mitigating measures. We refer to the mitigating effect of solution j on defect i as $m_{j,i}$ below.

Resource Allocation:

$$\text{minimize} \sum_{i=1}^{n} d_i * \left(1 - \sum_{j=1}^{m} s_j * m_{j,i} \right)$$

subject to:

$$\sum_{j=1}^{m} c_j * s_j \leq F$$

$s_j = 0,1$
where:

d_i is the priority of the ith defect
$m_{i,j}$ is the mitigating effect of solution j on defect i
c_j is the cost of solution j
F is the available funds.

When two or more solutions are dependent, they are evaluated as combinations. For example, if there are three solutions available to address a particular deficiency, we can define and evaluate the mitigating effect of each of the 2^3-1 combinations in the set of possible combinations. The combinations, rather than the individual solutions, are considered for implementation in the resource allocation, and a constraint is added to permit no more than one of these combinations to be implemented. There can be many such combination sets.

If *all* solutions were dependent and applicable to every deficiency, a limiting case, there would be 2^n-1 combinations to consider for each deficiency, a daunting task. The optimization would be trivial, as only one of the combinations can be included.

Finally, in the spirit of Taguchi's quality loss function described above, the objective function can be modified to consider the square of the remaining deficiencies, resulting in a non-linear optimization problem.

Quality Function Deployment and The House of Quality

In their article *The House of Quality*[8], John Hauser and Don Clausing describe how marketers and engineers can better talk to each other and, in the process, improve product and process design. The 'house of quality' (see Figure 13) is but one 'house' in a chain of houses that make up Quality Function Deployment (QFD), a management approach that originated in 1972 at Mitsubishi's Kobe shipyard site. QFD consists of planning and communication routines to design, manufacture, and market those goods and services that customers will want to purchase – those they judge to be high *quality*. But what can a large organization actually *do* to manufacture high quality products or services? The doing will involve people from throughout the organization, each performing specific *functions*. Putting these functions into action is called *deployment*. QFD addressed the *deployment* of organizational *functions* in order to produce *quality* products or services[9] The deployment requires communication between people having different functional responsibilities. There can be several transformations of 'inputs' to 'outputs', each performed in a 'house'[10] as depicted in Figure 13 and Table 3.

---

[8] Hausing, John R., and Clausing, Don, "The House of Quality", *Harvard Business Review*, May-June 1988, p 63-73.
[9] We can add – and that best meets organizational objectives.
[10] The word house is used because the transformation from inputs to outputs can be viewed as a matrix with a 'roof' representing interactions among outputs – the whole of which looks like a house.

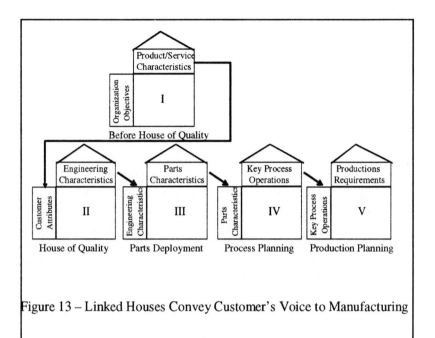

Figure 13 – Linked Houses Convey Customer's Voice to Manufacturing

Table 3 – Linked Houses

Input	'House'	Output
Organizational objectives	Before the house of quality	Product / service characteristics referred to as 'customer attributes'
Customer Attributes	House of quality	Engineering characteristics
Engineering characteristics	Parts deployment	Parts characteristics
Parts characteristics	Process planning	Key process operations
Key process operations	Production planning	Production requirements

An example of the transformation of organization objectives to customer attributes is given on page 340, in a house referred to as 'Before the House of Quality'. Corporate objectives are prioritized to determine the relative importance of market segments. These market segment priorities are then used to synthesize the product / service characteristics (referred to as 'customer attributes') of the market segments. The resulting customer attributes are the inputs to the next house, the House of Quality.

David Garvin noted that there are many dimensions to what a consumer means by quality and that it is a major challenge to design products that satisfy all of those at once.[11] Hauser and Clausing wrote:

"Before the industrial revolution, producers were close to their customers. Marketing, engineering and manufacturing were integrated – in the same individual.   Today's fifedoms are mainly inside corporations. Marketing people have their domain, engineers theirs." Usually, managerial functions remain disconnected, producing a costly and demoralizing environment in which product quality and the quality of the production process itself suffer.".... "Top executives are learning that the use of interfunctional teams benefits design. But if top management *could* get marketing, designing, and manufacturing executives to sit down together, what should these people talk about? How could they get their meeting off the ground?"[12]

The house of quality is a communication vehicle for marketing and design personnel that translates customer attributes or CA's (what customers say in describing desirable product characteristics) into engineering characteristics (EC's) that specify how the product (or service) can be designed to best meet what the customer means by quality. In other words, the marketing domain tells us what to do, the engineering domain tells us how to do it and the house of quality helps translate from the language of marketing to the language of the engineer.

Customer attributes appearing in the left part of the house of quality, can be grouped into bundles (and sub-bundles) of attributes, not all of which are

---

[11] David A. Gavin, "Competing on the Eight Dimensions of Quality," HBR November-December 1987, p. 101.
[12] Hausing, John R., and Clausing, Don, "The House of Quality", *Harvard Business Review*, May-June 1988, p 64.

equally important. Measures of the relative importance of the customer attributes must be obtained. Traditionally, this has been done by assigning values to the customer attributes from some arbitrary scale.. Difficulties in deriving accurate measures with such traditional approaches, particularly when more than just a few factors are involved, were discussed on pages 5 and 41. Measures derived with an AHP model will more accurately reflect the judgments of the participants, and will produce ratio measures as well. The AHP model alternatives are the individual customer attributes, clustered into groups and subgroups as necessary. The relative importance of the clusters can be determined by pairwise comparisons with respect to customers in general, or, if desired, with respect to prioritized market segments. (The priorities of the market segments being determined through pairwise comparisons with respect to organizational objectives in what Zultner calls before the house of quality (see Table 3, Figure 13, and 'Before the House', on page 340).

Along the top of the house of quality the interfunctional team lists those engineering characteristics that will best deliver the desired customer attributes. Designers often have to trade off one benefit against another. This tradeoff involves deriving priorities for the engineering characteristics with respect to the each of the customer attributes. This process, performed by an interfunctional team of marketing and engineering personnel – traditionally involves putting check marks or scores in the body of the house, but can be readily improved with an AHP model. The overall priorities of the engineering characteristics are determined by multiplying priorities of the engineering characteristics by the respective priorities of the customer attributes and then summing over the customer attributes – again part of the AHP process. This transformation of input measures into output measures in the house of quality, as well as in the other 'linked houses' depicted in Table 3 and Figure 13, require that the input measures and measures derived within each 'house' be ratio level measures. Otherwise, the results are mathematical meaningless and may distort the data and judgments used in the process (see discussion beginning on page 31. While we can be confident that priorities derived with AHP models are ratio level measures, we have no such confidence with the traditional approaches such as ordinal scales, check marks, or symbols to which arbitrary numbers are

assigned[13].   Since there is no reason to believe that these numbers or
symbols possess interval or ratio scale properties, the multiplication of these
numbers can produce mathematically meaningless results.

The 'roof' matrix of the house of quality helps engineers specify some
of the inter-relationships between the engineering features. In general there
can be numerous interactions between customer attributes and engineering
characteristics. For example, an engineer's change of the gear ratio on a car
window may make the window motor smaller, the door lighter, but the
window will go up and down more slowly. The Analytic Network Process
(ANP), discussed on page 324 is a powerful tool that has potential in
modeling such interactions.

A series of linked 'houses', shown in Figure 13, can convey the
customer's voice through to manufacturing. Each house having the 'whats'
in the rows and the 'hows' in the columns can be implemented with an AHP
model. For example, customer attributes, the rows of the house of quality
are used to prioritize engineering attributes, or the columns of the house of
quality. Subsequently, the 'hows' from our house of quality become the
'whats' of another house, one mainly concerned with detailed product
design. Engineering characteristics like foot-pounds of closing energy can
become the rows in a parts deployment house, while parts characteristics –
like hinge properties or the thickness of the weather stripping – become the
columns" or the 'hows'.   The process can continue to a third and fourth
phase as the 'hows' of one stage become the 'whats' of the next. Weather-
stripping thickness – a 'how' in the parts house- becomes a 'what' in a
process planning house. Important process operations, like 'rpm of the
extruder producing the weather stripping' become the 'hows.' In the las
phase, production planning, the key process operations, like 'rpm of the
extruder," become the 'whats,' and production requirements – knob
controls, operating training, maintenance – become the 'hows.' The linked

---

[13] Traditional quality function deployment uses numbers such as 1,3, and 9, or symbols to fill in the
matrix

houses implicitly convey the voice of the customer through to manufacturing[14].

Benchmarking

One aspect of a TQM effort that is instrumental in gaining or maintaining a competitive advantage is the comparison or benchmarking of *key business processes* with other best-of-breed companies and organizations[15]. Processes can be defined as key business activities that are needed to run an enterprise. Processes are activities that convert inputs, such as materials, resources, information, etc., into outputs (products and services) for the customer. In order to evaluate and assure that one has the best processes (and decide what improvements are needed), it is necessary to make comparisons with other best-of-breed companies and organizations. Comparisons should be made with the best regardless of industry membership or geography. Finding out what other companies are doing to operate their key business processes, setting the right goals, and achieving these goals, is a key strategy that will help put an enterprise on the road to being *best*.

It is important to thoroughly understand processes that are to be benchmarked before contacting companies with which to make comparisons. Without proper preparation, each member of a benchmarking team would have their own list of priorities to focus on and the utility of the results would be minimal. In order to maximize the return on benchmarking resources and achieve significant results, a consensus has to be developed as to what it means to be "best". This involves the evaluation and synthesis of many factors, both quantitative and qualitative. The AHP methodology was used by the IBM Rochester Minnesota's computer integrated manufacturing (CIM) process team to articulate what needed to be accomplished to be the best. The approach consisted of the following steps:.

1. Develop a hierarchical structure or model of the CIM processes and define relationships.

---

[14] Hausing, John R., and Clausing, Don, "The House of Quality", *Harvard Business Review*, May-June 1988, p73.
[15] Eyrich, H.G., "Benchmarking to Become the Best of Breed," Manufacturing Systems magazine, April 1991.

2. Compare the relative importance of hierarchical factors.
3. Synthesize the comparisons to arrive at overall weights for deciding what requirements are the most important for success.

The CIM hierarchy (see Figure 14) was developed by a team of leading experts at IBM Rochester. The expertise of the team members contributed significantly to the validity of the model. The goal of the hierarchical model (level 0), decided through consensus is *to be the best computer integrated manufacturer--globally.*

The level below the goal (level 1) contains four sub-goals that add substance to the main goal: quality (total quality control), responsiveness (timely customer solutions), flexible (adapting to changing business needs) and cost (product cost). The next level (level 2) contains the critical success factors for achieving the sub-goals: process (business activities needed to run an enterprise), methodology (key manufacturing techniques), integration (system solution for total enterprise), management systems (plans, controls, measurements, resources, support, etc), and technology (CIM architecture & technology). Because more granularity of the critical success factors was needed, the hierarchy was further decomposed by identifying requirements (level 3 of the hierarchy). This gave greater definition of what had to be done to achieve the sub-goals and main goal.

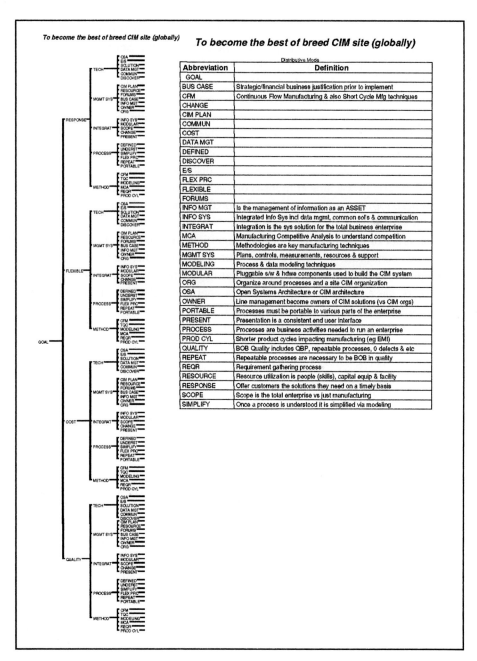

To become the best of breed CIM site (globally)

Distributive Mode

Abbreviation	Definition
GOAL	
BUS CASE	Strategic/financial business justification prior to implement
CFM	Continuous Flow Manufacturing & also Short Cycle Mfg techniques
CHANGE	
CIM PLAN	
COMMUN	
COST	
DATA MGT	
DEFINED	
DISCOVER	
E/S	
FLEX PRC	
FLEXIBLE	
FORUMS	
INFO MGT	Is the management of information as an ASSET
INFO SYS	Integrated Info Sys incl data mgmt, common sol's & communication
INTEGRAT	Integration is the sys solution for the total business enterprise
MCA	Manufacturing Competitive Analysis to understand competition
METHOD	Methodologies are key manufacturing techniques
MGMT SYS	Plans, controls, measurements, resources & support
MODELING	Process & data modeling techniques
MODULAR	Pluggable s/w & hdwe components used to build the CIM system
ORG	Organize around processes and a site CIM organization
OSA	Open Systems Architecture or CIM architecture
OWNER	Line management become owners of CIM solutions (vs CIM orgs)
PORTABLE	Processes must be portable to various parts of the enterprise
PRESENT	Presentation is a consistent end user interface
PROCESS	Processes are business activities needed to run an enterprise
PROD CYL	Shorter product cycles impacting manufacturing (eg EMI)
QUALITY	BOB Quality includes QBP, repeatable processes, 0 defects & etc
REPEAT	Repeatable processes are necessary to be BOB in quality
REQR	Requirement gathering process
RESOURCE	Resource utilization is people (skills), capital equip & facility
RESPONSE	Offer customers the solutions they need on a timely basis
SCOPE	Scope is the total enterprise vs just manufacturing
SIMPLIFY	Once a process is understood it is simplified via modeling

Figure 14 – CIM Hierarchy

After the hierarchy was established, a team of 10 people were hand selected for their expertise to perform the comparisons. Several people who designed the hierarchy were included on this comparison team in order to insure continuity. Interactive sessions were held in which both subjective and objective information were used to make the comparative judgments. The knowledge and experience of the participants were leveraged through consensus which resulted in the best possible judgments.

Finally, the relative importance of the *requirements* was evaluated for each critical success factor. Informative discussions took place among the CIM experts in reaching consensus on each of 350 pairwise comparisons. A synthesis of the priorities produced global priorities (priorities with respect to the goal) and is shown in Figure 15. Not only did these results tell us the rank order of requirements, but more significantly, we knew *how much* each would contribute to the goal. For example, the heavily weighted requirement *define*, which means to define business processes and identify owners, has a global priority of 0.099 or approximately 10% of the goal. As a result of structuring, we not only identified requirements, but we decided on what the priorities should be (on a ratio scale) for achieving the goal.

Benchmarking Effort Results

AHP helped provide structure to the benchmarking effort. It not only helped identify what had to be done to be best, but also helped prioritize (on a ratio scale) the importance of each critical success factor and requirement. Lacking this structure, each benchmarking member would have had their own list of priorities, or no list at all, making the teams much less effective. The AHP hierarchical model articulated what was required to become best. In addition to giving the benchmarking teams focus, AHP also assisted with identifying the best companies to benchmark and with setting benchmarking agendas. Finally the AHP results provided a framework to summarize the benchmarking teams' findings. A maturity index (not discussed here) facilitated comparison with other companies, making gaps clearly visible. Without a maturity index, it would have been difficult to make these comparisons from team notes, especially when comparing multiple companies. The maturity index also helped identify what companies to approach for follow-up visits. The structuring methodology described in this paper complemented the overall benchmarking developed at IBM Rochester, Minnesota. Once these processes were structured, the IBM Rochester model was used in making comparisons with leading companies around the world. The goals set and achieved from the benchmarking process enhanced IBM's ability to be the *best* in mid-range computers and played a significant role in IBM's winning the Malcolm Baldrige National Quality Award in 1990.

To become the best of breed CIM site (globally)

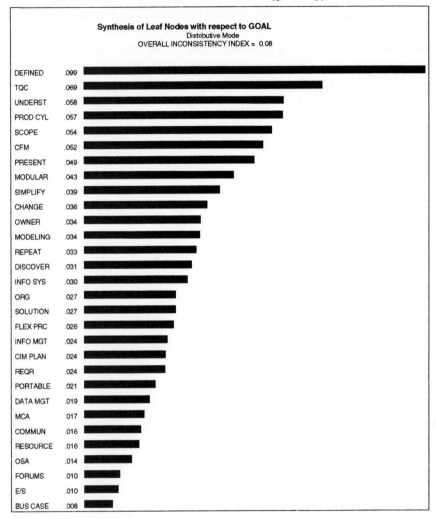

Figure 15 – Overall Priorities

Cause and Effect or Fishbone diagrams

A cause-and-effect diagram (also known as an Ishikawa diagram or Fishbone chart) is a tool for identifying possible causes of quality problems. In a sense, the Latrobe Steel Company system discussed above is very similar but serves to identified variables to improve yield rather than variables that are causing quality problems. Figure 16 is a fishbone chart for problems in airline customer service. When drawn with the lines on an angle, the shape of the diagram resembles the bones of a fish, hence the name fishbone chart. Each 'bone' represents a possible source of error. Certain 'bones' can have sub-bones. In essence, this is just an AHP diagram. The fishbone diagram in Figure 16 has four main categories applicable to many problems – these four 'M's are: material, machinery/equipment, manpower, and methods. Whereas fishbone diagrams like this are often used only as check lists, an AHP model of a fishbone diagram can be used to elicit expert judgment in order to derive priorities for the possible causes or to allocate resources if there are several causes, each requiring some intervention. Figure 17is a portion of a fishbone diagram for causes of Midway Airlines flight departure delay. This diagram is more specific than that in Figure 16 and contains an additional level of factors.

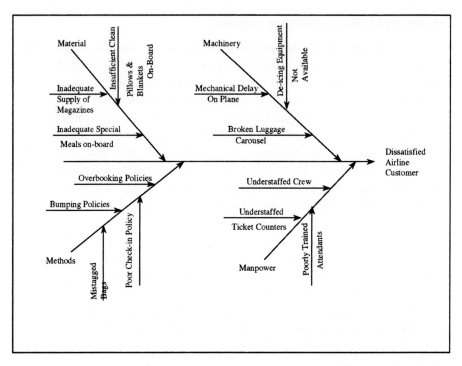

Figure 16 – Fishbone chart for problems in airline customer service

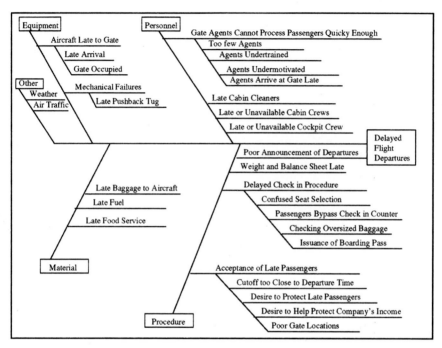

Figure 17 – Midway Airlines flight departure delay

Appendix II

Case Studies

AHP at the Inter-American Development Bank[1]

INTRODUCTION

In addition to its use in face-to-face meeting environments, the Analytic Hierarchy Process (AHP) has also been successfully used in distributed group decision support (DGDS) environments. This section presents one of several applications of AHP in DGDS environments at the Inter-American Development Bank (IDB).[2] The Bank appointed project managers and organized both advisory committees and project teams to work on these important procurement decisions:

- selection of the best alternative for the automation of its investment activities
- selection of the best alternative for the automation of its bank account reconciliation function
- selection of the best alternative for the implementation of an electronic image management system
- selection of an external audit company
- selection of a provider of VSAT (satellite) communications
- selection of a provider of Employee Health Insurance

The advisory committees were made up primarily of managers of the organizational units that would be interested in the solution to be implemented. The initial role of an advisory committee was to provide

---

[1] Lauro Lage-Filho. Dr. Lage, an expert in decision support works as a consultant for the Inter-American Development Bank. The opinions expressed in this paper are the author's, and do not necessarily reflect the views of the Inter-American Development Bank.

[2] The Inter-American Development Bank, the oldest and largest regional multilateral development institution, was established in 1959 to help accelerate economic and social development in Latin America and the Caribbean. In carrying out its mission, the Bank has mobilized financing for projects that represent a total investment of $240 billion. Annual lending has grown dramatically from the $294 million in loans approved in 1961 to $10 billion in 1998.

guidance to the project team about the project goal, the decision-making process, and the schedule to be followed. The advisory committee members were also responsible for assessing the relative importance of the selection criteria.

The project teams were composed of staff and external consultants working in the units represented in the advisory committees. Project team members had in-depth knowledge of the problem to be solved and were responsible for evaluating the preference for the alternatives regarding the criteria previously established or approved by the advisory committees. Subsequently, the advisory committees would review and approve the technical evaluations performed by the project teams and prepare recommendations to support the selected alternative. The account reconciliation project is presented next.

THE ACCOUNT RECONCILIATION PROJECT

The IDB had been performing its account reconciliation function through a manual process requiring seven officers working ten days each month. The process was complex and tedious owing to the large and growing number of accounts (about 250), a majority of them dealing in U.S., Canadian, Japanese, or European currencies.

In 1993, the Accounting Division proposed the automation of the reconciliation process after identifying the following benefits for the project: (1) savings of over $100,000 a year in staff time; (2) ability to cope with the expected increase of transactions without hiring additional staff; (3) faster resolution of outstanding problems; (4) daily account balancing for critical bank accounts; and (5) more effective managerial controls.

The following schedule of activities was developed for the project:

10/14	Introduce DGDS environment to participants
10/15	Implement computer conference
10/18-10/27	Attend vendors' demonstrations of the alternatives
10/19-11/04	Clarify Problem Statement and objectives
	Discuss alternatives' pros and cons
10/28-11/05	Structure AHP model

11/08   Approve AHP model
Establish relative importance of objectives (AC members, in-groups)
Establish preference for the alternatives (PT members, individually)
Consolidate evaluations (geometric means)

11/12   Discuss and approve results (PT)
Present recommendation to the AC

Decision Support Environment

The main components of the DGDS environment[3] used by the Bank are: (1) the method for the decision-making process, which is centered on the AHP and implements Herbert Simon's classic Intelligence, Design, and Choice Phases providing overall orientation to the decision-makers (see Table 1); (2) the Expert Choice computer program that helps to structure and solve decision problems; (3) the Lotus Notes computer program that supports the implementation of a computer conference and enables decision-makers to participate in the decision process at the time and location of their convenience; and (4) network and communications software.

The DGDS environment was presented to members of the advisory committee and project team in a four-hour, "hands-on" seminar. AHP concepts were presented as well as techniques for making the computer conference effective. To illustrate the method, participants were asked to tackle a personal decision problem using the proposed approach. The participants worked on the purchase of a new home being considered by one of them. The exercise was very realistic and was a positive motivator.

---

[3] Lauro Lage-Filho, *A Group Decision Support Environment Facilitating Decision-making Distributed in Time and Space. Doctoral Dissertation.* (Washington: The George Washington University, 1994).

Table 1 – Method

Intelligence Phase

- Discuss a preliminary problem statement to:
  obtain an enriched and consensual view of the problem.

Design Phase

- Discuss an initial list of alternatives to:
  obtain a revised list of alternatives;
  obtain an initial set of objectives/criteria.
- Discuss an initial set of objectives/criteria to:
  obtain a revised set of objectives/criteria.

Choice Phase

- Structure one or more AHP/Expert Choice models to:
  obtain common (group) Expert Choice model(s).
- Elicit individual judgments.
- Incorporate the geometric mean of the individual judgments into the
  combined Expert Choice model and synthesize the priorities.
- Discuss and approve the results and analyses.
- Document the decision for justification and control.

The intelligence, design and choice phases of the method are described next. The description, although focused on the account reconciliation project, also presents concepts applicable to generic decision problems.

Intelligence Phase

This phase, concerned with identifying the problem or opportunity, was conducted through a Lotus Notes computer conference. However, any mixture of face-to-face and computer conference sessions is possible. Regardless of the mode, it is important to give the group the opportunity to discuss, understand, and define the problem fully. During the intelligence phase, the group can reframe the problem or even define a new one. The problem statement resulting from the computer conference read:

> The team will evaluate and select an account reconciliation package to
> automate the reconciliation process conducted by the accounting section of
> the IDB. The system will match bank statement transactions received via
> SWIFT or manually entered from printed statements to cash transactions

recorded in the general ledger. This will help to identify discrepancies and assist in subsequent investigations. The system to be selected should also be able to handle other types of reconciliation but the initial scope of the project will be limited to the general ledger/bank statement reconciliation.

Design Phase

Here the group defined its objectives/criteria and alternatives. Some problems have a list of alternatives defined a priori as in this case, while other problems do not and will benefit from the definition of objectives before any alternative is even considered.

Five half-day vendor demonstrations of alternatives were made during a two-week period. Advisory committee and project team members attending these sessions used the computer conference to comment on the pros and cons of the demonstrated alternatives. They entered their comments as promptly as possible, preferably the same day of the session. A computer conference instruction advised participants to enter their own comments before reading the comments of others in order to better capture first impressions. An interactive exchange of ideas followed.

Choice Phase

The AHP served as the foundation of the choice phase. One of the strengths of the AHP is to provide a clear, organized, and logical view of the decision problem. However, there is no one 'right' view as a problem can be represented in several ways and the group members must exert some creativity[4].

The structuring of the AHP model started immediately after the demonstration period. There were four two-hour face-to-face meetings in addition to the highly active computer conferencing. Alternatives' pros and

---

[4] Thomas L. Saaty, "How to make a decision: The Analytic Hierarchy Process," *European Journal of Operational Research* 48, (1990): 9-26.

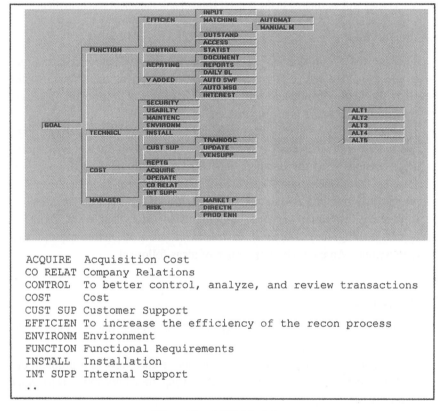

ACQUIRE   Acquisition Cost
CO RELAT Company Relations
CONTROL   To better control, analyze, and review transactions
COST   Cost
CUST SUP Customer Support
EFFICIEN To increase the efficiency of the recon process
ENVIRONM Environment
FUNCTION Functional Requirements
INSTALL   Installation
INT SUPP Internal Support
..

Figure 1 – AHP Model

cons discussed during the design phase were used to identify objectives to build the model. Participants offered preliminary versions of decision models and the ensuing discussion regarding these proposed models led to an improved, well understood, and agreed upon group model. The objectives were clustered into a hierarchical representation shown in Figure 1.

The goal, or first level of the model, was to select the best alternative to automate the Bank's account reconciliation process. Below the goal are levels that include the objectives and sub-objectives (or criteria) used to evaluate the relative preference for the alternatives.

The major objectives were functional requirements, technical requirements, cost, and managerial considerations:

Functional requirements covered the users' business needs, including specific requirements in Matching Efficiency, Control and Reporting. Additionally, *functional requirements* considered "value-added" features of the alternatives, such as automation of internal and external message creation, availability of daily balance reports, and interest calculation. The majority of these sub-objectives were further broken down to allow a full, detailed analysis.

Technical requirements addressed important system features, such as security, usability, maintainability, computing environment, installation process, customer support, and reporting capabilities.

Cost encompassed acquisition and operational costs. Acquisition cost is the cost of hardware and software required by the alternative. Operational cost is the cost to operate and support the system over a five-year period.

Managerial considerations focused on company relations, internal support, and risk appraisal. The *risk appraisal* sub-objective was further broken down into *market penetration, direction,* and *product enhancements.*

The lowest level of the model contained the alternatives to be evaluated: ALT1, ALT2, ALT3, ALT4, and ALT5.

Determination of the Importance of the Objectives

The determination of the relative importance of the first-level objectives (*Functional Requirements, Technical Requirements, Cost,* and *Managerial Considerations*) and of the sub-objectives related to *Cost* and *Managerial Considerations* was made by members of the advisory committee, grouped according to the organizational unit they represented: Cashier's Division (CSH), Accounting Division (ACC), and Financial MIS Division (IRM).

Members of each group worked together and used Expert Choice to derive the priorities of the objectives/sub-objectives. The geometric means of these priorities were calculated to represent the position of the advisory committee. The ACC group members established the relative importance of the sub-objectives under *Functional Requirements* and the IRM group members established the relative importance of the sub-objectives under *Technical Requirements*. In order to avoid influencing those evaluating the alternatives, the final priorities of the combined model were not calculated until preference for the alternatives had been established.

Evaluation of the Alternatives

After the advisory committee approved the AHP model, evaluations were made about the relative preference for the alternatives with respect to each of the lowest level sub-objectives. The evaluators, project team members, were grouped according to their area of expertise: functional requirements, technical requirements, cost, and managerial considerations. Prior to the evaluation, the group members organized the computer conference messages about the alternatives' pros and cons according to the relevant sub-objective(s). Additional information was added when appropriate. Guidance for the evaluation was provided via the computer conference. Evaluators were advised to maintain their focus on the sub-objective being considered and to refer to the computer conference discussions related to that aspect of the AHP model being evaluated. The computer conference database had 47 discussion items with 484 responses – a printout of the conference generated 146 single-spaced pages.

Group members worked sometimes jointly and sometimes separately in establishing their preference for the alternatives. Although there are advantages to making judgments in a group atmosphere, there are also, advantages in having the group members make judgments separately. For example, when working individually, the evaluators will have an opportunity to do their analysis and thus contribute their knowledge at their most productive time and pace, while being protected from any disturbing behavior of other members, common in group settings.[5] Furthermore, they will be able to use resources generally not available to them at meetings. Finally, they will become fully prepared to discuss their evaluations in a later group session.

Comparisons of the alternatives with respect to sub-objectives under *Functional Requirements* and *Technical Requirements* were made in two steps. First, the evaluators worked separately. Next, the participant's evaluations were combined by the geometric means of individual judgments. This established a convenient starting point for the group discussion that followed. The preferences for the alternatives reflected in the combined model were analyzed by the group members and compared with those in their individual models. This was done for each sub-objective immediately above the alternatives' level in the AHP models. There were two interesting possibilities. First, there were those situations when a majority of the evaluators established their preference in the "same direction" (i.e., alternative A is preferable to alternative B to some degree). In this case, the group usually readily accepted the geometric mean results. Nevertheless, it was desirable to ask the dissenters to explain their reasoning. The discussion often led to a deeper understanding of the subject and to a higher degree of consensus. Second, those rare occasions when the evaluators were divided into two (or three) groups according to their preference for an alternative. This indicated an incomplete or superficial discussion of the subject at the computer conference (or face-to-face meeting).

The evaluators chose to work together when establishing the preference for the alternatives under the other objectives of the AHP model - *Cost* and *Managerial Considerations.*

Validation of the Results

The project team held a two-hour meeting to synthesize, discuss, and validate the results. They reviewed the priorities of the main objectives derived by the advisory committee and discussed the results under each of

---

[5] Efraim Turban, *Decision Support and expert systems: Management support systems.* (New York: MacMillan, 1993).

these main objectives. The project team agreed that ALT5 should be selected. Figure 2 shows the results of the combined model. Later that day, in another two-hour meeting, the project team recommended ALT5 to the advisory committee. After thoroughly discussing the results under each of the main objectives in the model and making extensive use of the sensitivity analysis graphs, the advisory committee unanimously approved the recommendation.

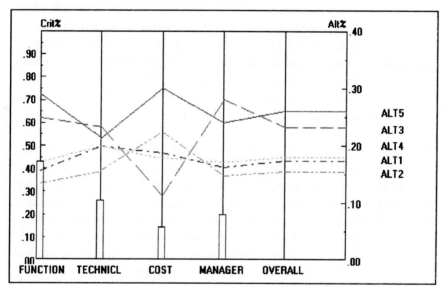

Figure 2 – Results of the AHP Model

CONCLUSION

Following the completion of the selection process, project participants compared the DGDS environment to the conventional, structured, face-to-face group decision-making process they had used before in similar projects. They perceived the DGDS approach as preferable to the face-to-face approach for group decision-making involving important and complex, real-world, decision problems. Specifically, the new approach contributed to[6]: (1) decreasing the time to reach a decision (a decision was made in little more than a month, whereas previously, project participants had been unable to make a similar decision in over a year); (2) increasing the depth of analysis; (3) increasing the degree of participation and consensus; (4) increasing task-oriented communication; and (5) decreasing the domination by a few members. The decision-makers perceived an increase in the quality of the decision and were more satisfied with the new group process.

Subsequent to this project, the approach described here has been used to support several other decisions by the Bank, including those related to the procurement of goods and services. Usually, the AHP model is included in the Request for a Proposal document and defines the structure of the proposal that the bidders will present. As a consequence, the proposals are homogeneous and comparable and the evaluation process is rational and transparent. The results have been well accepted internally as well as by the bidders -- no protests have been raised to the IDB. Also, as the approach became familiar to upper management, an increasing number of applications linked to the Bank's operations in its member countries is being made. In one such application, for example, Brazilian authorities used the approach to establish priorities for the preservation of Historic Cities and in another application the process was used by Venezuelan authorities to allocate resources for social projects.

---

[6] Lage-Filho, *Doctoral Dissertation.*

AHP For Future Navy Sea-Based Platforms[7]

In March of 1996, the Undersecretary of Defense for Acquisition authorized the Navy to enter concept exploration for a new sea-basing platform designated as CVX. The general missions of sea-based platforms are to:

- Provide credible, sustainable, independent forward presence during peace time without access to land bases;
- Operate as the cornerstone of a joint and/or allied maritime expeditionary force in response to crises; and
- Carry the war to the enemy through joint multi-mission offensive operations by:
    - Being able to operate and support aircraft in attacks on enemy forces ashore, afloat, or submerged independent of forward-based land facilities;
    - Protecting friendly forces from enemy attack, through the establishment and maintenance of battlespace dominance independent of forward-based land facilities; and
    - Engaging in sustained operations in support of the United States and its Allies independent of forward-based land forces.

To develop this sea-based aviation platform the Navy has created a long-term program to assess alternative platforms and technologies that balances risk and affordability and actively solicits Fleet and industry participation.

In order to support CVX development with an affordable and timely solution, the CVX Strategy-to-Task-to-Technology Process was adopted. The goal of this process is to develop an investment strategy for research and development that will support acquisition of a new class of carriers and

---

[7] Earl Hacker, Whitney, Bradley & Brown, Inc.,Vienna, VA 22182

meet the needs of the Navy in the 21st Century. This process embraces the concepts of Quality Function Deployment (QFD) . QFD is a systematic approach used by teams to develop products and the supporting processes based on the demands of the customer and the competitive marketplace. In developing a complex system such as an aircraft carrier, one of the most difficult tasks is to capture the warfighting needs in a series of specifications. The customer's vision is often different than what the engineer perceives are the requirements and priorities.

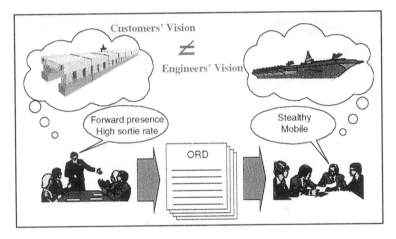

Figure 3 – Typical Problem

QFD is essentially a communication tool. If implemented properly, the engineer gains an in-depth understanding of the real needs and priorities of the "Fleet" (customer) and the problem is solved.

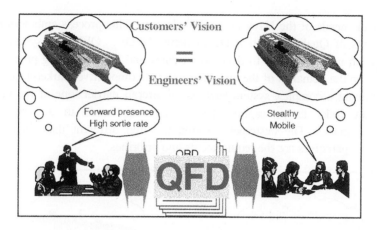

Figure 4 – Interfacing Customer and Engineering views with QFD

QFD is particularly useful for complex systems when there are multiple customers and users, conflicting user priorities, multiple feasible solutions, no quantified solutions in place, conflicting potential solutions, multiple disciplines involved, and no readily quantified user requirements. Such is the case with CVX. QFD is being used in the CVX process to document an objective definition of the users' need and priorities. As a result of early use of QFD in the investment strategy, the concurrent engineering process is strengthened through early definition of goals based on user needs, the visualization of complex system tradeoffs, highlighting of key issues, the gathering of "tribal" knowledge in a reusable database, early involvement of the Fleet and developers, and the early creation of teams and the facilitation of communications.

Figure 5 depicts the "house of quality" used in QFD.

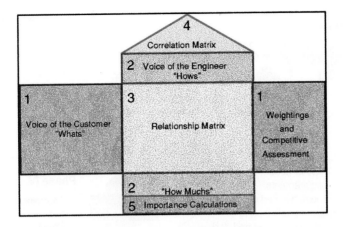

Figure 5 – House of Quality Methodology – AHP

The CVX process uses the Analytic Hierarchy Process (AHP) as a tool for capturing the voice of the "customer" -- the Fleet and integrating this with the voice of the design engineers and voice of the program management office. The methodology to accomplish this process consists of a thirteen-step process conducted in four phases as depicted in Figure 6.

The CVX Strategy-to-Task-to-Technology process (STT) establishes explicit linkage between "warfighter" needs and technology solutions by combining Strategy-to-Task methodology, functional attributes of CVX, and enabling research and development technologies in a prioritization process. Its output is used to help guide budget discussions and provide a framework for determining those technologies to apply to CVX research and development.

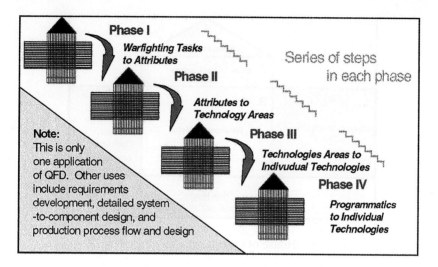

Figure 6 – Methodology Phases

To implement this process *Team Expert Choice* software was used to develop a linkage between and priorities of war fighting tasks and carrier attributes, technology areas, and technologies within each technology area. Once the individual technology priorities were developed, an investment strategy was adopted.

Carrier Attribute Prioritization

The STT methodology developed by RAND provides a linkage between our national goals and the tactical tasks that CVX must be capable of accomplishing in 2013. Figure 7 provides an overview of this STT linkage. The Rand STT was refined by the U.S. Army and then modified for the joint arena and adopted by the Joint Chiefs of Staff as the Universal Joint Task List(UJTL).

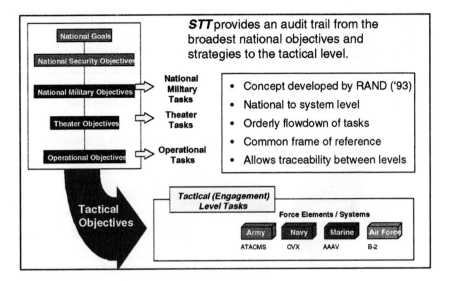

Figure 7 – Strategy-to-Task

Step 1 –Determine Appropriate CVX Tasks

In **Step 1** of the process, the UJTL tactical tasks were arranged in a hierarchy model as described in the UJTL. The appropriate level of detail generally ran to the 3rd level of the UJTL hierarchy. The structure is depicted in Figure 8.

Step 2 –Prioritize CVX Tasks

Two Fleet Process Teams (FPTs) were created to prioritize CVX tasks – one on the East Coast and one on the West Coast.

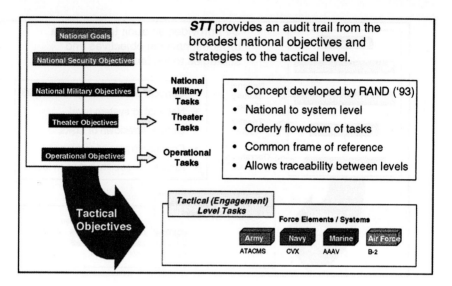

Figure 8 – CVX Tasks

Each FPT was made up of "war fighters" -- active duty officers experienced in a wide range of naval aviation and naval surface fields. Once the AHP hierarchy was established and the task definitions agreed upon and understood, the FPTs validated and prioritized the tasks.

East Coast FPT	West Coast FPT
• COMCARGRU 8	• COMNAVAIRPAC
• USS America	• COMHSWINGPAC
• USS Dwight D. Eisenhower	• COMSEACTLWINGPAC
• COMNAVAIRLANT	• COMAEWWINGPAC
• USS Enterprise	• COMCARGRU 7
• PEO CLA/PMA-378	• HQMC APP
• CINCLANTFLT	• USS Constellation
• PEO CLA/PMS-312	• SWATSCOLPAC
• COMCARGRU 4	• COMTHIRDFLT
• OPNAV N885	• COMNAVSPECWARGRU 2
• USS Theodore Roosevelt	• COMCRUDESGRU 1
• COMOPTEVFOR	
• COMSECONDFLT	
• HQMC APW	

Figure 9 – Fleet Process Team Participation

The Analytical Hierarchy Process (AHP), using Team Expert Choice with electronic scoring devices, supported the STT-to-Technology Process problem of prioritizing many tasks by arranging them into several levels and then guiding participants through a series of pairwise comparison judgments to express the relative priorities or importance of the CVX tasks and sub-tasks in the hierarchy. Each comparison began with discussion, led by a facilitator and keypads were used so that participants could enter their judgments simultaneously.

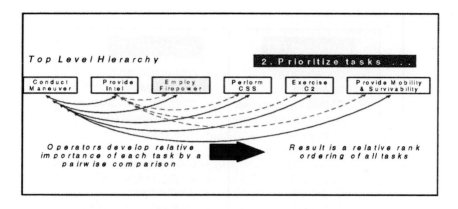

Figure 10 – Pairwise Comparison

The many judgments of FPT participants were synthesized to derive a single priority for each of the CVX tasks and sub-tasks. Metrics such as the geometric mean of each set of judgments, the geometric variance, the distribution of individual participant votes, and the consistency of the group as a whole were examined. These metrics were helpful in guiding discussion when large variations and wide distributions existed. An example screen is depicted in Figure 11. The number of participants and the discussions prior to voting kept the voting results very consistent throughout the entire voting process. Following any discussion, participants were allowed to revote. This was very beneficial by pointing out areas of concern and misconceptions and for providing "duty experts" an opportunity to voice their opinions if they differed from the initial voting results.

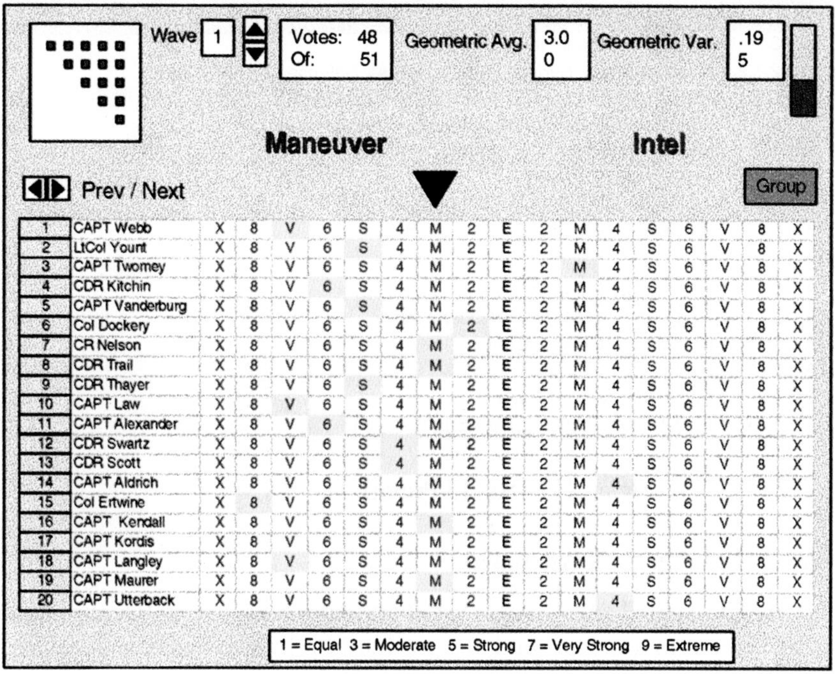

		Maneuver												Intel		
1	CAPT Webb	X	8	V	6	S	4	M	2	E	2	M	4	S	6	V	8	X
2	LtCol Yount	X	8	V	6	S	4	M	2	E	2	M	4	S	6	V	8	X
3	CAPT Twomey	X	8	V	6	S	4	M	2	E	2	M	4	S	6	V	8	X
4	CDR Kitchin	X	8	V	6	S	4	M	2	E	2	M	4	S	6	V	8	X
5	CAPT Vanderburg	X	8	V	6	S	4	M	2	E	2	M	4	S	6	V	8	X
6	Col Dockery	X	8	V	6	S	4	M	2	E	2	M	4	S	6	V	8	X
7	CR Nelson	X	8	V	6	S	4	M	2	E	2	M	4	S	6	V	8	X
8	CDR Trail	X	8	V	6	S	4	M	2	E	2	M	4	S	6	V	8	X
9	CDR Thayer	X	8	V	6	S	4	M	2	E	2	M	4	S	6	V	8	X
10	CAPT Law	X	8	V	6	S	4	M	2	E	2	M	4	S	6	V	8	X
11	CAPT Alexander	X	8	V	6	S	4	M	2	E	2	M	4	S	6	V	8	X
12	CDR Swartz	X	8	V	6	S	4	M	2	E	2	M	4	S	6	V	8	X
13	CDR Scott	X	8	V	6	S	4	M	2	E	2	M	4	S	6	V	8	X
14	CAPT Aldrich	X	8	V	6	S	4	M	2	E	2	M	4	S	6	V	8	X
15	Col Ertwine	X	8	V	6	S	4	M	2	E	2	M	4	S	6	V	8	X
16	CAPT Kendall	X	8	V	6	S	4	M	2	E	2	M	4	S	6	V	8	X
17	CAPT Kordis	X	8	V	6	S	4	M	2	E	2	M	4	S	6	V	8	X
18	CAPT Langley	X	8	V	6	S	4	M	2	E	2	M	4	S	6	V	8	X
19	CAPT Maurer	X	8	V	6	S	4	M	2	E	2	M	4	S	6	V	8	X
20	CAPT Utterback	X	8	V	6	S	4	M	2	E	2	M	4	S	6	V	8	X

Wave 1   Votes: 48   Of: 51   Geometric Avg. 3.0 0   Geometric Var. .19 5

◀▮▶ Prev / Next   Group

1 = Equal 3 = Moderate 5 = Strong 7 = Very Strong 9 = Extreme

Figure 11 – Typical Voting Screen

The prioritization of the tasks conducted on both coasts was merged into one model with one set of priorities and normalized. The resultant priorities of all the identified CVX tasks are a ratio scale. Figure 12 depicts the top 15 of the 63 lowest level CVX tasks and their relative priorities. The priorities shown in Figure 12 have been multiplied by 1,000 for readability.

Task		Priority
TA 3.3	Integrate Tactical Fires	86
TA 3.2.1.2	Conduct Strike, Surface, Subsurface, Air Defense / Aintiair Attack	74
TA 3.2.1.1	Conduct Fire Support / Close Air Support	47
TA 1.5	Coordinate Maneuver and Integrate with Firepower	44
TA 6.1	Maintain Mobility	42
TA 1.4.2	Occupy Combat Area	40
TA 6.3.1	Protect Against Combat Area Hazards	40
TA 4.3	Fix / Maintain Equipment	38
TA 4.1	Arm	30
TA 5.5	Employ Tactical C2W	30
TA 1.2	Negotiate Tactical Area of Operations	22
TA 5.1.1	Communicate Information	20
TA 4.2	Fuel	19
TA 3.1.2	Select Fire Attack System	18
TA 5.4.6	Synchronize Tactical Operations	18

Figure 12 – Top 15 Prioritized CVX

Step 3 –Develop CVX Attributes

Step 3 required developing a list of attributes for CVX. CVX attributes are the means to accomplishing the previously prioritized tasks and include design characteristics and capabilities that contribute to successful performance of the operational tasks.   The attributes were arranged into three groupings:

- Functions: characteristics or activities necessary in the performance of a task;
- Parameters: physical property that determines the behavior or capability to perform a task; and
- Operational Flexibility / Constraints: characteristic that effects the likelihood or degree of performing a task.

An initial attribute list was provided at the second meeting of the FPTs. The initial focus of this effort revolved around limiting the list to a workable number of attributes (30-40) and ensuring that the focus was broad and at the same level of detail. The FPTs met on each coast validating, adding, and deleting attributes.   Figure 13 lists the finalized attributes. To validate each attribute, participants were asked three questions:

- Is the prospective attribute a what or a how (means);

- Is the prospective attribute at the right level of detail; and
- Is the prospective attribute covered as part of another attribute?

Step 4 –Prioritize CVX Attributes

In **Step 4** the FPTs evaluated the degree of correlation between the attributes and the prioritized tasks through individual inputs. This was accomplished by using the ratings module of *Team Expert Choice*. Unlike pairwise comparison which is a relative measurement, the ratings module uses absolute measurement. To determine the degree of correlation between the attributes and the tasks, a set of standards or intensities are first developed. These intensities are shown in Figure 14 Strong, Medium,

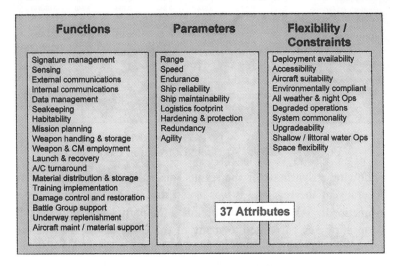

Figure 13 – Attribute Listing

Some, Tad, and None. The ratio scales below each intensity were developed through the normal pairwise comparison to establish their relative values. For example, a Strong (1.000) task-to-attribute correlation is approximately three times a Medium (.367) correlation. Participants then compared each attribute to each task by selecting one of the intensities. The selected intensity value is multiplied by weighting of the task and then summed for each task to arrive at a total value for each attribute. These values are shown in the TOTAL column. Figure 15 depicts the CVX war-fighting attributes and their relative priorities.

ATTRIBUTES	TOTAL	MANEUVER POSITION MOVEPREP	MOVE	TACPOSIT	NEGOTIATE	NAVIGATE	DOMINATE CTRFIRES
1	Aircraft Turnaround	0.605	0.251	0.441	0.441	0.340	0.144	STRONG
2	Data Management	0.737	0.388	0.332	0.332	0.396	0.616	0.680
3	Internal Communications	0.793	0.474	0.443	0.443	0.583	0.764	0.729
4	External Communications	0.825	0.565	0.587	0.587	0.560	0.704	0.879
5	Habitability	0.255	0.243	0.180	0.180	0.260	0.173	0.147
6	Launch and Recovery	0.640	0.357	0.644	0.644	0.756	0.238	STRONG
7	Material Distribution	0.339	0.574	0.277	0.277	0.141	0.106	0.391
8	Mission Planning	0.700	0.355	0.454	0.454	0.455	0.557	0.910
9	Seakeeping	0.438	0.489	0.928	0.928	0.813	0.683	0.873
10	Sensing	0.630	0.365	0.650	0.650	0.910	0.789	0.976
11	Signature Management	0.482	0.271	0.511	0.511	0.668	0.332	0.855
12	Training Implementation	0.319	0.285	0.283	0.283	0.264	0.326	0.456
13	Wpns & CM Employment	0.563	0.205	0.645	0.645	0.668	0.125	0.976
14	Wpns Handling & Storage	0.480	0.533	0.338	0.338	0.298	0.056	0.867
15	Endurance	0.470	0.528	0.827	0.827	0.729	0.411	0.964

(Maneuver | Position | MovePrep)
(Strong 1 (1.000) | Medium 2 (.367) | Some 3 (.150) | Tad 4 (.062) | None 5 (.000))

Figure 14 – Task / Attribute Correlation Example

Following a synthesis of the results, discussion developed concerning the accuracy of the results. It was noted that the top six attributes were cross-functional. As discussions continued the participants understood that these top attributes correlated to many of the CVX tasks; whereas launch and recovery was more specific to firepower and underway replenishment. The point taken was not that launch and recovery was unimportant, but that attributes like external communications cut across most of the tasks the carrier must be capable of accomplishing.

No.	CVX Attribute	Warfighting Priority	No.	CVX Attribute	Warfighting Priority
1	Reliability	0.837	20	Aircraft Suitability	0.478
2	External Communications	0.825	21	Aircraft Maint/Material Spt	0.472
3	Internal Communications	0.793	22	Endurance	0.470
4	All Weather/Night Capability	0.762	23	Logistics Support Footprint	0.442
5	Data Management	0.737	24	Seakeeping	0.438
6	Mission Planning	0.700	25	Shallow/Littoral Ops	0.436
7	Launch and Recovery	0.640	26	UNREP	0.433
8	Sensing	0.630	27	Hardening & Protection	0.414
9	Degraded Operations	0.625	28	Agility	0.374
10	Aircraft Turnaround	0.605	29	Range	0.366
11	Wpns & CM Employment	0.563	30	Speed	0.364
12	Ctl / Restore Damage	0.559	31	Material Distribution	0.339
13	System Commonality	0.545	32	Training Implementation	0.319
14	Maintainability	0.537	33	Habitability	0.255
15	Battle Group Support	0.533	34	Space Flexibility	0.239
16	Redundancy	0.510	35	Accessibility	0.217
17	Upgradeability	0.492	36	Deployment Availability	0.082
18	Signature Management	0.482	37	Environmental Compliance	0.056
19	Wpns Handling & Storage	0.480			

Figure 15 – Prioritized CVX Attributes

NAVSEA engineers will use previously cataloged potential technology investments to determine those technologies, which if pursued, could provide major increases in carrier effectiveness or efficiency. This will be accomplished by correlating the degree to which potential technology investments contribute to the prioritized CVX attributes. This list of relative technology priorities will aid in determining which potential enabling technologies can provide the best value for design of the CVX. Subsequently, AHP will be again applied to develop a strategy for funding technology investments within the constraints of CVX research and development.

Figure 16 - Prioritized CVX Attributes

NAVSEA engineers will use previously optimised potential technology investments to determine those technologies, which if pursued, could provide major increases in carrier effectiveness or efficiency. This will be accomplished by correlating the degree to which potential technology investments contribute to the prioritized CVX attributes. This list of relative technology priorities will aid in determining which potential enabling technologies can provide the best value for design of the CVX. Subsequently, AHP will be again applied to develop a strategy for funding technology investments within the constraints of CVX research and development.

Index

Absolute judgment, 40, 144, 145, 154
Accuracy, 38, 39, 41, 45, 51, 63, 66, 71, 139, 141, 213, 215, 217, 296, 363, 398
Activity Level Resource Allocation, 276
Alternatives - Pros and Cons, 27
Analogs and Adages, 9
Analytic Network Process, 323, 324, 329, 330, 364
Analytical Planning (The Forward/Backward Process), 230
Artificial Clustering of Elements – Linking Clusters, 143
Assessing the Voice of the Customer, 340
Benchmarking, 365
Benefit/Cost, 181, 184, 251, 261, 262, 278
Benefit/Cost/Risk, 184
Benjamin Franklin, 28
Beyond Weights and Scores, 45
BOGSAT, 5, 6
Brainstorming, 17, 19, 127, 133
Categorizing and Combining, 129
Cause of Rank Adjustment, 153
Causes of Inconsistency, 47
Channel Capacity, 38
Channel capacity and short term memory, 38
Choosing a Coast Guard Weapon Patrol Boat Fleet, 82
Closed and Open Systems, 154
Cognitive Decision Rules, 8
Cognitive limitations, 6
Common Simplistic Strategies, 7
Comparison Modes, 66
Compensatory and Non-Compensatory Decision-making, 49
Compensatory decision models, 49
Competitive Value Analysis, 347
Competitive Value Pricing, 348
Complete Hierarchy, 179
Contemporary Management Trends, 333
Converting to Pairwise, 141
Creativity, 17, 128, 296

Critical Path Method, 202
Decision Making, 5, 6, 11, 12, 18, 51, 111, 185, 188, 316, 322, 324
Decision-making Concepts & Methodologies, 27
Deriving Probability Distributions, 205, 218
Deriving Scenario Likelihoods, 205, 228
Developing a Decision Hierarchy, 54
Discrete Alternative Resource Allocation, 244
Dissatisfaction with outcomes of meetings, 300
Eigenvalues and Eigenvectors, 63
Empowered for the Future, 331
Establishing Priorities, 62
Evaluation and Choice, 137, 147
Expert Choice, 43, 53
Feedback, 12, 185, 309, 316, 323, 324, 325, 327, 328, 330
Forecasting, 44, 205, 213, 216, 217, 222, 223, 226
Forecasting - The Forward Process, 213
Forecasting Alternative Outcomes, 205, 222
Forecasting models interacting with choice model(s)., 226
From Brainstorming to Structuring to Evaluation and Choice, 127
Graphical judgments, 68
Groups and meetings, 291
Herbert Simon, 18
Ideal and Distributive Synthesis Modes (Preventing or allowing rank reversals), 151
Inconsistency Ratio, 92
Incremental improvement, 113
Integer Programming, 205
Integrating with Quantitative Methodologies, 190
Inter-American Development Bank, 375
Introduction
Management Decision-Making Today, 1

401

Judgments
  Verbal, 40, 41, 72
Levels of Measurement, 32
Linear Programming, 190
Meeting Model, 301
Meeting Outcomes
  Relational as well as Task, 302
Meetings, Meeting Facilitation and
  Group Support Systems (GSS), 291
Methodology Overview, 239
Misuse of Numbers, 31
Musts and Wants, 111
Narrowing Down, 129
Navy Sea-Based Platforms, 386
Numerical judgments, 67
Other decision-making 'recipes', 111
Other Topics / Refinements, 139
Pairwise Comparison Modes, 66
Pairwise Comparisons versus MAUT
  Swing Weights, 187
Principles and Axioms of the Analytic
  Hierarchy Process, 50
Problem Solving, 3, 15, 18, 111, 296
Problem Solving and Decision-Making,
  15
Queueing Models, 198
Rank Adjustment/Reversal, 151
Ratings Approach, 144
Ratings Approach for A Large Number
  of Alternatives, 59
Reducing Inconsistency, 95
Relative judgment, 29, 72, 88, 144, 154,
  222, 348
Requisites for Change, 11
Resistance to Change, 11
Resource Allocation, 235, 243, 244, 268,
  276, 287, 358
Resource Allocation Summary, 287
Retirement Places Rated, 114

Satisficing, 6, 7, 8
Scarcity and Abundance, 154
Selecting a Forecasting Method, 205,
  217
Sensitivity, 79, 80, 83, 104, 106, 108,
  109, 150, 224
Seven Step Process for Choice, 109
Short Term Memory, 38
Silverlake Project, 236, 239, 241
Strategic Planning, 333
Structural adjustment, 175
Structuring, 121, 133, 134, 136, 137
Summary of the benefits of AHP, 113
Synthesis, 13, 22, 78, 79, 101, 102, 103,
  156, 159, 166, 167, 169, 170, 171,
  172, 174, 223, 225, 314, 315, 318,
  319, 320, 344
Synthesizing Forecasting Methods for a
  Composite forecast, 205, 215
The Analytic Hierarchy Process, 13, 14,
  19, 39, 43, 44, 45, 46, 71, 139, 152,
  153, 154, 182, 192, 230, 234, 268,
  316, 322, 357, 379
The Need for Better Decision-making, 2
Total Quality Management, 334
Tradeoffs, 5
Transformation of data, 141
Typical application
  Choosing Coast Guard Weapon Patrol
    Boat Fleet, 82
Unfreeze, change, refreeze, 10
Unimportant vs. Crucial Decisions, 10
Using Hard Data, 140
Validation study, 71, 73, 383
Value Based Value Pricing, 344
Verbal judgments, 68
Voting, 130, 395
Weights and Scores, 37
What is a meeting, 300